# Environmental Law and Policy in Wales

# Environmental Law and Policy in Wales

## Responding to Local and Global Challenges

*Edited by*
*Patrick Bishop*
*and*
*Mark Stallworthy*

University of Wales Press
Cardiff
2013

© The Contributors, 2013

All rights reserved. No part of this book may be reproduced in any material form (including photocopying or storing it in any medium by electronic means and whether or not transiently or incidentally to some other use of this publication) without the written permission of the copyright owner except in accordance with the provisions of the Copyright, Designs and Patents Act 1988. Applications for the copyright owner's written permission to reproduce any part of this publication should be addressed to the University of Wales Press, 10 Columbus Walk, Brigantine Place, Cardiff CF10 4UP.

*www.uwp.co.uk*

*British Library Cataloguing-in-Publication Data*
A catalogue record for this book is available from the British Library.

ISBN 978-0-7083-2580-3
e-ISBN 978-0-7083-2581-0

The right of the Contributors to be identified as authors of this work has been asserted in accordance with sections 77, 78 and 79 of the Copyright, Designs and Patents Act 1988.

Typeset by Prepress Projects Ltd, Perth, UK
Printed by the MPG Group, Bodmin, Cornwall

# Contents

|   |   |   |
|---|---|---|
| *Foreword* | | *vii* |
| *Preface* | | *ix* |
| *Contributors* | | *xi* |

1   Introductory: expressing Welsh law perspectives on environmental protection    1
*Patrick Bishop and Mark Stallworthy*

2   Debatable ground: the devolution settlement and environmental law in Wales    7
*Karen Morrow*

3   Nuisance law in industrial Wales – local and national conflicts (part one): copper smelting in a pre-regulatory era    25
*Mark Wilde*

4   Nuisance law in industrial Wales – local and national conflicts (part two): oil refining, the common law and regulation    43
*Mark Wilde*

5   Nature conservation in Wales    63
*Lynda M. Warren*

6   Badgers, bovine tuberculosis and the role of science in the formulation of Welsh environmental and agricultural policy    83
*Patrick Bishop*

| | | |
|---|---|---|
| 7 | The Food Strategy for Wales: a soft law instrument?<br>*Robert Lee* | 105 |
| 8 | Sustainable communities in Wales: developing a new governance approach to local sustainable development in Wales's most deprived areas<br>*Victoria Jenkins* | 123 |
| 9 | Climate change law in Wales: realizing the value of participation<br>*Mark Stallworthy* | 143 |
| 10 | Made in Wales: devolving and evolving environmental policy making<br>*Elen Stokes* | 167 |

*Bibliography* *183*
*Index* *195*

# Foreword

I am delighted to have the opportunity to set the context for this important publication, which draws on the expertise in environmental law based in our Welsh universities.

It reflects the very distinctive role that Wales is playing in meeting the pressing environmental challenges that are faced by societies around the world. This role was established in law under the Government of Wales Act, which requires Welsh Ministers to set out how they propose to promote sustainable development in the exercise of their functions. It will be further strengthened by new legislation in the shape of a Sustainable Development Bill, which will deepen and extend this duty across the whole of the devolved public sector in Wales. The Bill will be set alongside other legislation covering environmental impacts and will coincide with the establishment of a new single environment body, Natural Resources Wales.

These changes are designed to use the new legislative powers to refresh, simplify and modernize a range of legislation that has grown through accretion since 1945. This represents a key stage in the devolution process, establishing a framework for sustainable development which is clear, connected and consistent, provides certainty, and focuses on the long term.

At a time when global solutions to our environmental challenges seem a long way off, it is critical that we improve our capacity to govern for the long term at a national, regional and local level. It is worth remembering that the UN Rio+20 summit estimated that states and regions are responsible for 70–80 per cent of everything that needs to be done, with much of the real progress of the last twenty years resulting from leadership at this level. Regional and local governments are closer to the action, with the capacity to expand ambition and drive change in partnership with business and communities, incubating new ideas, and to scale up action and replicate success.

This book, then, is a very timely contribution from environmental lawyers in the 'Welsh academy' and is itself another sign of a growing strength and vitality in

Welsh contributions to environmental problem solving more widely. The selection of papers tackles some of the major environmental challenges and explains how the principles and processes of the law are applied, offering fresh insights into how law can be deployed most effectively in the development of environmental policy goals. *Environmental Law and Policy in Wales: Responding to Global and Local Challenges* is welcome as a fresh, thought-provoking contribution to continuing and urgent environmental debates.

Peter Davies
Sustainable Futures Commissioner for Wales

# Preface

The catalyst for this collected volume was the powerful feeling that, with a significant dynamic towards a devolved Wales now in train (a key element within which is environmental law and policy), this was an opportune moment to reflect on aspects of our shared engagement with those same challenges. To this end a colloquium was held at Swansea University in April 2011, during which colleagues were asked to address a range of legal quandaries affecting the goals of environmental protection from a Welsh perspective. Most of all, the sessions that followed afforded the opportunity to pause and reflect on the conceptual foundations of what we are about, and to view both technically and critically the tools of our trade. Many of the papers there, and themes introduced therein, have been subsequently developed into the chapters collected here.

At the same time, we were agreed that our discussions were taking place within what can be categorized as both a mature and an emerging Welsh legal jurisdiction. Speakers were informed by a timely sense of being rooted in 'place', also recognizing a notably complex law and policy context on account of its many cross-cutting and multi-dimensional environmental themes. It will, we hope, be seen that contributions presented here variously engage with such challenges in an expansive spirit, sharing recourse to black letter law whilst also alive to the limitations in the sort of reductionist thinking that envisages a neat segmentation of problems within narrow doctrinal (or disciplinary) confines. Two final points: first, as editors, we have sought to see relevant law and policy reflected here in early 2012; and, second, we are much indebted both to our publishing editor, Sarah Lewis, for her forbearance and her unflinching support for this project, and to an anonymous reviewer whose wise and constructive suggestions have helped make this volume a much improved academic effort on all our parts.

Patrick Bishop and Mark Stallworthy
Swansea, May 2012

# Contributors

**Dr Patrick Bishop** is a lecturer at the School of Law, Swansea University, and a member of the Centre for Environmental and Energy Law and Policy (CEELP). His research to date has focused on numerous aspects of environmental law, including the utility of private law as a method of environmental protection, environmental ethics, environmental crime, and regulatory approaches and enforcement. His publications reflect these varied interests.

**Dr Victoria Jenkins** is a lecturer at the School of Law, Swansea University, and deputy director of the Hywel Dda Institute for the promotion of 'Legal Wales'. In research terms, she is broadly interested in public environmental law, but particularly in legal approaches to the achievement of sustainable development and the impact of devolution on environmental protection in the UK.

**Professor Robert Lee** is at Cardiff Law School (where he was Head of School 1996-9), and a codirector of the Economic and Social Research Council (ESRC) Centre on Business Relationships, Accountability, Sustainability and Society (BRASS), which works on issues of business and sustainability/social responsibility. He is a professional development consultant with the Environment Products and Regulation Group of Freshfields Bruckhaus Deringer. He is editor of *Environmental Law Monthly*, coeditor of Analysis for the *Journal of Environmental Law* and environmental editor for the *Journal of Business Law*. He was specialist adviser to the House of Commons Welsh Affairs Committee on the National Assembly for Wales (Legislative Competence) (Environment) Order 2009 and author of the Food Strategy for Wales.

**Professor Karen Morrow** is at the School of Law, Swansea University, and is codirector of the School's Centre for Environmental and Energy Law and Policy. Her research interests include the theory of environmental law, environmental governance, environmental torts, and environment and gender. She is coeditor of the *Journal of Human Rights and the Environment* and serves on the editorial board of the *Environmental Law Review*. She is deputy convener of the Environmental Law section of the Society of Legal Scholars.

**Professor Mark Stallworthy** is at the School of Law, Swansea University, where he is also codirector of the School's Centre for Environmental and Energy Law and Policy. He sits on the Climate Change Consortium of Welsh Universities (C3W) Scientific Management Board, as deputy director of the C3W 'human dimensions' group, and on the editorial boards of the *Journal of Environmental Law* and *International Company and Commercial Law Review*. His main research interests focus on law responses to the problem of climate change, including in terms of policy effectiveness and securing environmental justice.

**Dr Elen Stokes** is a City Solicitors Educational Trust Lecturer in Property Law at Cardiff Law School, and an Associate Member of the ESRC Research Centre for Business Relationships, Accountability, Sustainability and Society (BRASS), Cardiff University. Her research interests include the regulation of health and environmental risks, particularly those associated with new technologies.

**Professor Lynda M. Warren** is a marine biologist and environmental lawyer and has worked for most of her career as a university academic. She holds an emeritus professorship in environmental law at Aberystwyth University and teaches on its LLM course in environmental law and management. Her main research interest has been how law and science are used in developing and implementing environmental policy and she has focused on two main areas: nature conservation and radioactive waste management. She is a member of a number of government bodies, including the Royal Commission on Environmental Pollution, and is deputy chair of the Joint Nature Conservation Committee. She also chairs the Wales Coastal and Maritime Partnership and is the chairperson of the Wildlife Trust for South and West Wales.

**Dr Mark Wilde** is a senior lecturer at the School of Law, University of Reading. He conducts extensive research in environmental law and tort and has published widely in these areas. As regards environmental liability he has published on the theme of genetically modified organisms (GMOs), radiation and maritime oil pollution. He also has a keen interest in the regulation of atmospheric emissions and the interplay between law, technology, policy and economics. This research has now been expanded into the sphere of climate change, where he is involved in interdepartmental projects.

# Chapter 1

# Introductory: expressing Welsh law perspectives on environmental protection

*Patrick Bishop and Mark Stallworthy*

Those concerned to see a coherent and effective development of environmental law (especially including policy makers and legal advisers as well as researchers, teachers and students) share a broad awareness of two critical features. First, there is the wide-ranging nature of those problems that can be viewed as 'environmental' in character; second, those law and policy fields with which environmental lawyers are required to engage are both multi-faceted and polycentric.

A 2009 article in the *Journal of Environmental Law* by Elizabeth Fisher *et al.* marked a notable contribution to a maturing environmental law discourse. The authors generally posed the question of why environmental law continued to be 'so darn difficult as an intellectual enterprise', and sought more specifically to classify the main methodological challenges they saw as confronting all engaged within this sub-discipline's broad jurisprudential church.[1] The challenges were organized within four main interconnecting strands, namely interdisciplinarity, policy dynamics, governance fragmentation and jurisdictional multiplicity.

To a greater or lesser extent, the various chapters in this collection represent exemplars of the methodological challenges highlighted by Fisher *et al.* A few non-exhaustive examples may serve as illustrations. The concept of behavioural change, integral to Stallworthy's analysis (chapter 9) of climate law in Wales, requires an interdisciplinary engagement with aspects of behavioural economics and cognitive psychology. Further, the legal response to climate change has occurred across numerous jurisdictional levels, including the international community, the European Union, the UK and Wales. Such jurisdictional multiplicity is not unique to the legal response to climate change; the control and eradication of bovine tuberculosis considered by Bishop (chapter 6) is the subject of EU, UK and Welsh legislation and thus a central feature of such a crowded law and policy arena is governance fragmentation. Indeed, such fragmentation is arguably an inevitable consequence of devolution whereby various competencies are divided between London and Cardiff. However, this may be justified on the premise that it is desirable that decisions be taken as close as possible to those affected on the ground, as illustrated by Jenkins's (chapter 8) discussion of sustainable communities and the importance of public engagement at the local and community level.

Although not explicitly considered by Fisher *et al.*, it is possible to add a fifth methodological challenge, namely the extensive diversity of legal instruments that may be used to tackle environmental problems. Those interested in contract are generally firmly embedded in the law of obligations; similarly, an administrative lawyer's centre of gravity will be located in institutional structures and relations, and principles of judicial review. We could continue with a plethora of further examples. The essential point is that environmental lawyers are faced with a myriad of distinct legal instruments, borrowed from, *inter alia*, public law, property law, EU law, international law and criminal law. Further, while one might be tempted to think of environmental law as predominantly a branch of public law (broadly defined), Wilde's historical evaluation (chapters 3 and 4) of nuisance serves as a useful reminder that, even in a regulatory era, private law mechanisms are not moribund. The nature of the various mechanisms available to policy makers and legislatures is equally diverse, including traditional 'command-and-control' regulation supported by sanctions for non-compliance; economic instruments such as taxation designed to discourage environmentally damaging activities; and non-regulatory approaches such as those designed to 'nudge' actors towards beneficial conduct.[2] Thus, in the post-modern legal world characterized by a diminishing regulatory monopoly on the part of the state,[3] environmental lawyers are faced with a regulatory landscape in which the distinctions between formal and informal mechanisms in law and policy have become blurred. The foregoing analysis is encapsulated by Lee's analysis (chapter 7) of the food strategy for Wales as a soft law instrument.

Accordingly, as editors we present in this volume not only illustrations of the fundamental challenges that confront environmental lawyers, but also a range of responses to such challenges from within the Welsh environmental academy. There follows a brief *tour d'horizon* of the kinds of problems that fall within the categories identified above, which we in turn challenged contributors to take into consideration in their work here.

First, from an interdisciplinary perspective, environmental lawyers confront a wide range of ethical and regulatory choices, often in areas dominated by complexity and knowledge gaps. This requires working with mixes of both traditional and emerging principles, and related lessons and obstacles presented from other, non-legal perspectives.

Second, in respect of policy dynamics, in which optimum solutions often appear contingent and subject to continual review, environmental lawyers must work with regulatory responses, which variously reflect either established or more radical alternative instrumental and normative influences. In each respect, intradisciplinary tensions can be said to arise, including on such questions as rationale, purpose and efficacy.

Thence, Welsh perspectives can be most readily identified in relation to the remaining challenges: those of governance fragmentation and jurisdictional multiplicity. Regarding the third element, fragmentation, this is reflected in the deployment of evolving regulatory regimes, and the wider engagement of actors, through public–private partnerships and otherwise. To these ends legal categories are not closed, and methods rely on soft as well as hard law approaches, just as use is made of supplemental, extra-legal techniques geared towards meeting policy objectives. An important element lies in the harnessing of expanding public law understandings and approaches, manifested in greater formalization of legal inputs. These occur typically through proceduralized, rather than substantive, controls, alongside cognate developments relating to information and transparency, public participation and access to justice.

The fourth, and perhaps most prescient, challenge before the writers contributing here relates to the quandaries that result from jurisdictional overload, a condition complicated somewhat by the impetus, charted in this present volume, towards addressing environmental issues from a Welsh perspective. Both vertical and horizontal issues require resolution, as distinct levels of jurisdiction seek to impose themselves (or indeed shy away from) environmental problems. Yet such interrelationships remain 'under-explored and scholarly debate on the proper methodology for undertaking such analyses remains virtually non-existent'.[4] This demands an engagement with a complex of interjurisdictional connections, as the conditions for conflict arise and call for resolution.

At a basic level, an interjurisdictional analysis might address the question of the extent to which Welsh environmental law and policy is different from its English counterpart. It is submitted that a more interesting question is the extent to which a divergent approach is desirable. Morrow (chapter 2) charts the development of devolution in Wales and acknowledges that the process is one of evolution, not revolution. Nevertheless, the devolution settlement in Wales, both prior and subsequent to the 'yes' vote in the referendum to determine whether or not to activate the powers contained in Part IV of the Government of Wales Act 2006, unquestionably opens windows of opportunity for distinctive Welsh approaches. However, in the context of environmental protection, such openings may be narrower than might otherwise be the case, on the basis that the impetus for a significant proportion of environmental legislation is provided by the EU. An illustration of the tendency towards homogeneity as a result of EU action is provided by Warren's analysis (chapter 5) of nature conservation, noting that Wales is similar to the rest of the UK in the way it addresses habitat and species protection, partly because of the influence of European and international commitments which take effect at a UK level.

Yet despite such limitations on autonomy one may acknowledge that policy makers in Wales are able to adopt a distinctive, even unique, approach to environmental protection. It does not automatically follow that, merely because divergence is possible, Welsh policy makers ought to strive for it. Even in a climate of streamlined and enhanced law-making powers for the National Assembly, it might continue to be the case that Welsh environmental law and policy is not inherently dissimilar to the rest of the UK. To this end Stokes (chapter 10) adopts a cautionary tone, warning that over-enthusiastic legislative activity on the part of the National Assembly might lead to less credible policy formulation.

The above challenges are very much 'live', in the sense that answers to environmental problems by reference to the logic of greater centralization have often proved out of reach. That said, although international environmental law frameworks are beset by the realities of interstate division and conflict, as politically conceived state interests are prioritized, indications of positive progress do exist. Thus, first, they can contribute to agenda setting, albeit that progress generally requires elaboration and delivery at national (and, in the EU's case, supranational) levels. Second, there have been notable success stories: for instance in relation to the development of international mechanisms to address damage to the ozone layer. This demonstrated that especially where geopolitical conditions are right (there, for instance, including a restricted specific goal, the ready availability of alternative technologies and multilateral willingness to commit to both financial support and trade sanctions) even at this level success can be achieved. Otherwise, it is typically at regional levels of governance, and below, that workable legal mechanisms to meet environmental threats are more likely to be found.

So the chapters that follow are situated within and across a variety of legal categories, and explore a range of applicable techniques. In these specific contexts, it is argued that, in the search for effective approaches, it is crucial that policy makers be aware of the possibilities and limitations of legal mechanisms. Furthermore, in the face of the complexities and value conflicts that often characterize environmental problems, tools of risk assessment in the field of environmental degradation have developed more nuanced characteristics (such as 'best environmental techniques' within 'integrated pollution prevention and control') than a crude adoption of cost–benefit analysis might otherwise suggest. Indeed the modern predilection for target setting (long-term) and problematic juxtaposition with day-to-day politics (short- to medium-term) is also now beginning to be translated into legal terminology, and questions of juridification will also increasingly arise here.

Meanwhile, new 'environmental' principles have emerged, from the frankly amorphous and practically unworkable 'polluter pays' to the highly contested but nevertheless cogent (especially within an EU framing) idea of 'the precautionary principle' and the principle of 'restoration at source'. More problematic, given its chameleon-like potentialities for policy makers, is the principle of 'sustainable development', but even such ubiquity is tending to alter the terms of debate.

Foundational questions for legal discussion in the field of the environment are ultimately about where balances between recognized interests are to be struck. Environmental laws, whether in their instigation or in their elaboration and interpretation, are underpinned by powerful, purposive elements that reflect decision makers' choices. This poses immense challenges for environmental lawyers, conceived in Tim Jewell and Jenny Steele's admonition by reference to whether an '"assimilation" of environmental decision-making to the very patterns of thought which have given rise to environmental problems' will give rise to 'no more than an admission of defeat'.[5] Conversely, attention to the coherent elaboration of environmental law offers the potential, both normatively and by instrumental development, for fresh ways of viewing problems and their resolution.

We assert here that there is value in acknowledging distinctions between the physical materiality of places where environmental impacts are actually felt and the abstract nature of our legal tools and constructs (including, for instance, our notions of property and boundaries).[6] On a deeper level, therefore, immense challenges arise for an environmental law discourse that ultimately depends on the policy context within which it must operate, but also, importantly, which it is able to influence. Conflicts arise in a variety of situations, often masked by the adoption of narrow tools of analysis. These include, for instance, the choices at work in the interpretation of recognized common law stances. An illustration can be seen in the privatization context, where judicial adherence to traditionally separate corporate identity principles can result in a narrowing of potential liability for compulsory clean-up of contaminated land.[7] Similarly, in a case involving a question of whether more than formal compliance was required for effective EU and domestic transposition of international obligations (under the 1973 *Convention on International Trade in Endangered Species*), the Court of Appeal prioritized adherence to the principle of commercial certainty in protecting the interests of an importer despite an apparent lack of veracity of the formal documentation underpinning the regime. There, dissenting, Laws LJ, noting that exercises in statutory interpretation are 'hardly ever entirely value-free', favoured a more purposive construction, in accord with environmental objectives underpinning the regulatory regime.[8]

The urgency of many environmental debates can therefore be characterized by reference to how we determine optimal solutions. Not only should responses change as new threats present themselves (or are alleviated), but they should not be arbitrarily decoupled from discussions about alternative governance choices and applications.[9] That the focus here is on environmental issues at work within the Welsh polity does not betoken any wilful blindness towards the significant externalities that characterize the picture on a wider canvas, including wider pressures from competing policy priorities. Nor does it presuppose any ignoring of wider governance and jurisdictional complexities. It is our central proposition that a critical application of Welsh environmental law perspectives can add a valuable localized framing of the challenges that arise. Indeed, a selection of such perspectives makes up the substance of this volume.

Accordingly, rooted within a distinctive perspective of 'place' and 'community', this volume has sought to make a coherent contribution to ongoing debates, giving voice to Welsh perceptions of environment and law, and forging valid links between the two.

## Notes

1 E. Fisher, B. Lange, E. Scotford and C. Carlane, 'Maturity and methodology: a debate about environmental law scholarship', *Journal of Environmental Law*, 21 (2009), 213–50.
2 R. H. Thaler and C. R. Sunstein, *Nudge: Improving Decisions about Health, Wealth, and Happiness* (New Haven, CT: Yale University Press, 2008).
3 N. de Sadeleer, *Environmental Principles: From Political Slogans to Legal Rules* (Oxford: Oxford University Press, 2002), p. 245.
4 Fisher *et al.*, 'Maturity and methodology', 241–2.
5 T. Jewell and J. Steele, *Law in Environmental Decision-Making: National, European and International Perspectives* (Oxford: Clarendon Press, 1998), p. 25.
6 N. Graham, *Lawscape: Property, Environment and Law* (Abingdon: Routledge-Cavendish, 2010).
7 Also reflected in traditional common law positions: see, for instance, concerning the potential for rules of corporate succession to negate liability for clean-up of contaminated land, *R. (on the application of National Grid Gas plc formerly Transco plc) v. Environment Agency* [2008] Environmental Law Rep. 4.
8 *R. v. Secretary of State for Environment, ex p. Greenpeace* [2002] EWCA 1036.
9 See D. C. Esty, 'Toward optimal environmental governance', *New York University Law Review*, 74 (1999), 1495–1574.

# Chapter 2

# Debatable ground: the devolution settlement and environmental law in Wales

*Karen Morrow*

## Devolution and constitutional reform

The implementation of devolution across the UK in the late 1990s, while only one manifestation of an intense period of broader constitutional reform, perhaps represents one of its most significant expressions.[1] Indeed it is arguable that, in a system long regarded by commentators as substantially more political than legal, devolution, the one area of constitutional change motivated by popular pressure, has brought statute law more markedly to the fore than had previously been the norm in our constitutional arrangements.[2] The devolution legislation introduced in the UK in the late 1990s differentiated clearly between Scotland and Northern Ireland on the one hand and Wales on the other. In the former, broadly parliamentary status was accorded to the new governing bodies, while in the latter something more akin to a glorified form of local government was on offer. The motivation for this aspect of what is often termed 'asymmetrical devolution' was attributed to a relatively lukewarm response by the Welsh electorate to the initial referendum on devolution. It would, however, be fair to say that asymmetrical devolution could also be justified in part by the fact that Wales, unlike Scotland and Northern Ireland, did not exhibit a marked separate pre-devolution legal identity.[3] As events have played out, devolution in Wales has gained considerable traction in comparatively short order.[4] This has resulted in its incremental expansion, making the principality something of a constitutional field laboratory as, given the constraints imposed on the initial form of devolution that was employed in Wales, it arguably represents the most relevant model for possible future reconsideration of the vexed question of devolution to the English regions. Having said this, as will be apparent from the discussion that follows, the story of devolution in Wales so far could equally be seen as revealing the difficulties inherent in keeping a devolved system within tight bounds.

Furthermore, it may be taken to illustrate the necessarily dynamic response to governance that is involved in this area in the absence of a more concrete federal constitutional model and the presence of differentiated devolutionary settlements within the UK legal system. The Welsh experience then raises a number of issues, not least relating to the political momentum generated by introducing even a curtailed form of devolution and the implications for its practical/political (if not legal) entrenchment.[5] This had already been observed in the context of the comparatively limited form of what is often referred to as administrative or executive devolution that had become operational in Wales from the mid-1960s onwards, despite entrenched opposition in Whitehall.[6] It is interesting to note for present purposes that, while the Welsh Office held no 'environment' administrative remit as such at this time, the related areas of agriculture and housing and local government were, for a variety of reasons, the subject of particular civil service resistance to devolving competences.[7] These areas overlap with mainstream 'environmental' issues as they share common features and often raise similar concerns. Also significant, in terms of the emergence of a distinctive Welsh approach to governance, was that, even under this very constrained model of devolution, some 'policy divergence' began to become apparent, for example in respect of land reclamation.[8]

Once the current, executive devolution process was inaugurated, the fact that the post-2004 Labour-majority Welsh Assembly Government (WAG) was actively seeking to carve out its own distinctive niche in policy terms, demonstrating 'clear red water' between the regimes in London and Cardiff, exerted a distinct impetus for change.[9] Thus, regardless of the initial justification of the Welsh devolved administration or intention for it to operate in a fashion that was distinct from its Scottish and Northern Irish counterparts, pressure emerged to secure the relatively rapid evolution of the initial Welsh devolution settlement into something much more commensurate with the devolutionary approaches applied in Scotland and Northern Ireland. Indeed, Beatson queries whether there are in fact greater difficulties attached to a 'staged' rather than a 'wholesale' approach to constitutional reform more generally and this question appears to be particularly apposite when considering the impact of the several significant changes that have had to be made in respect of the Welsh devolution settlement in just over a decade.[10]

This chapter considers the developing nature of the general devolution settlement for Wales, moving on to discuss a number of fundamental matters that shape provision for the environment. It then reflects on whether or not a case can be made for identifying 'legal distinctiveness' in environmental law in Wales in legislation, case law and policy. The chapter concludes by contemplating the significance of the outcome of the 2011 referendum for the future development of environmental law in Wales.

## The changing landscape of the devolution settlement

### *The Government of Wales Act 1998*

The Government of Wales Act 1998 (GoWA 1998) was adopted following a referendum with a turnout comprising 51.5 per cent of the electorate, which expressed the narrowest of margins of victory; the 'yes' campaign registered 50.3 per cent of the vote.[11] The Act conferred a range of powers on the Welsh Assembly, including considerable capacity relating to the environment. The initial delegation was achieved by the Transfer of Functions Order (TFO) 1999 and further powers were added by later UK legislation.[12] It must be noted that the powers accorded to the Assembly at the outset were primarily executive, rather than legislative in nature.[13] In fact, all primary legislative power remained vested in the Westminster Parliament. The Assembly's delegated powers were limited to areas delineated in Schedule 2 to the GoWA 1998 and broadly comprised those formerly enjoyed by the Secretary of State for Wales under individual statutes.

According to the Rt Hon. Ron Davies AM, the last pre-devolution Secretary of State for Wales, the selection of the executive devolution model under the GoWA 1998 owed more to pragmatic political compromise within the Labour government than to principle.[14] Nonetheless, despite its inherent limitations the GoWA 1998 did allow 'sufficient scope to deliver a distinctive policy agenda for Wales – albeit with some specific constraints, which were more significant in some portfolios than others.'[15] Where environment and planning are concerned, WAG placed early emphasis on developing policy distinctiveness, and enjoyed a degree of success in obtaining new powers in UK primary acts with reference to the Wales Spatial Plan, local authority municipal waste strategies and flood defence.[16] The Welsh Assembly Government also gained an ability to exercise influence on certain non-devolved decisions. Nonetheless, it is arguable that much of this progress was in spite of the devolution settlement rather than because if it. Despite these developments, pressure points emerged in the environmental devolution context, for example with respect to power generation.[17]

In terms of day-to-day environmental governance, although the Environment Agency's remit ostensibly applies without differentiation to England and Wales, the Agency's regional approach to regulation and the fact that it also enjoys the status of a Welsh Government-sponsored body have allowed Asiantaeth yr Amgylchedd Cymru to attain and continue to develop a degree of administrative distinctiveness.[18]

The original devolution settlement created a single body corporate to carry out both legislative and executive functions, based on the then-prevailing local government model. This was, however, comparatively rapidly displaced by the Assembly's institutional practice, which effectively developed a functional separation of powers modus operandi, with the Assembly delegating executive functions to WAG.[19] In July 2003, with a more proactive agenda in mind, the Commission on the Assembly's Powers and Electoral Arrangements (the Richard Commission) was set up to examine, amongst other things, the clarity and breadth of the powers of the Welsh Assembly and the implications of devolution for the operative arrangements in UK policy making relating to Wales.[20] The Richard Commission's final report was published in 2004 and gained considerable support from civil society and the Welsh press.[21] In response to the report, in 2005 the Secretary of State for Wales, in collaboration with the Assembly's First Minister, produced a White Paper, *Better Governance for Wales*, which focused on institutional reform (specifically introducing formal separation of powers between the Assembly and the Welsh Assembly Ministers), the need to rationalize/streamline the legislative process, and electoral reform.[22] This document ultimately set the scene for the adoption of new primary legislation in respect of the devolution settlement for Wales, albeit in narrower terms than those that had been advocated by the Richard Commission.[23] Subsequent changes to the legislative process represent the most significant developments for current purposes. The White Paper envisaged striking 'a new balance of legislative authority for Wales as between Parliament on the one hand and the Assembly on the other', but at the same time emphasized the continuing significance of Westminster's contribution to the legislative environment in Wales (in terms of 'Wales-only' legislation, and laws applicable to England and Wales or the whole United Kingdom).[24]

## *The Government of Wales Act 2006*

Unlike the 1998 devolution legislation, the initial changes introduced by the Government of Wales Act 2006 (GoWA 2006) were not the subject of a referendum, arguably because of their largely technical nature. The modifications introduced predominantly served to bring governance arrangements in Wales more into line with those applicable in the other devolved administrations and at Westminster. That said, the additional provisions contained in Part IV of GoWA 2006, geared towards augmenting the legislative settlement applicable to the Welsh Assembly, were conditional on endorsement by the electorate in a referendum and these will, as discussed below, ultimately prove to be of much greater significance in both principle and practice.

It is undoubtedly significant that the then government, in mooting its initial changes to the GoWA 1998 relating to the law-making process for Wales, did not view what was proposed as representing essential change in the existing settlement.[25] Rather, what was envisaged was a means to remedy delay in the law-making process in Wales that was contingent on the need for Welsh provisions to slot into the Westminster legislative calendar. The first significant feature of the GoWA 2006 was its provision for formal separation of powers between the legislature and the executive, providing official sanction for what was by then well-established institutional practice. Of much greater import, however, was its attempt to introduce a more rationalized legislative process applicable to devolved areas. In the first instance, change focused on extending provision for Orders in Council – specifically Legislative Competence Orders (LCOs) – to expand the Assembly's law-making powers in devolved fields.[26] Where the environment is concerned, this would be achieved through amendment of Part 6 of Schedule 5 to the GoWA 2006. However, despite the developments introduced, the procedure remained decidedly cumbersome, comprising seven distinct phases: a request for enhanced powers by the Assembly; discussion (between WAG, the Assembly and Whitehall); a proposed draft order; pre-legislative scrutiny (in Parliament and the Assembly); a draft order being sent to the Assembly for approval (no changes being allowed at this stage); and (approval being forthcoming) a request for an Order in Council being made to the Secretary of State.[27] Finally, if it was to proceed, this would be subject to the Affirmative Resolution Procedure for statutory instruments, thus requiring approval by both Houses of Parliament.[28] In controversial areas, this process could take years; see, for example, the not atypical three-year course of National Assembly for Wales (Legislative Competence) (Environment) Order 2010, which is considered below.[29] Although the Order in Council process, supplemented by Devolution Guidance Note 16, was undoubtedly ponderous, with only fourteen government-proposed orders and two member-proposed orders being completed in the four years that this regime was in place, it provided for clearly structured and substantial engagement between the Assembly and Parliament.[30] Though its nature precluded the procedure from offering equality between actors, it did at least ensure a full and active role for the Assembly throughout the process from initiation to conclusion.

The GoWA 2006 also made provision to extend devolved powers through the inclusion of 'framework powers' in Westminster primary legislation. The augmentation of primary legislation and Westminster's continuing sovereign ability to legislate for the devolved nations even in devolved areas does not, however, offer such formalized and (relatively) predictable interaction between the actors as that outlined above. In this area, a combination of constitutional convention and a variety of agreements and guidance operate to facilitate interaction between Westminster, Whitehall and the devolved legislatures.[31] Furthermore, the devolved legislatures employ legislative consent motions (LCMs, also known as Sewel motions in Scotland) in order to give express consent for Westminster to legislate on devolved matters.[32] In light of these factors, demarcation issues will inevitably continue to arise in the devolution context under the UK constitutional model, regardless of refinements to the enabling legislation.

Finally, while interaction between Westminster and the devolved legislatures is of central importance, Whitehall too plays a key role in devolution, and a great deal of the associated activity is helped or hindered by UK civil servants. Studies show that attitudes within Whitehall vary considerably across departments but it is undoubtedly significant for present purposes that the Department of Environment, Food and Rural Affairs and the then Department for Transport, Local Government and the Regions, two of the Departments most concerned in environmental governance, have in the past been singled out as being amongst the most obstructive in the context of devolution.[33]

## Contextualising environmental issues in the Welsh devolution settlement

From the outset, the Welsh devolution settlement uniquely placed sustainable development (with environment as a component therein alongside social and economic concerns) centre-stage by making WAG subject to a sustainability duty, now contained in Section 79(1) of the GoWA 2006.[34] The duty arguably attempts to shift sustainability from debatable principle to (achievable?) practice. Section 79(1) states that:

> The Welsh Ministers must make a scheme setting out how they propose, in the exercise of their functions, to promote sustainable development.

The adoption of the sustainability scheme requires consultation, publication, monitoring (by means of an annual report) and review. As a result of the s79 requirement, sustainability is widely integrated into WAG's activities, in particular policy testing, operational planning and expenditure review. The GoWA 2006 adds an additional dimension to this cross-cutting approach by introducing a 'Wellbeing' Power in s60(1), which authorizes the Welsh Ministers to:

> do anything which they consider appropriate . . . to promote or improve one or more of the economic, social and environmental wellbeing of Wales.

The GoWA wellbeing power is broader than both the duty bearing the same name imposed by the Local Government Act 2000 and the extended version introduced in the Sustainable Communities Act 2007.[35] Nonetheless, it could be regarded as potentially enabling an atomistic approach to develop towards the concept of sustainability by allowing its constituent economic, social and environmental elements to be treated as distinct from one another, rather than as inherently connected. However, in the Welsh context, it would appear that this is an empty threat, as the wellbeing power must be read in conjunction with the overarching provision of the sustainability duty.

The sustainability duty has other far-reaching implications in terms of the way in which the devolved administration views and presents itself. In its 2009 sustainable development scheme, *One Wales: One Planet*, WAG adopts its own definition of sustainable development, tackling the problem of the inherent lack of precision in the term itself, in the following terms:

> In Wales, sustainable development means enhancing the economic, social and environmental wellbeing of people and communities, achieving a better quality of life for our own and future generations:
> - In ways which promote social justice and equality of opportunity; and
> - In ways which enhance the natural and cultural environment and respect its limits –
>
> using only our fair share of the earth's resources and sustaining our cultural legacy.[36]

Furthermore, sustainable development is not confined to influencing WAG's domestic activities. In the Ministerial Foreword to the sustainable development scheme, the then First Minister stated that:

> Our Scheme for Sustainable Development gives Wales an opportunity to show leadership and ambition, and to learn from the past. It gives us the opportunity to show how we are playing our full role as a global citizen, within the context set by the UN Millennium Development Goals.[37]

This international dimension is taken very seriously and has been vigorously pursued, notably in the wake of the 2002 World Summit on Sustainable Development, in part through Wales's role as a founder of and participant in nrg4SD (the network of regional governments for sustainable development).[38] These examples, then, illustrate the proactive approach taken by WAG towards sustainability in terms of internal policy and external presentation. While they may be viewed by the cynical as merely making a virtue out of necessity, such an observation fails to acknowledge the degree of 'buy-in' that WAG has exhibited in this regard in developing committed and innovative high-level policy approaches and an integrationist agenda that go far beyond tokenism, though the practical implications of this require further consideration and are further discussed below.[39]

## Devolution, the environment and legal distinctiveness

### Legislation

As one of the purposes of devolution is to enable the delivery of 'local solutions to local problems' in devolved areas, so differences in approach towards devolved matters are perhaps to be expected. This potential distinctiveness can emerge in a number of ways, notably through specific provision for Wales in 'Wales-only' Westminster legislation or the much more numerous Wales-oriented clauses in UK or England and Wales legislation. Discussion here, however, will focus on the Assembly's own, devolved, environmental legislation. As pointed out above, under the initial regime laid out in the GoWA 2006, central importance was accorded to Legislative Competence Orders and for this reason, and because the post-referendum regime has only begun to be made manifest, the National Assembly for Wales (Legislative Competence) (Environment) Order 2010 (the environment LCO) will provide the core material for discussion.[40] First, the broader context in which the Environment LCO functions requires consideration. In this area, while broad responsibility is devolved under Schedule 5 of the GoWA 2006, such is the superstructure imposed by EU and international law, with their attendant obligations on the UK, that legislative room to manoeuvre in this regard is necessarily significantly curtailed.[41] Having said this, the acknowledged need for environmental law to respond to local conditions necessitates some degree of legislative latitude; this coincides with the state sovereignty-based incorporation of flexibility that characterizes most transnational law provision in this area. Notably, both of these elements are strongly reflected in the marked preference for legislation in the form of Directives in EU environmental law, binding Member States with regard to the ends to be achieved while according them considerable discretion about the means through which these are effected. It is also worth observing that, while in this context the devolved administrations are functioning subject to the same constraints as the UK government as a whole, their ability to influence international and EU law-making priorities is at best variable and ultimately (as nation states, rather than their constituent parts, are normally the key actors in both of these contexts) limited by domestic constitutional and political constraints.[42]

Moving on to consider the possible distinctiveness of environmental measures adopted thus far by devolved administrations in the UK, this may be considered in theory as falling into three main categories. First, there may be differences that do not import a distinctive approach on the substance of the law, but accommodate other aspects of jurisdictional difference, including structural factors (for example, reflecting institutional differences), administrative goals (for example, integration with other provisions, or rationalization) and matters of procedure. Second, temporary differences in substantive legal coverage, rooted in political decisions/practicalities on the timing of implementation of UK- or EU-rooted obligations, are possible across the devolved administrations. Such differences would necessarily be subject to inbuilt temporal constraints as they are subject to deadlines imposed in the parent legislation. Third, and more significantly, though it is argued considerably less frequently given the parameters referred to above, differences are possible in the substance of the law relating to jurisdiction-specific powers and duties.

Ross and Nash's study on the interface between devolution and EU environmental law suggests that only limited distinctiveness of approach has yet emerged in environmental law across the devolved administrations.[43] Nonetheless, to say that distinctiveness is not marked is not to deny its existence. While limitations in distinctiveness may be attributed in part to the constraints imposed by EU and, to a lesser extent, international law, they may also be explained by the fact that environmental variation on the ground within the UK is often for the most part restricted. In any case, thus far it appears that any differences in legislation that have emerged across the devolved administrations are legally rather than environmentally motivated, though this is not to say that the latter type of distinctiveness cannot emerge in the future.

Where devolution has led to differences in legal provision, this has already prompted litigation, notably in Case C-428/07 *Horvath v. Secretary of State for Environment, Food and Rural Affairs* [2009] OJ C220/4 12.9.2009. This case was concerned with whether Member States were permitted to include requirements relating to the maintenance of public rights of way in their standards for good agricultural and environmental conditions (GEAC) under Article 5 and Annex IV of Regulation 1782/2003. Furthermore, and of central importance to the discussion in hand, the court was called upon to consider whether or not it was discriminatory for the devolved administrations to have different (in this case less demanding) GEAC standards from those applicable in England. The UK Secretary of State for the Environment had appealed unsuccessfully against the case's referral to the European Court of Justice (ECJ), on the grounds that it would open up a very wide-ranging investigation into the nature and content of devolved legislation within the framework of EC law generally. He had argued that the referral was not justified because Article 5 of Regulation 1782/2003 permitted Member States to implement the required provision at a regional level and that therefore differential implementation did not need to be objectively justified for the purposes of the principle of equality and non-discrimination. He had further argued that, for these purposes, implementation by a devolved authority was to be treated as if it were implementation by the Member State. The ECJ, broadly agreeing with the Secretary of State's argument, determined that Member States could adopt differentiated implementing provisions, in so far as they contributed to the retention of rights of way as landscape features/habitats. More importantly for present purposes, the Court took the view that, where the constitutional system of a Member State provides that devolved administrations are to have legislative competence, the fact that those administrations adopt different standards does not constitute discrimination contrary to Community law. This reasoning recognized the freedom of Member States to allocate powers internally and implement Community acts that are not directly applicable by means of measures adopted by regional or local authorities, provided that this achieves correct implementation. If such obligations are not correctly implemented, attribution of legal responsibility and (following the Lisbon Treaty) potential liability for fines is hugely significant and ensures that the UK government is likely to keep both a close eye and a tight rein on the activities of the devolved administrations in this area.[44]

## Legislative Competence Orders and Assembly measures and the environment

As outlined above, LCOs have played an important role in transferring specific powers to WAG in order to facilitate the adoption of Assembly measures. The first LCOs came on stream in 2007, and their use gradually gained in momentum in the period until 2011, with a total of eighteen being recorded across this period.[45] This figure, however, needs to be seen in the context of over 900 Wales statutory instruments made between 2007 and 2011.[46]

The only environment-specific LCO adopted in the period between 2007 and 2011 was the National Assembly for Wales (Legislative Competence) (Environment) Order 2010 (the environment LCO), though other LCOs, for example the National Assembly for Wales (Legislative Competence) (Housing and Local Government) Order 2010 and the National Assembly for Wales (Legislative Competence) (Agriculture and Rural Development) Order 2009, do inevitably raise some environmental considerations.[47] Despite the fairly broad environmental powers encapsulated in the GoWA regime and subsequent Westminster statutes, the need for the LCO was described by the Parliamentary Under-Secretary of State for Wales during the scrutiny process in the following terms:

> Welsh Ministers currently have a broad range of Executive powers relating to the environment, but they are piecemeal, and gaps prevent the Assembly Government from delivering particular policies or restricting reforms to specific areas of environmental regulation.[48]

Arguably this is the perennial problem of devolution, in which the allocation of accumulated powers on paper rarely fits well with needs on the ground. This problem is particularly acute where environmental issues are concerned, as they are inherently interconnected and cross-cutting, both internally and in regard to other contexts such as energy, and it is therefore difficult, if not impossible, to attribute responsibility for them between different levels of government in such a way as to account for all eventualities.

The Environment LCO was actually one of the first that WAG sought to have introduced in 2007 but the final instrument was not made until 2010.[49] The length of the process is in part explained by the fact that the draft was subject to alteration by the National Assembly for Wales Legislation Committee No. 4, the House of Commons Welsh Affairs Select Committee and the House of Lords Constitution Committee.[50] The changes related to structure, drafting and of course substance.

The LCO itself runs to only three sections, though it was supported by an eighty-two-paragraph memorandum from the Minister for Environment, Sustainability and Housing.[51] The latter document provides a useful guide to what WAG envisages as resulting from the rather terse legislative provisions. It also explicitly ties the LCO into a broader legal context, locating it in 'a distinct policy agenda in Wales, centred on a vision of a truly sustainable environment and focused on Welsh priorities and needs' and referring to the *One Wales: One Planet* agenda and the *Environment Strategy for Wales*, 2006.[52] Article 2 of the LCO extends the Assembly's legislative competence by inserting a number of matters into field 6 of Part I to Schedule 5 of the GoWA 2006. The areas covered include aspects of waste (Matters 6.1 and 6.2; the two-part approach was adopted in response to the challenges posed by the need to cover aspects of marine waste whilst avoiding the necessity of adopting a dual definition of the term 'Wales'); protecting/improving the environment in respect of pollution (Matter 6.3); and some particularly interesting provisions on protecting/improving the environment in relation to nuisances (Matter 6.4).[53] Each of these is subject to detailed exceptions, and Article 3 of the LCO makes necessary alterations to Part 2 of Schedule 5 to the GoWA 2006 to effect these. Potential topics for Assembly measures under the Environment LCO include promoting recycling; reducing waste to landfill; strengthening air, light or noise pollution controls; and tackling specific nuisances (such as graffiti, dog fouling and invasive plant species). Among these, waste management is the current priority.[54]

Assembly measures are WAG's designated form of legislation and, unlike the essentially enabling provisions of LCOs, have the potential to directly change the law on the ground. In the period from 2007 to 2011 there were thirteen completed government-proposed Assembly measures (with another four in progress); two completed member-proposed measures (with another eight proposed, including one on recycling which was later withdrawn); four that were rejected by the Assembly; and three in various stages of progress.[55] There have also been a completed Assembly Commission-proposed measure and one completed Committee-proposed measure. This rather modest total must be viewed in light of the fact that measures require specific legal foundation, in a TFO, UK legislation or a LCO. Of the completed measures, only one deals directly with the environment, namely the Waste (Wales) Measure 2010 (the Waste Measure), which is concerned with waste reduction and management.[56] Rather more encouraging is the fact that the Waste Measure itself was adopted relatively swiftly, being first proposed in late February 2010 and receiving Royal approval by mid-December of the same year.[57]

The Waste Measure takes its policy context from WAG's 2010 Overarching Waste Strategy Document for Waste, *Towards Zero Waste*, and to that end focuses on four areas: a mandatory single use carrier bag-charging and environmental project revenue scheme (to be used if voluntary initiatives fail to deliver);

municipal waste-recycling and composting targets (with provision for penalties if these are not met); additional landfill controls; and augmenting the s54 Clean Neighbourhoods and Environment Act 2005 provision for construction/demolition site waste management plans (including introducing fees and charges for them).[58]

The Waste Measure is fairly brief, comprising twenty-two sections and a single short schedule. Once again, though, the explanatory material is considerably longer than the legislation itself; the Waste Measure's explanatory notes weighs in at eighty-two paragraphs and the Minister for Environment, Sustainability and Housing's explanatory memorandum totals a formidable 101 pages.[59] While the explanatory material is not part of the law, it does a great deal to explain the Measure's context and aims. That said, the reasons for such elaborate underpinning in the instruments discussed in this chapter may owe as much to the complex nature of the constitutional gavotte that applies in the context of the GoWA 2006 devolution provisions, where each step benefits from (and indeed may require) clear articulation in order to reach the statute book in the first place, as to the substance of the provisions involved.

However, following the 'yes' vote in March 2011 on activating provision for the transfer of primary law-making powers, contained in Part IV of the GoWA 2006 (discussed below), to the Welsh Assembly, the initial elaborate GoWA regime that we have discussed has been rendered otiose as new more direct recourse can be made to legislative power. It remains to be seen whether such intricate justificatory documentation will feature under the next iteration of the devolution settlement that we have recently embarked on. It is, however, at least arguable that explanatory and supporting material may be scaled back where the newly minted Welsh Government feels itself to be on a firmer legal and political footing and where it will no longer, for the most part, be necessary to go 'cap in hand' to Westminster for extended powers and to trace the pedigree of each provision in minute detail in order to insulate it from potential political and legal challenge.

## Legal proceedings

An interesting by-product of devolution more generally emerged in a broadly environmental law context in the case of *R. (on the application of Deepdock Ltd) v. Welsh Ministers, Anglesey CC v. Welsh Ministers* [2007] EWHC 3347. This case involved explicit consideration of where proceedings arising from a devolved context should be heard; specifically whether judicial review proceedings between the claimant mussel farmers and the respondent public authorities should be held in Wales or London. The facts were as follows: the Assembly, having called in a planning application, had given planning permission for the building of a marina. The Minister then gave the developer permission to deposit materials on the seabed, which was necessary for the construction works to proceed. Deepdock, fearing that the deposits in question would harm the marine environment, and in particular mussel beds, brought judicial review proceedings.

The parties disagreed about the best venue for the case: the ministers preferred Wales, while Deepdock preferred London (arguing for this on the basis of the convenience of the parties and their legal representatives and the general importance of the case to all British mussel farmers and fishermen). Hickenbottom J directed that the proceedings should be heard in Wales. He viewed Deepdock's preference for London as the venue as based on the false assumption that, if the hearing was held in Wales, then it could only be in Cardiff, and a failure to consider that the most convenient venue for all of the parties was north-west Wales. Although Deepdock had instructed solicitors from England and retained London counsel, the judge did not deem the convenience of legal representatives to be the weightiest factor to be considered. Moreover, the judge took the view that the devolution settlement had transferred political accountability for the decision in question to the organs of devolved government in Wales, and that challenges to any devolved decisions should therefore be dealt with in Wales. Finally, the fact that the case raised substantial local environmental and employment issues also played a significant part in the court's decision.

The reasoning adopted on where devolved cases should be heard in *Deepdock* laid the foundations for future devolved cases in Wales generally, and for environmental claims in particular. This approach is broadly in line with developments within the legal community in the wake of devolution, which, while falling well short of any claims that Wales represents a separate jurisdiction, are supportive of its developing what has been termed a distinctive 'legal personality'.[60] The judicial approach adopted in *Deepdock* seems to be being borne out in an emerging home-grown environmental case law that is not only originating from but also being heard in Wales; see, for example, *Western Power Distribution Investments Limited v. Welsh Ministers* [2010] EWHC 800 (Admin) and *Smout v. Welsh Ministers and others* [2010] EWHC 3307 (Admin). At this relatively early stage it remains to be seen whether the 'legal personality' being developed is confined to the location of litigation or affects its substance – though the latter would arguably go beyond what the architects of the devolution settlement for Wales originally intended.

## *The Welsh environmental policy context*

Although it has latterly picked up pace, it is apparent that, thus far, Welsh Assembly legislation in general and in respect of the environment in particular has been comparatively slow to emerge. However, law does not provide the only opportunity for developing distinctiveness of approach in a devolved context; policy too has an important role to play in giving characteristic shape and direction to law as implemented. This role is arguably particularly significant in the absence of distinctive legal provision. Though some commentators point to a marked degree of policy innovation in Wales in the wake of devolution in a number of spheres, others have taken the view that this does not appear to be the case where environmental provision is concerned.[61] It would, however, seem to be the case that, in terms of the development of policy processes in a wider sense, and in particular in terms of inclusiveness and engagement, there is at least an arguable case for distinctiveness in this area. In fact, environmental policy (and the related areas of planning and sustainability) has, to date, at least in terms of consultation, been by far and away the most prolific area of WAG activity, accounting for over twice as many such exercises as any other area in the past and continuing to dominate the ongoing consultation agenda. On the eve of the 2011 referendum, out of a total of 921 closed consultation exercises, the environment accounted for 231; town and country planning for fifty-five; and sustainable development for five.[62] Of forty-nine open consultations, twenty-eight concerned environment and three town and country planning, though interestingly there were none on sustainable development. While it would go far beyond the scope of this chapter to conduct content analysis on the consultation documents in order to identify any significantly Welsh slant in them and in the final policies adopted, at the very least we can conclude that, for WAG, environment and related issues do account for a significant proportion of their public-facing consultation activity. If anything, the figures suggest that environment is actually gaining in significance in this regard, accounting for approximately 25 per cent of past consultation exercises and over 50 per cent of open ones.

## The shape of things to come: the 2011 referendum and its implications

The final issue to be considered in this chapter involves an attempt to predict the shape of things to come in respect of environmental law in Wales. The previous section suggests that the environment and related fields are likely to remain prominent amongst the Welsh Government's priorities, a view augmented by the inclusion of the Environment and Sustainable Development portfolio in the current Welsh Cabinet.[63]

The outcome of the referendum held on 3 March 2011, to determine whether or not to activate the powers contained in Part IV of the GoWA 2006, though admittedly featuring a low turnout of 35.4 per cent of the electorate, was very much more definite in its outcome than the 1997 poll on the original devolution settlement, with a 'yes' vote of 63.5 per cent.[64] As a consequence, the Welsh Government now enjoys potentially augmented political standing and accompanying legislative powers, most significantly in being able to adopt legislation without the approval of Westminster, that are much more akin to those of the Scottish Parliament and the Northern Ireland Assembly. Despite this, Carwyn Jones, the First Minister, was at pains to point out that the new legislative settlement would not herald swift change, commenting that 'The first thing you don't do is produce a raft of legislation just for the sake of it.'[65] Thus, in terms of immediate legislative priorities for the Welsh Government in so far as the environment is concerned, these can be represented as a further example of evolution, not revolution. Given how recently it was made, it would seem to be reasonable to suppose that the matters honed and prioritized over a period of years as expressed in the Environment LCO will, at least in the short to medium term, represent the central foci for devolved legislative activity. This view is supported by ongoing activity to make the Waste (Wales) Measure operational, notably the making of the Recycling, Preparation for Re-use and Composting Targets (Definitions) (Wales) Order 2011 (laid before the Assembly on 1 March 2011, just pre-dating the referendum) and the Preparation for Re-use and Composting Targets (Monitoring and Penalties) (Wales) Order 2011 (approved by the Assembly and laid just after the referendum on 7 March 2011).[66]

Nonetheless, in the longer term the blanket grant of powers in devolved areas that replaces the previous regime necessitating case-by-case petitioning of Westminster has both practical and symbolic implications. In the case of the former, the exercise by the Assembly of direct legislative powers will facilitate a timelier and more tailored legislative response to Welsh priorities. In the latter area, the 'yes' vote provides direct endorsement for an enhanced Welsh devolution settlement, on a footing that is more akin to (though still considerably less extensive than) that enjoyed by the other devolved administrations than hitherto, which boosts the Assembly's claims to legitimacy.[67] The legal profession has already begun to speculate on what the latest incarnation of the devolution settlement for Wales will mean in practice, with opinions ranging from viewing it primarily as a rationalizing provision, through those seeing an opportunity to lobby, to those envisaging more radical consequences with ramifications for local government in Wales.[68]

## Notes

1 See J. Beatson, 'Reforming an unwritten constitution', *Law Quarterly Review*, 126 (2010), 48–71.
2 Ibid., pp. 60, 49; V. Bogdanor, 'Our new constitution', *Law Quarterly Review*, 120 (2004), 242–62.
3 See Professor R. Rawlings's comments in the Report of the Commission on the Powers and Electoral Arrangements of the National Assembly for Wales (Richard Report) (2004), p. 14, para. 41, at *http://www.richardcommission.gov.uk/content/finalreport/report-e.pdf* (accessed 4 July 2011), though his observations on the continuing nature of this unity arguably require re-examination in light of subsequent developments.
4 E. Royles, *Revitalizing Democracy? Devolution and Civil Society in Wales* (Cardiff: University of Wales Press, 2007).
5 Bogdanor, 'Our new constitution'.
6 Richard Report, p. 7, paras 14–16. The argument underpinning this stance (which was ultimately proved correct) was that, once the Welsh Office was created, there would be ongoing momentum for further transfer of powers.

7 Ibid., p. 7, para. 15.
8 Ibid., p. 9, para. 20.
9 J. Bradbury and J. Mitchell, 'Devolution: between governance and territorial politics', *Parliamentary Affairs*, 58, 2 (2005), 287–301, pp. 293–5; R. Morgan, 'Clear red water', speech to the National Centre for Public Policy, Swansea, 11 December 2002, at *http://www.sochealth.co.uk/Regions/Wales/redwater.htm* (accessed 29 March 2011).
10 Beatson, 'Reforming an unwritten constitution', 51.
11 Electoral Geography 2.0, 'Wales: devolution referendum 1997', at *http://www.electoralgeography.com/new/en/countries/w/wales/wales-devolution-referendum-2007.html* (accessed 28 March 2011). For a discussion of the reasons behind the result and its implications, see L. McAllister, 'The Welsh devolution referendum: definitely, maybe?', *Parliamentary Affairs*, 51, 2 (1998), 149–65.
12 Five further TFOs were made between 1999 and 2004, though the others were concerned with updating and correcting the 1999 Order; Richard Report, pp. 183–4.
13 Note that the Secretary of State held some powers to make delegated legislation.
14 Richard Report, p. 10, para. 27.
15 Ibid., p. 88, para. 17.
16 Ibid., pp. 106–8.
17 Ibid., pp. 186–8.
18 See *http://www.environment-agency.gov.uk/aboutus/default.aspx?* (accessed 28 May 2012).
19 A. Cole, *Beyond Devolution and Decentralisation: Building Regional Capacity in Wales and Brittany* (Manchester: Manchester University Press, 2006), pp. 62–86.
20 Richard Report, p. 1, para. 1; Commission on the Assembly's Powers and Electoral Arrangements, Terms of Reference, at *http://www.richardcommission.gov.uk/content/termsref/index.htm* (accessed 4 July 2011).
21 *http://www.richardcommission.gov.uk/content/finalreport/report-e.pdf* (accessed 20 March 2011); Bradbury and Mitchell, 'Devolution', pp. 293–4.
22 Welsh Office, *Better Governance for Wales*, Cm 6582 (Cardiff: TSO, 2005); Chapter 3, in particular, 3.5–6. The separation of powers mirrored the Assembly's own internal *de facto* separation of powers (in so far as this was possible within the original devolution settlement) alluded to above, adopted in 2002 following an internal review; ibid., 1.17, 2.5.
23 Bradbury and Mitchell, 'Devolution', 294–5.
24 *Better Governance for Wales*, 3.7, 3.9. The White Paper proposed that a new, more coherent approach, giving a more pronounced consultative role to the Assembly, be applied in this area; see 3.12–13.
25 Ibid., 3.14.
26 Ibid., 3.16, 3.19.
27 For details see Devolution Guidance Note 16, 'Orders in Council under Section 95 of the Government of Wales Act 2006', at *http://www.justice.gov.uk/guidance/docs/dgn16.pdf* (accessed 15 March 2011). LCOs could be proposed by the Welsh Assembly Government, an Assembly Committee or an individual Assembly member winning a ballot (in much the same way as a Private Member's Bill at Westminster); see National Assembly for Wales, 'Legislative Competence Orders', at *http://www.assemblywales.org/bus-home/bus-legislation/bus-legislation-guidance/bus-legislation-guidance-lco.htm#lcodiagram* (accessed 28 March 2011).
28 Wales Office, 'Devolution settlement', at *http://www.walesoffice.gov.uk/devolution/* (accessed 9 March 2011).
29 SI 2010/248; National Assembly for Wales, 'Archive page: progress of legislative competence orders and measures', at *http://www.assemblywales.org/bus-home/bus-legislation/bus-legislation-progress-lcos-measures/bus-legislation-progress-lcos-measures-archive.htm#environment* (accessed 23 March 2011).

30 Devolution Guidance Note 16, at *http://www.justice.gov.uk/guidance/docs/dgn16.pdf* (accessed 29 March 2011).
31 In particular, the Devolution Guidance Notes (formerly the responsibility of the Department of Constitutional Affairs, now under the remit of the Ministry of Justice), notably 1, 'Common working arrangements', at *http://www.justice.gov.uk/guidance/docs/dgn01.pdf* (accessed 29 March 2011), 4, 'The role of the Secretary of State for Wales', at *http://www.justice.gov.uk/guidance/docs/dgn04.pdf* (accessed 29 March 2011), and 9, 'Post-devolution primary legislation affecting Wales', at *http://www.justice.gov.uk/guidance/docs/dgn09.pdf* (accessed 29 March 2011).
32 For example, in the environmental field, 'Legislative Consent Memorandum: Energy Bill', January 2011, at *http://www.assemblywales.org/sub-ld8354-e-2.pdf?langoption=3&ttl=SUB-LD8354%20-%20LEGISLATIVE%20CONSENT%20MEMORANDUM%3A%20ENERGY%20BILL* (accessed 29 March 2011).
33 Cole, *Beyond Devolution and Decentralisation*, p. 81.
34 Originally s121 GoWA 1998. No similar provisions apply to the Scottish and Northern Irish devolved regimes.
35 K. Morrow, 'Actualising sustainability in the United Kingdom: recent developments in devolved and local government', in K. Bosselmann, R. Engel and P. Taylor (eds.), *A Guide to Governance for Sustainability: Issues, Challenges and Successes*, Environmental Policy and Law Paper No. 70 (Bonn: IUCN, The World Conservation Union, 2008), pp. 171–83, at *http://cmsdata.iucn.org/downloads/eplp_70_governance_for_sustainability.pdf* (accessed 25 July 2011).
36 Welsh Assembly Government, *One Wales: One Planet – the Sustainable Development Scheme of the Welsh Assembly Government*, at *http://wales.gov.uk/docs/desh/publications/090522susdevsdspage0115en.pdf* (accessed 28 March 2011), p. 8. A. Ross, 'Why legislate for sustainable development?', *Journal of Environmental Law*, 20 (2008), 35–68, cites the GoWA 1998 as good practice in legislating for sustainable development, at p. 60.
37 WAG, *One Wales: One Planet*, p. 5.
38 WAG provides the secretariat for nrg4SD; *http://www.nrg4sd.org/* (accessed 28 March 2011).
39 Morrow, 'Actualising sustainability'.
40 SI 2010/248.
41 See S. Tierney, 'Giving with one hand: Scottish devolution within a unitary state', *International Journal of Constitutional Law*, 5 (2007), 730–53.
42 Wales participates in EU regional and international policy networks. Ministers from the devolved administrations, in contrast with sub-national bodies in other Member States, have been allowed to participate at Council meetings (see Cole, *Beyond Devolution and Decentralisation*, p. 73), though they must represent the position of the UK as a whole. More generally, Schedule 3 to the GoWA 2006 deals with UK legislation in pursuit of EU law in devolved areas.
43 A. Ross and H. Nash, 'European Union environmental law & who legislates for whom in a devolved Great Britain', *Public Law*, July (2009), 564–94, p. 589.
44 For a discussion of this in an environmental law context, see B. Jack, 'Enforcing Member State compliance with EU environmental law: a critical evaluation of the use of financial penalties', *Journal of Environmental Law*, 23 (2011), 73–95.
45 Legislation.gov.uk at *http://www.legislation.gov.uk/all?title=Legislative%20Competence%20Order%20* (accessed 13 July 2011).
46 Legislation.gov.uk, 'Wales statutory instruments', at *http://www.legislation.gov.uk/wsi* (accessed 13 July 2011).
47 SI 2010/248; SI 2010/1838, dealing, for example, with sustainable homes; SI2009/1758.
48 Fourth Delegated Legislation Committee, Draft National Assembly for Wales (Legislative Competence) (Environment) Order 2010 19/01/2010.

49 See *http://www.assemblywales.org/bus-home/bus-legislation/bus-leg-legislative-competence-orders/bus-legislation-lco-2007-2-2/bus-legislation-lco-2007-2-lco.htm* (accessed 1 April 2011).
50 J. Davidson, 'Memorandum from the Minister for Environment, Sustainability and Housing. Constitutional law: devolution, Wales. The draft National Assembly for Wales (Legislative Competence) (Environment) Order Wales 2010', at *http://www.assemblywales.org/lco-ld7799-em-e.pdf* (accessed 29 March 2011), paras 67–78.
51 Davidson, 'Memorandum from the Minister for Environment, Sustainability and Housing'.
52 Ibid., paras 4–10 and 11–23 respectively; quotation from WAG, 'A summary of the Environment Legislative Competence Order (LCO)', at *http://wales.gov.uk/docs/desh/policy/100222environmentlcosummaryen.pdf* (accessed 28 March 2011); WAG, *Environment Strategy for Wales*, 2006, at *http://wales.gov.uk/docs/desh/publications/100621wastetowardssummaryen.pdf* (accessed 1 April 2010).
53 Ibid., para 72.
54 WAG, 'A summary of the Environment Legislative Competence Order (LCO)'.
55 The proposed Shipment of Waste for Recovery (Community Involvement Arrangements) (Wales) Measure was withdrawn on 17 March 2010; see *http://www.assemblywales.org/bus-home/bus-legislation/bus-leg-measures/bus-legislation-measures-proposed_recycling.htm* (accessed 28 March 2011).
56 SI 2010 nawm 8.
57 WAG, 'A summary of the Environment Legislative Competence Order (LCO)'.
58 *http://wales.gov.uk/docs/desh/publications/100621wastetowardssummaryen.pdf* (accessed 1 April 2011).
59 J. Davidson, Minister for Environment Sustainability and Housing, 'Explanatory memorandum to the proposed Wales (Waste) Measure 2010', at *http://www.assemblywales.org/ms-ld7924-em-e.pdf* (accessed 31 March 2011).
60 G. Langdon-Down, 'How more devolved powers in Wales could affect the law', *Law Society Gazette*, 20 January 2011, at *http://www.lawgazette.co.uk/features/how-more-devolved-powers-wales-could-affect-law* (accessed 29 March 2011).
61 Cole, *Beyond Devolution and Decentralisation*, pp. 71–2; Ross and Nash, 'European Union environmental law'.
62 Data extracted from *http://wales.gov.uk/consultations/?lang+en&statusclosed* and *http://wales.gov.uk/consultations/?lang+en&statusopen* (accessed 31 March 2011).
63 'Who are the Welsh Government cabinet ministers and what are their ministerial responsibilities?', at *http://wag-en.custhelp.com/app/answers/detail/a_id/109* (accessed 7 July 2011).
64 BBC, 'Welsh referendum analysis: Wales united in clear vote', at *http://www.bbc.co.uk/news/uk-wales-12653025* (accessed 31 August 2012).
65 BBC, 'Carwyn Jones says no rush to pass laws after Yes vote', at *http://www.bbc.co.uk/news/uk-wales-politics-12653410* (accessed 28 March 2011).
66 SI 2011/551 (W. 77); *http://www.legislation.gov.uk/wsi/2011/551/introduction/made?view=plain* (accessed 1 April 2011); SI 2011/1014 (W. 152); WAG, 'The making of the Preparation for Re-use and Composting Targets (Monitoring and Penalties) (Wales) Regulations 2011', at *http://wales.gov.uk/publications/accessinfo/drnewhomepage/drlegislation/2011/reusetargetregs/?lang=en* (accessed 1 April 2011).
67 R. Scully, 'What will Wales powers referendum result mean?', at *http://www.bbc.co.uk/news/uk-wales-12587227* (accessed 28 March 2011).
68 Langdon-Down, 'How more devolved powers in Wales could affect the law'.

## Chapter 3

# Nuisance law in industrial Wales – local and national conflicts (part one): copper smelting in a pre-regulatory era

*Mark Wilde*

### Introduction

This and the following chapter focus on the role of the common law as a means of environmental protection and the key role that certain Welsh cases played in forging the law of nuisance as it currently stands. Certain cases, drawn from two industries that have played major parts in the industrial heritage of Wales, are used as historical case studies with the intention of drawing lessons for the future.

South Wales was at the forefront of the industrial revolution; this created land use conflicts on a hitherto unknown scale. In the nineteenth century the antiquated law of public and private nuisance was called upon to resolve, for example, disputes between coppermasters and landowners and farmers arising from the damage caused by 'copper smoke'. In the twentieth century the oil industry arrived in south west Wales with the construction of a number of oil refineries near Milford Haven. Once again the impact on the local environment was substantial.

The present chapter and the following chapter constitute a two-part analysis of these industries and focus on the copper and oil-refining industries respectively. The case studies raise somewhat different, although related, issues regarding the relationship between common law and public regulation. The copper cases were brought at a time when there was no public regulation of industrial activities to speak of. Those who were aggrieved by the evils of copper smoke had nowhere to turn but the common law. This exposed the weaknesses of the common law in terms of the difficulties of balancing competing land uses and the procedural obstacles associated with pressing home a successful action in the courts. By the time the oil industry arrived in Pembrokeshire in the 1950s and 1960s the legal landscape had changed and industrial emissions were the subject of regulatory regimes. Here the issue was whether the common law should be afforded the space to correct regulatory failures stemming from inadequate standards or poor enforcement or the scope for common law actions should be closed down on the basis that localized harms would already have been weighed against the national interest as part of the planning process. Although these industries were very different in terms of their modes of operation and the regulatory climates that pertained in their respective epochs, a number of common themes emerge. In both cases, economic interests came to the fore and had a major effect on the development of nuisance. The Welsh copper-smelting cases (e.g. *Bankart v. Houghton*) were precursors of the seminal House of Lords decision in *St Helens Smelting v. Tipping*, which established that harm had to be judged by reference to the character of the neighbourhood.[1] Clearly, industrialization had irrevocably changed the character of the neighbourhood in certain areas. The ability of nuisance to provide redress in respect of environmental harms caused by industrialization was further curtailed as a result of the House of Lords decision in *Allen v. Gulf Oil Refining*.[2] Here it was held that an Act of Parliament authorizing the construction of an oil refinery could give rise to a statutory authority defence. This was despite the fact that the Act was silent on the actual operation of the plant and even though the Act made no provision for compensation as regards nuisances caused by the plant.

In these cases the ability of nuisance law to protect the local environment was severely curtailed by these doctrinal developments. As regards the wider themes raised by these cases, an interesting aspect is that the public interests, adduced as reasons for limiting the scope of nuisance, were driven by the 'national' interest as determined by London. In one copper-smelting case it was famously argued that the Royal Navy would suffer if it could not obtain copper cladding for its ships. In *Allen* it is clear that domestic oil refining was regarded as being in the 'national' economic interest and there appeared to be no consideration of the impact on the village of Waterston.

In relation to the wider themes it is important to note that the chapters go beyond a strictly doctrinal analysis of the cases and delve into the legal history of the issues. To this end the author has made use of archival evidence, contemporary newspaper accounts and even the personal recollections of a lawyer involved in the *Allen* case. Such an approach is necessary because a doctrinal analysis can take us only so far in terms of understanding how a case came about and the ramifications that flow from it. A case report is no more than a snap shot of a dispute which may have been running for some years before it gets near the courtroom door. Furthermore, owing to the peculiarities of civil procedure, case reports rarely furnish us with the outcome of a dispute. Many points of law are settled as a result of interlocutory appeals on preliminary issues. The case may never actually proceed to a full trial of the facts. Historical sources can fill in the gaps by shedding light on how a case came about, the motivations of the parties and what actually happened 'on the ground' following a ruling by the court. In this respect these techniques have been used to help answer important questions regarding the relationship between common law and public regulation in an environmental context; for example, the extent to which civil juries may have been swayed by public interest arguments in the copper-smelting cases and the extent to which the *Allen* litigation resulted from the failure of planners and regulators to address the concerns of local residents.

It should also be noted that many of these themes are not merely of historic interest and may contain lessons for the future. A number of major infrastructure projects are currently in the pipeline, ranging from High Speed 2 to nuclear power stations and vast wind farms on the Welsh coast. However, in recent times the view has often been expressed that, whereas there was once a distinct lack of public scrutiny regarding major infrastructure projects, the pendulum has now swung too far the other way. The notorious public inquiry into Heathrow Terminal 5 is often held up as an example of the cumbersome nature of the planning system relating to the delivery of major infrastructure projects.[3] Given the current economic climate and the desire by the current UK coalition government to build its way out of recession by promoting major infrastructure projects, there is an appetite for less regulation and expedited planning procedures.[4] In fact, moves towards the streamlining of the planning system, in terms of the authorization of major infrastructure projects, pre-date the latest policy announcements. The Planning Act 2008 is intended to smooth the path for infrastructure projects by offering a simplified procedure. Moreover, it expressly preserves the defence of statutory authority that was at the heart of the *Allen* case. Statutory powers and procedures are often predicated on the assumption that there is no room for the common law, in that the regulatory machine would have apprised the decision maker of all he or she needs to know regarding the localized impacts of development. Cases such as *Allen* serve as salutary lessons regarding the dangers of making such assumptions.

## The copper industry

Even by the standards of the Industrial Revolution the copper industry was notorious for the highly toxic nature of its emissions. Thus it is fitting that the industry gave rise to perhaps the best-known case in nuisance, *St Helens Smelting v. Tipping*, which established the fundamental concept of character of the neighbourhood.[5] Henceforth, a degree of relativism was introduced into the law of nuisance in that, in the absence of physical damage, only harm that was exceptional given local circumstances would be actionable. There was one important proviso, however, namely that nuisance causing physical harm would remain actionable per se. In other words, physical harm would remain unreasonable irrespective of how widespread and 'normal' that type of harm was in the area. Nevertheless, as we shall see, it is not always easy to draw a neat distinction between this tangible and intangible harm. In fact Tipping was not the first person to take on the might of the coppermasters; there had been earlier cases centring upon the much bigger south Wales copper industry. The historical context of these cases sheds some light on how the land use conflicts resulting from the Industrial Revolution brought about the doctrinal developments established in *Tipping*.

## A brief history of copper mining and smelting in the UK

In fact the roots of the UK copper-smelting industry were established centuries before the Industrial Revolution. Copper ore has been abstracted and smelted in Britain since the Bronze Age, although smelting on an industrial scale did not commence until the Elizabethan era.[6] In 1568 the Mines Royal Society was incorporated with the objective of unlocking the mineral wealth of the realm, largely for military purposes. The Society imported all the requisite skills and expertise from Augsburg in Germany, the acknowledged world leader in copper-smelting technology at the time. Initial smelting operations were established in Keswick but by the 1590s the main base of the nascent industry had shifted to south Wales, where the industry took root in the Neath and later the Tawe valleys. There were various logistical reasons for the move including the abundance of fuel for the furnaces in the form of coal and timber, and that copper ore could be shipped across the Bristol Channel from Cornwall. Furthermore, it is surely no coincidence that one of the parties who stood to gain most from the move was William Herbert, the First Earl of Pembroke and a major Mines Royal shareholder.[7]

The Mines Royal Society laid the foundations of one of south Wales's most important industries, and the region remained a major world centre for copper smelting until the decline of the British industry in the late nineteenth century. In the interim a smaller copper-smelting centre emerged in a hitherto rural part of Lancashire.[8] The isolated St Helen's Chapel gave its name to the industrial town that grew there. A concatenation of circumstances led to the development of copper smelting in Lancashire. The first copper smelters were built following the discovery of copper ore in Parys Mountain on Anglesey, from which the ore could be easily shipped to north west England, where the smelters were fed by abundant resources of local coal. In fact the coalmasters actively courted the mineral refiners by offering cheap land near the coal mines to build the smelters and supplies of coal at preferential rates.[9]

By the late eighteenth century, copper was in high demand for manufacturing all manner of objects from pots and pans to copper cladding for ships of the Royal Navy. When combined with zinc, a highly versatile alloy was produced in the form of brass. The Industrial Revolution created demand for copper and brass on an unprecedented scale. The malleable and heat-resistant properties of the materials rendered them ideal for manufacturing the intricate components of steam engines. However, this increased demand hastened the depletion of domestic reserves of copper ore and nearly led to the premature demise of the British smelting industry. In 1825 the industry was revived by a decision to reduce the duty payable on imported copper ore.[10] The existing copper-smelting plants were situated near great ports, which facilitated their reliance upon imported ore. The south Wales industry was supplied by ore shipped into Swansea, and St Helens was fed by Liverpool, to which it was now connected by canal.[11] Henceforth British copper smelting went from strength to strength and consolidated the fortunes of the small number of family firms who had come to dominate the industry. Foremost amongst these were the Cornish mining dynasties, including the Vivians and the Grenfells, who had diversified into smelting.

The St Helens copper industry received a further boost from the close links that it was able to forge with the alkali industry thanks to a fortuitous synergy in production processes.[12] The St Helens alkali industry used the highly polluting Leblanc process to produce caustic soda, a vital ingredient in the manufacture of soap and glass. The production process used salt and sulphuric acid, which were chemically combined and later burnt with coal and chalk. The cost of sulphuric acid reached extortionate levels because of shortages of Sicilian sulphur, and an alternative was needed. The industry's chemists discovered that sulphur could be extracted from pyrites. It so happened that the copper industry had begun importing high-grade pyretic ores from Cuba following the reduction in excise duty. This led to the development of the 'wet copper' refining process whereby a chemical process was used to produce copper sulphate. Once the copper had been abstracted from this solution the residual sulphuric acid could be supplied to the alkali industry.

Copper smelting was one of the most polluting activities in industrial history, and the surrounding countryside and farmland paid a heavy price for the economic benefits generated by the coppermasters. The refining process involved 'roasting' or, to use the technical description, 'calcining' the ores to burn off impurities including sulphur and arsenic. The deathly white smoke was known as 'copper smoke' and its harmful nature was apparent from the earliest days of the industry. On an industrial scale the fumes poisoned animals, scorched crops and denuded trees. The calcining process had to be conducted several times before the smelting process could even be commenced, and the latter process was highly polluting in its own right. The damage was vividly described by Thomas Williams, a local doctor who carried out extensive research into the effects of copper smoke and published a book on the subject:

> Subjected for 150 long years to the corrosive agency of sulphurous vapours, a smiling valley has at length, indeed, been transformed into a desert scene of ashes and lifeless gravel tracts. The mountains of scoriae ... and other refuse products which spread over many superficial acres in the vicinity of the works, are utterly infertile. Black and uninviting to the eye, they are capable of lodging no single form of life.[13]

In 1821 a number of local landowners, including the Duke of Beaufort and the Earl of Jersey, were sufficiently moved by the problem to establish a prize fund and launched a competition to find a method to:

> Obviate all inconvenience arising from the smoke produced by the calcining and smelting of copper ores, and at the same time to preserve much valuable matter that now is lost by escaping through the flues of the furnaces.[14]

The competition attracted only a limited number of contenders, one of whom was the current incumbent of the Vivian's smelting business, John Henry Vivian. J. H. Vivian's father had invested heavily in his son's education. The investment had paid off in that J. H. Vivian was renowned as one of the world's leading metallurgists. It was, perhaps, his passion for science, rather than the relatively modest prize of £1,000, that motivated him to participate in the competition. Indeed, he spent far more than this in his attempts to find a solution. The competition is also interesting in that the wording of the notice links a cleaner process with a more efficient process which captures valuable particles that might otherwise escape up the flue along with less desirable elements. Indeed, the fact that cleaner technologies are often more efficient technologies is a recurrent theme in the history of pollution abatement technology. From a commercial perspective this phenomenon would also have been of great interest to Vivian.

Despite the expertise and resources that Vivian had to throw at the problem, the solution proved elusive.[15] He experimented with shower chambers at the Haford works whereby water sprays were used in an attempt to condense the harmful materials. Although the method dealt with certain chemicals, it failed to deal with the key harmful ingredient, sulphur dioxide. His rivals' experiments, which included attempts to vaporize the harmful matter by feeding the gases through long horizontal flues heated to extreme temperatures, fared little better. The trials were abandoned and Vivian reverted to the age-old dispersal method and built tall chimneys at the Haford works. Vivian was in no doubt that this would disperse and dilute the fumes to the extent that they could do no harm; this view proved to be overly optimistic. With no regulator to call upon and no solution forthcoming from the industry itself it was only a matter of time before the common law would be called upon to resolve the matter.

## Copper smelting and the common law of nuisance

The celebrated case of *St Helens Smelting v. Tipping* has focused attention on copper smelting in the St Helens area. However, earlier litigation focused upon the much larger south Wales industry, where major actions had already been pursued by local farmers, a prominent member of the landed gentry and an affluent newcomer with dreams of establishing an idyllic rural retreat.

### *The Llansamlet farmers*

The tall smokestacks installed at the Haford works did not enable the sulphurous acid gas to clear the neighbouring hills in the manner in which Vivian had intended. The fumes were channelled up the valley by the prevailing winds and, because the gas was heavier than air, it would sit over the valley in a white cloud when pinned down by temperature inversion. In 1833 a group of farmers upwind from the Haford works at Llansamlet pooled their resources and succeeded in filing a bill of indictment in public nuisance against the Vivians.[16] J. H. Vivian was especially aggrieved in that he had devoted more time and investment to solving the copper smoke problem than any of his fellow coppermasters. The indictment was perceived as a threat to the future of the copper-smelting industry and the family was determined to crush the action by engaging perhaps the most heavyweight and talented advocate of the day, Sir James Scarlett KC, who commanded a fee of 400 guineas for taking the case.[17]

The trial was held at Carmarthen Quarter Sessions in March 1833, and the prosecution produced a stream of witnesses who attested to the damage to crops and livestock caused by the copper smoke. However, the jury was swayed by Scarlett's famed oratory and his portrayal of 'the club' (as he termed the farmers' collective formed to pursue the action) as rude agriculturalists intent upon destroying an industry of vital importance to the local economy. He even went so far as to suggest that the action jeopardized the defence of the realm in that closure of the industry would deprive the Royal Navy of copper cladding for its ships. In his summing up, Patteson J directed the jury that they should put aside issues of public utility, but to no avail, the jury finding such arguments irresistible. A number of farmers made a further attempt to hold the coppermasters to account and in 1834 brought an action in private nuisance against the Grenfells' Middle Bank Works. On this occasion the jury was not persuaded by the public utility argument and it was accepted that the activity amounted to a nuisance. However, it was a pyrrhic victory in that minimal damages were awarded on the basis that the bulk of the damage was due to poor farming methods and animal husbandry.[18]

One might ask why the poorly equipped farmers were at the forefront of the early nuisance campaigns when much of the adversely affected land formed part of great estates owned by the Duke of Beaufort and the Earl of Jersey. Indeed, at the Carmarthen trial Sir James Scarlett asked the jury why such figures had not pursued actions if the issue was of such great magnitude.[19] In fact the answer is simply that the local landowners had been instrumental in the development of the copper smelting industry. This is why the Earl of Jersey first attempted to find a solution through promoting a competition rather than pursuing the confrontational approach offered by the courts. In fact, with no solution forthcoming, Lord Jersey was eventually driven to take legal action. However, he found that his legal position was seriously compromised by the involvement of his forebears, and indeed his personal involvement, in the industry.

## *The Earl of Jersey v. Williams and others*

In 1814 George Child Villiers, the Fifth Earl of Jersey, gained ownership of the Briton Ferry Estate as a result of a complex series of property transactions within the family.[20] The estate encompassed much of the Tawe Valley, where copper smelting was at its height. A number of Lord Jersey's forebears had been involved in the development of the local industry and in 1828 the Earl himself leased land to the Grenfells upon which they built the Middle Bank Works. The Middle Bank works were later to become the focus of the Llansamlet farmers' private nuisance action referred to above. By the 1830s those parts of the estate that remained in agricultural use were suffering the effects of the copper smoke. Much of the damage was attributed to the Williams and Foster families' giant Morfa works, which had been built immediately adjacent to the Vivians' Haford works. The plants were to remain bitter rivals for decades to come until the merger of the businesses in a restructuring of the industry that took place in the twilight years of British copper smelting.[21] However, both the plots upon which these plants stood had been leased from the Duke of Beaufort, to whom the land had earlier been devised by one George Lord Vernon and one William Augustus Henry Villiers. The latter was the Earl's younger brother and immediate predecessor in title.[22]

The Morfa works were expanded throughout the 1830s yet the Earl held back from legal action, possibly conscious of his awkward connections with the industry. However, by 1840 the situation was so severe that Lord Jersey was moved to commence an action in private nuisance in the Court of Queen's Bench. He sought the enormous sum of £20,000 in respect of damage to his reversionary interest in farmland leased to Charles Henry Smith. It was claimed that the works emitted 'divers large quantities of deleterious and noxious matters' that had 'corrupted' the lands of several farms and 'impregnated' the walls of dwelling houses.[23] The defendants turned to equity in order to prevent the legal action from proceeding on two main grounds. First, it was argued that the Earl and his family had been heavily involved in the very activity of which complaint was made. Second, it was argued that the Earl's failure to bring an action for several years amounted to at best acquiescence and at worst active encouragement in the expending of large sums of money in extending the works. As regards the first argument, Lord Jersey argued in his demurrer that any transactions made by his predecessors in title could not result in any restrictive covenants running with the land that precluded successors in title from pursuing actions in nuisance. On appeal the Lord Chancellor declined to rule on this issue, finding there was sufficient evidence of acquiescence or encouragement arising from Lord Jersey's delay in bringing the action.[24] Thus the action was nipped in the bud and the substantive issues of law were never tried.

By the close of the 1840s the coppermasters had defeated both the farmers and the landed gentry. There was to be one further major reported action, this time brought by a new product of Victorian society: the successful professional city gentleman seeking a rural retreat.

## Houghton v. Bankart

Dugdale Houghton was a successful land agent and surveyor from Birmingham and in the early 1850s he set about upgrading an estate to the east of Neath that he had inherited some years earlier. His intention was to create a rural idyll to which he could retreat at weekends and eventually retire. To this end he acquired modest numbers of livestock and set about improving the land. However, the bucolic dream began to sour following his decision to acquire the leases of two farms at Coed-y-Arl Uchaf and Coed-y-Arl Ishaf.[25]

The farms were situated in the vicinity of the Red Jacket Copper Works, which had been recently acquired by Frederick Bankart, a solicitor by profession from London. When Houghton first viewed the properties in 1853 there was no sign of damage to the land. This may have been because at the time Bankart was experimenting with the wet copper process, which reduces the number of calcining operations. However, shortly after Houghton acquired the lease the experiments were abandoned on the grounds that the process was too costly and the plant reverted to dry smelting. Furthermore, the capacity of the plant was increased by the construction of additional furnaces. Before long Houghton noted the deleterious effect upon crops and livestock. Crops failed and livestock died, including two prized horses, Beauty and Comet. The animals had succumbed to an array of symptoms including swollen heads and tongues, ulcers on their jaws, tumours in their throats, swollen joints and brittle bones.[26]

In 1858 Houghton commenced an action for damages in nuisance, and the case was heard at the Carmarthen Summer Assizes of that year.[27] Houghton was represented by William Grove, both a lawyer and a scientist of some note, who used his expertise to build a scientific case linking the damage to the copper smoke from the Red Jacket works.[28] To this end he engaged the services of William Herepath, Professor of Analytical Chemistry at the Bristol Medical

School. Herepath produced compelling evidence that large blood and water blisters on the lungs of afflicted animals were caused by the inhalation of sulphurous fumes. Further damage to joints and so forth was consistent with the ingestion of contaminated grass. The jury rejected a somewhat speculative and unscientific defence argument that sought to cast doubt on the causal link, namely that the land was afflicted by a sort of malaise or miasma in which plants and animals could not flourish. This was attributed to the salt marshes and stagnant waters at the mouth of the estuary.[29] The jury was not convinced and found in favour of Houghton, awarding him £450.[30]

Nevertheless, Bankart was not yet ready to concede defeat and filed a bill in Chancery seeking an injunction to restrain Houghton from recovering the damages on the grounds that he had acquired the farm leases in full knowledge of the existence of the plant. Romilly MR held that the magnitude of the harm was far greater than Houghton could have foreseen when he took on the leases and he was thus not guilty of unconscionable conduct.[31] Thus Houghton was entitled to his damages; however, the Master of the Rolls also observed that had it been Houghton seeking an injunction the relief would also have been denied on the facts. In other words there was a lack of unconscionable conduct on both sides and the case was not, therefore, one in which equity ought to intervene.

Houghton's victory had no effect on the operation of the Red Jacket works. In fact, pollution actually increased as more and larger furnaces were installed. In 1860 the parties were back in court in a further nuisance action brought by Houghton, this time at the Swansea Summer Assizes of July 1860.[32] On this occasion Houghton sought the very large sum of £8,000 in respect of damage to everything from trees and prized cattle to 'copper smoke rabbits'. Once again Houghton was represented by William Grove, who repeated the meticulous scientific arguments that formed the mainstay of the first case. On this occasion the defendant's case was presented by Montague Chambers, who somewhat wrong-footed Grove by not engaging the plaintiff on the causation front at all. Chambers told the jury that they should consider whether the copper smelting had been conducted in a fit and proper place, in a fit and proper manner, and should also consider the interests of trade and commerce. Indeed, the public benefit argument had held sway with the jury in the Llansamlet case some years earlier. In summing up, the judge, Bramwell B, cast doubt on whether the activity had been conducted in a fit and proper place. He suggested that the Tawe Valley, which had already been damaged beyond repair, might have been a more suitable location. However, the judge was scathing regarding the level of damages claimed. In the event, the jury held that the case in nuisance had been made out but awarded a mere £175 in damages. Houghton later pressed ahead with an attempt to gain injunctive relief but eventually conceded to an order, by mutual consent, that the defendant should be at liberty to purchase his interest in the afflicted farms instead.[33] Houghton returned to the Midlands with his dreams of a rural idyll in tatters but with the consolation of being able to afford a splendid mansion in Worcestershire.

The references to 'fit and proper place' and 'public utility' that had been made in the Swansea trial were highly significant. They reflected major developments occurring in the law of private nuisance regarding the extent to which such considerations should be allowed to determine whether an activity was to be actionable. These debates culminated in litigation that was unfolding in the United Kingdom's second copper-smelting centre, St Helens.

## *St Helens Smelting v. Tipping*

William Whitacre Tipping, a retired cotton spinner from Wigan and eccentric recluse, purchased New Bold Hall and considerable surrounding land in about 1860. The purchase included some 1,300 acres of land, comprising parkland, pleasure grounds, plantations, ornamental gardens and farmland, and a number of livestock. The land had once formed part of the vast Bold estate but had been broken up by the family to reduce the costs of upkeep and to realize the capital value.[34] In an earlier transaction a neighbouring plot had been leased for industrial use and by the time Tipping arrived a copper smelter was in operation. The smelter had been recently acquired by a consortium led by Mr Walter R. Critchley and Lord Alfred Henry Paget, trading under the name the Commercial Copper Smelting Company. The new owners improved and extended the plant and before long the familiar effects of copper smoke were apparent on Tipping's property. Attempts to reach an amicable settlement failed and proceedings in nuisance were commenced.

The case was tried before Mellor J at Liverpool in August 1863 and considerable scientific evidence was adduced in order to establish the causal link between the emissions from St Helens Smelting (as the business had by now been renamed) and Tipping's losses.[35] The plaintiff's main expert witness was Professor Frederick C. Calvert FRS, Professor of Chemistry at the Manchester Royal Institution, who used kites to take atmospheric samples. Witness testimony was provided by William Hill, a gardener at Bold Hall for thirty years, who attested that the damage to trees and plants coincided with the recent expansion of the facility. Similar evidence was provided by other agriculturalists, horticulturalists and market gardeners whose businesses had been affected by the copper smoke. However, in common with the earlier *Houghton v. Bankart* case, the issue turned on whether the activity had been conducted in a fit and proper place rather than causation. The jury found that the smelting had not been conducted in a fit and proper place and awarded Tipping damages of £361 18s. 4½d.

The case exposed a growing area of uncertainty in the law of nuisance, namely what was meant by the term 'fit and proper place' and to what extent public utility was relevant to making this determination. On this there were two inconsistent recent authorities, both of which conveniently concerned harm caused by smoke from brick kilns. In *Hole v. Barlow* the trial judge, Byles J, linked the issue of fit and proper place with public utility by stating that industry would be 'greatly injured' if all those in the neighbourhood could maintain an action in nuisance.[36] The decision was upheld by the Court of Common Pleas, where Willes J further muddied the waters by stating it was also appropriate to consider whether the plant had been 'reasonably conducted'. This appeared to introduce a fault requirement into the issue of 'reasonable user'. In *Bamford v. Turnley* the Court of Exchequer Chamber rejected the fault requirement and took a much more restrictive view of the relevance of locality and the economic benefits of industry.[37] It soon became clear that Tipping's action would become a test case for resolving how the law of nuisance should be adapted to cope with the growing problem of land use conflict after the Industrial Revolution.

In the House of Lords the leading judgment was delivered by the Lord Chancellor, Lord Westbury.[38] His Lordship stated that a neighbourhood largely devoted to manufacturing might well be a 'fit place'. However, he rejected the Appellant's assertion that this would allow the activity to be continued with impunity no matter how severe the ensuing damage. The Lord Chancellor went on to hold that there was a difference between 'material injury to property' and 'sensible personal discomfort'. The latter type of harm would be actionable only if it was over and above what would be expected in a locality of that nature. Material injury would remain actionable notwithstanding how much damage had already been caused to the locality by the activity. Public utility arguments were invoked in order to justify the insertion of this additional requirement in respect of harm falling short of 'material injury'. Henceforth, the 'locality doctrine' became enshrined as a central pillar of nuisance, despite the fact that, as Simpson has observed, Lord Westbury's discussion of this issue was strictly *obiter* in that only physical damage was at issue in the case.[39] Furthermore, it has never been entirely clear where the border lies between 'material injury' and 'trifling inconveniences'. There has been an assumption that 'material injury' must mean physical damage in the sense of damaged crops or buildings; the effect of this has been to neutralize many claims that were far from trivial yet failed to meet this threshold of tangibility.[40]

Of course, so far as Tipping himself was concerned, these considerations were of no importance in that the damage which his estate had sustained fell squarely within the tangible category. However, the victory did not resolve the matter and the pollution continued unabated. Before long, Tipping returned to court in order to pursue an application for injunctive relief in Chancery. It should be noted at this point that Tipping's case was very similar to that of Dugdale Houghton in that both men knowingly acquired land in the vicinity of copper smelters. In both cases production dramatically increased shortly after the new owners took possession with the result that the harm was greater than they could have foreseen.

However, whereas the court indicated that Houghton would have been precluded from injunctive relief, in *Tipping*, Wood VC had no hesitation in granting the relief. The decision was upheld on appeal to the Court of Appeal in Chancery, where Knight-Bruce LJ held that where a nuisance has been established and damages awarded 'a Court of Equity should grant an injunction to prevent the continuance of the nuisance'.[41]

## Conclusion: the decline and fall of the UK copper industry after *Tipping*

As the St Helens litigation reached its climax, major developments were afoot regarding pollution abatement technology for the copper-smelting industry. By now the Vivian family business was in the hands of J. H. Vivian's son, Hussey H. Vivian, who continued his father's attempts to find a solution to the copper smoke issue. H. Vivian acquired the patent to a system developed by the German metallurgist Moritz Gerstenhofer. Gerstenhofer calciners condensed the acid gas and converted it to sulphuric acid.[42] This was in itself a valuable by-product and could be sold for use in fertilizer manufacturer and to the local tinplate industry for use in the pickling process. Vivian invested £60,000 installing Gerstenhofer calciners at the Haford works and proselytized widely about the technology.[43] The existence of a viable technology combined with Tipping's recent victory seemed set to force major changes in the UK industry. Indeed, there was an early victory when English Copper capitulated and installed Gerstenhofer calciners in response to a nuisance action commenced by Nash Edwards Vaughan MP in respect of damage to his Rheola Estate in the Nedd Valley.[44] Nevertheless, Vivian's fellow coppermasters resisted change and were deeply suspicious of Vivian's motives on the grounds that he just happened to own the patent to one of the leading pollution abatement technologies.[45]

By the 1860s the legislature had begun to get to grips with acidic industrial emissions and in 1863 the first Alkali Act was passed, which imposed emission limits for hydrochloric (or muriatic) acid released by the alkali industry. The Act resulted from the findings of the House of Lord Select Committee on Noxious Vapours.[46] The emission limits had been made possible by the invention of Gossage towers, which condensed most of the acidic emissions.[47] However, sulphur dioxide from the copper industry was less readily condensed and the lack of a viable technical solution dissuaded the Committee from recommending that the copper industry should be included within the regime.

In 1878 the Royal Commission on Noxious Vapours returned to the issue of whether the copper-smelting industry should be brought within the regulatory regime established by the first Alkali Act.[48] The Commission noted that there had been considerable advances since the Select Committee of 1862 concluded that there were no viable means of arresting the copper smoke. The Royal Commission accepted that emission limits could be imposed at plants using the cleaner wet copper process. However, despite Vivian's spirited evidence in support of his Gerstenhofer system, the Commission concluded that there was no economically viable method of dealing with copper smoke from dry smelting. In this respect the Commission accepted the evidence of Vivian's competitors to the effect that such large costs should not be imposed upon an industry that was struggling to compete in a now global business. For example, Chili, which had hitherto exported its ores to south Wales, had by now established its own refining facilities. Thus the Commission concluded:

> On the whole, therefore, although we are much impressed with the magnitude of the escape of acid vapours from copper works, we think that in the present state of the trade, the adoption of the best practicable means now could not be generally enforced without danger to the continuance of the works, and consequent injury to the many persons directly and indirectly dependent on them.[49]

This statement was highly significant in that it signalled that the legislature had no intention of stepping in and providing a regulatory regime to remediate the harms brought to the fore by the *Tipping* litigation. Once again, the common law was left to hold the fort and it would be many years before the copper industry was brought within the fold of the Alkali regime.

In any event, the industry was already in decline, although there was a late revival of the industry following the discovery of nickel in the Sudbury basin in Ontario and Ludwig Mond's decision to build his plant at Clydach.[50] The Mond plant survives to this day as a small refiner of specialist nickel products, although it is the last remnant of the Swansea industry. The old family firms were merged, nationalized and eventually bought by ICI before fading into history.

## Notes

1 (1860) 27 Beav. 425, 54 E. R. 167; (1865) 11 H. L. C. 642, 11 E. R. 1483.
2 [1981] A. C. 1001 (HL).
3 See, for example, B. Kelly, 'The Planning Bill: implications of the proposals for a new regime for major infrastructure for democracy and delivery', *Journal of Planning and Environment Law*, 13 (2008), 1–12.
4 The autumn statement of 2011 by the Chancellor of the Exchequer, George Osborne, was largely devoted to a major increase in funding for major infrastructure projects as a means of stimulating the economy. Headline figures that grabbed the media's attention included a commitment to devote an additional £5 billion to capital projects, forming part of a wider package of measures amounting to some £30 billion. See H. M. Treasury, 'Autumn statement 2011', Cm 8231 (2011). For media commentary see Patrick Wintour, Larry Elliott and Hélène Mulholland, 'George Osborne's £5bn gamble to stave off recession', *The Guardian* (London), 28 November 2011, 1.
5 (1865) 11 H. L. C. 642, 11 E. R. 1483.

6 P. T. Craddock, 'Bronze age metallurgy in Britain', *Current Archaeology*, 99 (1986), 106–9; for the leading account of the Elizabethan copper industry see M. B. Donald, *Elizabethan Copper: The History of the Company of Mines Royal 1568–1605* (London: Pergamon, 1955).
7 See R. Rees, *King Copper: South Wales and the Copper Trade 1584–1895* (Cardiff: University of Wales Press, 2000), p. 5.
8 See T. C. Barker and J. R. Harris, *A Merseyside Town in the Industrial Revolution: St Helens 1750–1900* (Liverpool: University of Liverpool Press, 1954), ch. 7.
9 Ibid. For example, the coalmaster John Mackay attracted the Parys Mine Company to his Ravenhead estate with the offer of all the brick clay they desired to build the plant and all the coal they required at the rate of 5/– per ton (30 cwt).
10 Ibid., p. 240.
11 Ibid. Between 1828 and 1839 annual imports of copper ore into British ports rose from a mere 282 tons to 30,000 tons.
12 Ibid., pp. 243–4. See also B. W. Clapp, *An Environmental History of Britain* (London: Longman, 1994), pp. 26–7.
13 Thomas Williams, *Report on the Copper Smoke, Its Influence on the Public Health, and the Industrial Diseases of Coppermen* (Swansea, 1854), pp. 12–13. For an in-depth historical account of the damage caused by copper smoke see E. Newell, 'Atmospheric pollution and the British copper industry, 1690–1920', *Technology and Culture*, 38 (1997), 655–89.
14 The competition was advertised in these terms in *The Times*, 21 November 1821, 2. See also Rees, *King Copper*, p. 66.
15 For an account of the trials conducted by the contenders see Rees, *King Copper*, pp. 67–74.
16 See Rees, *King Copper*, ch. 5. His account of the trial is drawn from reports of the proceedings in the *Cambrian* (8 and 16 March 1833) and the *Welshman* (8 March 1833).
17 Scarlett had served as Attorney General under Wellington. His compelling manner over both juries and judges was renowned at the bar, where a joke circulated that he had invented a machine for making judges nod. See G. F. R. Barker, rev. Elisabeth A. Cawthon, 'Scarlett, James, first Baron Abinger (1769–1844)', in H. C. G. Matthew and Brian Harrison (eds.), *Oxford Dictionary of National Biography* (Oxford: Oxford University Press, 2004); online edn., ed. Lawrence Goldman, January 2009, at *http://www.oxforddnb.com/view/article/24783* (accessed 5 September 2012).
18 See Rees, *King Copper*, ch. 5, citing the report of the trial in the *Cambrian* (9 August 1834).
19 Ibid., p. 83.
20 The intricacies of these transactions are not necessary for present purposes, but they are set out in detail in a reported case of a property dispute involving the Fifth Earl: *Smith v. Earl of Jersey* (1821) 3 Bligh P. C. 290, 4 E. R. 610.
21 See Rees, *King Copper*, pp. 20–1.
22 The above transactions are set out in a case report of the Chancery proceedings: *Williams and Others v. the Earl of Jersey* (1840) 4(16) *The Legal Guide* 246.
23 Ibid.
24 *Williams and Others v. The Earl of Jersey* (1841) CR. & PH. 91, 94; 41 ER 424, 425.
25 For an account of the background to the case see Rees, *King Copper*, ch. 7.
26 Ibid., p. 117. These were the classic symptoms of *efryddod*, as the condition was termed by the Welsh farmers.
27 For an account of the trial see Rees, *King Copper*, pp. 115–21, citing reports of the proceedings in the *Cambrian* (6 and 13 August 1858).
28 Ibid., p. 116. Grove had recently acted as one of the defence counsel in the Dr Palmer (William Palmer) poison case, which excited a great deal of public interest in 1856. It had been his task to challenge the prosecution's scientific evidence. Nevertheless, the

defendant was found guilty and hanged at Stafford Gaol on 14 June 1856 before 35,000 spectators.
29 Ibid., p. 120.
30 Ibid., p. 121.
31 *Bankart v. Houghton* (1860) 27 Beav. 425, 54 E. R. 167.
32 For an account of the trial see Rees, *King Copper*, pp. 121–6, citing reports of the proceedings in the *Cambrian* (27 July 1860) and the *Swansea and Glamorgan Herald* (25 July 1860).
33 There is one further reported case involving the parties, relating to the valuation of the estate: *Houghton v. Bankart* (1861) 3 D. E. G. F. & J. 16, 45 E. R. 783. Note the unwitting premonition of twentieth-century Coasean analysis; see chapter 4, p. 55.
34 For the definitive historical account of the case see A. W. B. Simpson, 'Victorian judges and the problem of social cost: *Tipping v. St Helens Smelting Company*', in A. W. B. Simpson (ed.), *Leading Cases in the Common Law* (Oxford: Clarendon Press, 1995). By the 1850s the estate was in the hands of Sir Henry Hoghton, the eighth baronet, who had acquired his late wife's family seat at Hoghton Tower near Preston. Having decided to take up permanent residence at Hoghton Tower, he set about divesting himself of the Bold estate in 1858. After he failed to sell the estate as a single lot the land was broken up into smaller lots, which were auctioned off from 1859.
35 A full account of the trial was set out in the *Liverpool Mercury* (28 August 1863).
36 (1858) 4 C. B. (NS) 334, 140 E. R. 1113.
37 (1862) 3 B. & S. 66, 122 E. R. 27.
38 (1865) 11 H. L. C. 642, 11 E. R. 1483.
39 Simpson, *Leading Cases in the Common Law*, pp. 189–90.
40 Ibid.
41 (1865) L. R. 1 Ch. App 66.
42 See Rees, *King Copper*, pp. 128–30.
43 In 1865 *The Times* published an article on Vivian's acquisition of the Gerstenhofer patent and reported that the firm hoped to produce 1,000 tons of sulphuric acid per week; 'The copper smoke question', *The Times*, 21 August 1865.
44 See Rees, *King Copper*, p. 131. Vaughan made some reference to the damage to his estate a letter to *The Times* in September 1865; he discovered that a large wood of 400 acres was 'pining' and after sending samples to 'one of the most eminent analytical chymists in London' was told that 'the specimens gave sulphuric acid and recognizable quantities of arsenic'; N. Edwards Vaughan, Letters to the Editor, 'Copper smoke', *The Times*, 11 September 1865.
45 See Rees, *King Copper*, pp. 131–2.
46 *Report from the Select Committee of the House of Lords on Injury from Noxious Vapours* (C (1st series) 486, 1862). The Earl of Derby, a former prime minister and influential political figure, was largely responsible for instigating the enquiry. He owned estates in the area that had been affected by the emissions but Baker and Harris cite evidence that suggests that his actions were also a personal favour to his friend Sir Robert Gerard, a major benefactor of Lord Derby's earlier political campaigns. The Gerards were also great landowners in the area and had invested considerable resources in pursuing private actions against the alkali industry. See J. P. S. McLaren, 'Nuisance law and the industrial revolution: some lessons from social history', *Oxford Journal of Legal Studies*, 155 (1983), 194–5; Simpson, *Leading Cases in the Common Law*, p. 185.
47 The eponymous inventor was one William Gossage, who invented the technique in 1836 at his works in Stoke Prior in Worcestershire. The hydrochloric acid was condensed in towers packed with damp brushwood, which absorbed the acid. However, this produced a weak acid solution that in itself created a new 'waste stream', which was very often discharged into rivers. Thus the need to adopt an integrated approach to pollution

management was discovered at a very early stage. See Clapp, *An Environmental History of Britain*, p. 24.
48 Report of the Royal Commission on Noxious Vapours (C (2nd series) 2159).
49 Ibid., 16–19.
50 See R. O. Roberts, 'The development and decline of the non-ferrous metal smelting industries in south Wales', in W. E. Minchinton (ed.), *Industrial South Wales 1750–1914: Essays in Welsh Economic History* (London: Frank Cass & Co, 1969).

# Chapter 4

# Nuisance law in industrial Wales – local and national conflicts (part two): oil refining, the common law and regulation

*Mark Wilde*

### Introduction: from copper refining to oil refining

As the copper-refining industry withered and eventually died out, another form of mineral refining, namely oil refining, was on the ascendancy further along the coast in Pembrokeshire.[1] However, by this stage the legal landscape had altered in that a more comprehensive system of environmental regulation had evolved. Atmospheric emissions from industrial facilities such as oil refineries were subject to the control of the Alkali Inspectorate (an anachronistic title given that the industry from which it had taken its name had largely died out by this time) and local authorities, which had statutory nuisance powers under the Public Health Acts. However, the Alkali Inspectorate was notorious for its cosy relationship with industry and the opacity of its decision-making processes. It was not greatly in evidence regarding the problem of atmospheric emissions from the oil-refining industry, and this may have been one of the factors that compelled local residents to seek a remedy under the common law in *Allen v. Gulf Oil Refining Ltd.*[2]

The fact that public law regulation had by now occupied territory that had largely been the domain of the common law at the time of the copper-smelting cases created new tensions between public and private laws. This centred on the extent to which public powers should be permitted to abrogate existing private rights. Of particular concern was the defence of statutory authority, which effectively established immunity from civil liability in respect of nuisances caused by activities authorized under statute. The defence is largely based on an assumption that the legislature must have foreseen possible nuisances yet deemed them to be an acceptable price to pay for the economic benefits flowing from the land use. If such a calculation has been made it would be morally repugnant to require the unfortunate local residents to shoulder the costs of the unwanted by-products of the scheme such as pollution without compensation. However, this is the outcome of the only reported case to emerge from nuisance disputes regarding the UK oil-refining industry, *Allen v. Gulf Oil Refining Ltd.*

As will be seen, the issue remains of contemporary importance in that statutory authority has been expressly preserved by the latest planning legislation. As noted in the general introduction to this two-part analysis, this is a cause for concern in the light of the proposed spending on large-scale infrastructure projects. Given the centrality of statutory authority in this context, it is necessary to consider the origins and scope of the defence in some detail.

## The statutory authority defence in nuisance and *Rylands v. Fletcher*

The defence of statutory authority applies in public and private nuisance and *Rylands v. Fletcher*.[3] In short, where a development has been sanctioned by legislative powers, such as a private Act of Parliament, the promoter is empowered to cause harm that *inevitably* flows from the use of those powers. Such harm would otherwise constitute an actionable nuisance or liability under *Rylands v. Fletcher*. The defence arose as a direct result of the 'railway revolution' in the nineteenth century. In *R. v. Pease* the Court of Kings Bench acknowledged that a railway could not be operated without causing certain nuisances; the startling of horses by steam locomotives in this case.[4] As the enabling Act expressly authorized the operation of steam locomotives, it was safe to assume that, by conferring those powers, Parliament had intended to bestow a degree of immunity upon the promoters in respect of that type of harm.[5] This new defence of 'statutory authority' was later invoked in respect of all manner of railway nuisances including the famous 'railway sparks cases' used by Pigou and Coase to illustrate the contrasting economic analyses of law.[6]

The defence was not used in an environmental context until the case of *Manchester Corporation v. Farnworth*, which concerned crop damage caused by a new coal-fired power station.[7] The House of Lords interpreted the defence in a narrow manner and held that the defendant would have to show that the plant could not have been better designed. In this case it was clear that the plant should have been built with taller chimneys to disperse the pollutants. An injunction was granted and then suspended in order to facilitate the investigation of pollution abatement options. There are no further reports of legal proceedings, although the historical record shows that the height of the chimneys was raised.[8] This was despite vigorous assertions made in the litigation to the effect that reconfiguring the plant in this way would be too costly and impracticable. The House of Lords would not visit the subject of statutory authority, in the context of nuisance and infrastructure projects, until some fifty years later.

## *Allen v. Gulf Oil Refining Ltd*

### *The historical context of the case*

In the mid-1960s, Gulf Oil Refining Ltd was authorized to construct an oil refinery at Milford Haven as part of a massive expansion of its European operations. The plant was built on a 450-acre greenfield site, comprising mainly farmland, between the shoreline and the village of Waterston situated half a mile inland. It is important to note that there were two aspects to the planning process. Having taken legal advice, Gulf elected to promote a private Bill to authorize certain aspects of the scheme. This resulted in the enactment of the Gulf Oil Refining Act, which authorized the acquisition of land and the construction of a railway branch connecting the plant to the main line and berthing facilities (including a number of large jetties) to enable tankers to deliver the crude oil. Second, planning consent was sought from Pembrokeshire County Council in respect of the erection of the main refinery. The Bechtel International Corporation was contracted to build the refinery and an integral petrochemicals plant. Work started soon after the Act received the Royal Assent. It was opened by Her Majesty the Queen on 10 August 1968.[9]

The new plant towered over the village and significantly disrupted the lives of the villagers from the moment it was put into operation.[10] The local authority (Haverfordwest Rural District Council) and the refinery general manager (R. J. Horsak) began receiving complaints almost as soon as the boilers were fired up for the first time during commissioning work in May 1968.[11] Residents suffered from substantial nuisances including loud roaring and whistling noises, vibration, foul odours, gas flares and the emission of noxious gases including sulphur dioxide.[12] Certain residents also complained that the fumes induced nausea and caused sleepless nights and that they lived in perpetual fear of an explosion at the refinery. The fear of explosions was far from fanciful. A major fire had broken out during commissioning work just weeks before the royal opening ceremony, much to the alarm of the villagers, who witnessed workers running for their lives and scaling the perimeter fence.[13] The change to the neighbourhood brought about by the construction of the refinery is most vividly described by one villager in the following terms: 'This lane was once a quiet secluded area, which is why I decided to live here sixteen years ago – now it resembles an active volcano.'[14]

In the 1960s there was no formal requirement to conduct an environmental impact assessment or anything of the like. Nevertheless, such atmospheric pollution and the effect on nearby populations was not unforeseeable. Pollution caused by other refinery projects, especially in the Thames estuary, had been a cause for concern and had led to questions and debates in Parliament, largely at the instigation of Mr Bernard Braine, the Member of Parliament for Billericay. In 1953 Mr Braine was assured by the then Minister for Housing and Local Government, Mr Harold Macmillan, that the Alkali Inspectorate had the matter well in hand.[15] In 1958 the residents of Leigh-on-Sea (coincidentally organized by another Mrs Allen) submitted a petition with 5,800 signatures to Mr Braine, which he forwarded to the Minister for Housing and Local Government, which by this time was Mr Henry Brooke.[16] Mrs Allen had also collated letters from local residents, which were submitted with the petition. These catalogued adverse effects from oil refining that precisely anticipated those later reported by the residents of Waterston. The discomforts and nuisances endured by residents in the Thames Estuary included headaches, nausea, sleepless nights and glare from gas flaring and floodlighting. The Minister echoed his predecessor's confidence that the Alkali Inspectorate was on top of the problem.[17] However, by the mid-1960s it seems that the situation was little improved.[18] The archival evidence regarding the Gulf project suggests that concerns of this nature were barely addressed at any stage in the planning of the refinery at Waterston.

The Ministry of Fuel and Power was strongly in favour of the Gulf scheme and provided substantial advice and support to the promoters.[19] The development of domestic oil-refining capacity was deemed to be in the public interest and a vital means of improving the nation's balance of payments. The Welsh Office viewed the new refinery as a welcome boost to a depressed local economy and a source of new jobs. Overall, the government of the day was anxious not to stand in the way of the Bill and it was noted with some relief that there was insufficient opposition to merit a public enquiry. Petitioning against a private Bill in order to force an enquiry was a complex and costly process necessitating the use of expensive Parliamentary Agents. This would have provided the only opportunity for raising public health or environmental concerns; however, no objections of this nature appear to have been received. As regards the planning application, public health and environmental concerns were voiced during a meeting of the planning committee, although the matter was not debated at length.[20] Nevertheless, the concerns did at least result in the inclusion of a planning condition to the effect that 'arrangements be made for the purpose of avoiding any nuisance from air pollution, smell, noise, dust or effluent.'[21]

Whatever arrangements were put in place, and it is not clear what form they took, they were clearly insufficient to avoid the harm. The early complaints raised by the villagers were dismissed as teething problems associated with commissioning work. However, the problems persisted once the plant was put into full-scale production. Nevertheless, the local authority expressed confidence that Gulf had done everything that could be done to mitigate the nuisances. There is no indication that the Alkali Inspectorate was approached and at no point did the local authority consider instigating proceedings in public nuisance or using its powers under the Clean Air or Public Health Acts.[22] By 1972, conditions had deteriorated to such an extent that the local public health inspector proposed that Gulf Oil Ltd should purchase every property in the village and pay for the construction of a new settlement some distance away.[23] This solution raised the spectre of the economic analysis of tort whereby the polluter is able to buy out conflicting land uses – although, in this case, conditions had become so intolerable that the villagers actively supported the proposal.[24] The solution would have been relatively straightforward in that most of the villagers were council tenants. Thus, moving the village would simply have entailed paying the council to build a new development of council properties rather than engaging in individual negotiations with each householder. Initially, Gulf also expressed support for the proposal, and for a time it seemed that a solution had been found; however, without warning the company adopted a much more hard-line attitude. Not only did Gulf reject the proposal to move the village, it denied any liability in respect of the nuisances.[25] The company did, however, agree to construct blast barriers, consisting of mounds of earth commonly used at munitions factories, to direct the blast from the village should an explosion occur.[26]

## The litigation

Thus the proposal to move the village never came to pass and in 1975 over 50 villagers commenced proceedings in nuisance; one of those actions was brought by Elsie May Allen and this was selected as a test case.[27] Having lost on a preliminary point of law in pre-trial proceedings, on the grounds that Gulf Oil had a defence of statutory authority under the 1965 Act, the case was appealed to the Court of Appeal, where the matter was heard by Lord Denning MR and Cumming-Bruce LJ.[28]

Lord Denning was heavily influenced by the Victorian railway nuisance cases referred to above.[29] He noted that the defence of statutory authority was available only where the Act which authorized the construction of the railway line also extended to the operation of locomotives upon that railway; otherwise damage caused by a locomotive would be without prejudice to existing common law rights. This restrictive approach may have been due to the fact that the legislation did not usually provide for any alternative means of compensation. Turning to the 1965 Act, Lord Denning noted that those parts that enabled the construction of the main refinery and the railway branch line and jetties were silent on the operation of the refinery. In contrast, a provision on subsidiary plant and equipment including machines, pumps, buildings and railway sidings made express reference to the use of such equipment; furthermore, the provision included a right to compensation in respect of harm caused by such use. Lord Denning concluded from this that the draughtsman was well aware of the importance of the distinction between building and operating a plant. Where it was felt necessary to restrict existing common law rights in order to facilitate operation, this was explicitly set out and the possible hardship was offset by a statutory right to compensation. The fact that no similar right to compensation was included in those parts of the Act dealing with the main refinery, railway lines and jetties demonstrated that there was no intention to oust common law remedies.[30]

The most interesting aspect of Lord Denning's judgment concerns the observations he made regarding how such statutes should be interpreted in future. In short, he stated that, where statutes do not allow for compensation, they should be construed as operating without prejudice to the common law unless express words are used to justify the harm. In the worst-case scenario, such as a major accident not attributable to any negligence on the part of the operator, Lord Denning clearly felt that it would be extraordinary if injured parties were left without a remedy on the grounds that such harm was authorized:

> So in this case I would hold that if there should be an explosion at this refinery, the defendants are bound to compensate those who are killed or injured or whose property is damaged: and it is no answer for the defendants to say, 'We are sorry. We were very careful. We used all the latest safety precautions. But yet it happened.' Justice demands that, despite those protestations, compensation should be paid by the defendants to those who suffered by the operations.[31]

This is a telling statement, as it shows that Lord Denning was aware of a serious flaw in the legislation in that it did not provide for adequate compensation. By emphasizing the risk associated with the activity, Lord Denning justified interpreting the legislation in a manner that would allow the common law of nuisance to subject the plant to strict liability.[32] This reflects the classic justification for strict liability, which is that the person who creates a risk by conducting a hazardous activity should bear the risk of accidents irrespective of whether they are attributable to any fault on his or her part.[33]

Cumming-Bruce LJ agreed that the wording of the 1965 Act did not establish a statutory authority defence in respect of the operation of the refinery; thus, on this ground, Allen was successful in her appeal. However, although he was conscious of the narrow issue upon which the court was required to rule, in *obiter* comments Cumming-Bruce LJ was anxious to address wider issues that he considered would be of importance if the case were to proceed to a full trial of the facts. In short, he noted that Allen's claim did not allege 'material' damage to property and it would thus fall to be determined whether the refinery was out of keeping with the character of the neighbourhood according to the test enunciated by Lord Westbury in *St Helens Smelting v. Tipping*.[34] In this respect Cumming-Bruce LJ proposed that the fact that Parliament had authorized the construction of a refinery, which is a large-scale infrastructure project, meant that Parliament must have intended there to be a change in the character of the neighbourhood.[35] This view later received some support in a number of cases regarding the effect of planning permission on the character of the neighbourhood.[36] However, the nuisances endured by the villagers in Waterston amounted to a substantial interference with the use and enjoyment of property, although they fell just short of the material damage threshold demanded by the 'character of the neighbourhood' test. In fact, the arbitrary nature of the distinction between 'material damage' and 'sensible personal discomfort' is clearly exposed by applying the test to the facts of this case. It seems extraordinary to suggest that nausea, sleep deprivation and fear of explosions should be regarded as the reasonable consequences of living in the shadow of an oil refinery that has arrived uninvited upon one's doorstep. Yet the material damage threshold trivialized these significant harms. Had the case proceeded to a full trial then would evidence of a few dead plants in Mrs Allen's back garden have tipped the harm across the material damage threshold? In fact the archival evidence reveals that certain residents could have made out a case of physical damage. One complainant pointed to the fact that it was impossible to tell that her cottage had been recently whitewashed because of the deposition of dirt and soot.[37] Harm of this nature constitutes physical damage for the purposes of private nuisance, although, from the claimants' perspective, the noise, vibration and sleep deprivation would probably have seemed the most serious harms. Notwithstanding the existence or lack of physical damage in this particular case, it has been questioned whether, in *Tipping*, Lord Westbury intended to set out a general proposition to the effect that 'material damage' must always denote physical loss; an alternative explanation is that 'substantial interference' could meet the material threshold.[38]

The Court of Appeal was mindful of the fact that by ruling in favour of the plaintiff it was clearing the way for proceedings that could conceivably result in the granting of an injunction forcing the closure of the plant. However, Lord Denning suggested that, given the economic benefits of the facility, this was a case in which it would be appropriate for a court to exercise its discretion to grant damages in lieu of an injunction in respect of the ongoing harm.[39] In the event the need for a court to make this determination was removed by a successful appeal to the House of Lords on the scope of the statutory authority defence.[40]

Whereas the Court of Appeal had subjected the text of the 1965 Act to close scrutiny, the majority in the House of Lords adopted a broad-brush 'common sense' approach. Lord Wilberforce stated that the extension of statutory authority to the operation of the plant was a 'necessary implication' of the power to acquire lands and build upon it.[41] The ability of a resident to restrain Gulf from operating the plant would have 'remarkable consequences' in that the company would be left with a useless multimillion-pound refinery on its hands on land that could not be used for any other purpose.[42] In similar vein Lord Diplock added, 'Parliament can hardly be supposed to have intended the refinery to be nothing more than a visual adornment to the landscape in an area of natural beauty.'[43] Lord Roskill agreed that the respondent's restrictive interpretation of the Act would lead to a 'most curious' and 'illogical' result.[44] Lord Edmund-Davies concluded that the limited provision for compensation under the Act could not be regarded as conclusive evidence that Parliament had not intended the Act to operate without prejudice to common law remedies.[45] Furthermore, the majority expressed the view that any ambiguities in the text regarding Parliamentary intent could be ironed out by the preamble, which referred to the necessity of providing oil-refining facilities in the UK.[46]

Only Lord Keith, in dissent, adhered to a strict application of the *contra proferentem* rule whereby statutory provisions that are alleged to further the interests of the promoter are subject to a strict construction. As his Lordship put it, 'It will not do to slip through Parliament provisions which do not on the face of them express reasonably clearly the intention to take away the rights of others.'[47] Lord Keith also argued that the existing authorities should have made it clear how to draft the Act to avoid any ambiguity regarding the scope of the defence. As the appellants 'may reasonably be taken to have had access to the best legal advice' and as 'the reported cases show clearly the route to be taken in order to avoid any doubt about its [the statutory authority defence's] availability' it was logical to conclude that a conscious decision must have been made to limit the scope of the defence.[48] His Lordship continued that, had the Act expressly set out an all-inclusive statutory authority defence, 'Parliament may well have insisted on provisions for compensation.'[49]

It is clear that the majority of the House of Lords were greatly concerned about the possibility that construing the Act in a manner that excluded the defence could potentially result in the granting of an injunction preventing the continued operation of the refinery. Lord Wilberforce stated that once liability had been established the plaintiff would be entitled to injunctive relief 'subject only to a precarious appeal to Lord Cairns' Act.'[50] The House of Lords evidently did not share Lord Denning's view that the court could readily exercise its discretion in favour of awarding damages in lieu of an injunction on the basis of a balance of convenience test.[51] Tromans was highly critical of the House of Lords for allowing this issue to colour its judgement.[52] In effect, the plaintiff was denied one remedy because it was too drastic and another remedy because it was not drastic enough; as he dryly observed, 'the Allens of this world pay dearly for the judicial insistence that the plaintiff get nothing but the best by getting nothing at all.'[53] Furthermore, as the outcome of the *Farnworth* case demonstrated, even where an injunction is granted it does not automatically follow that this will force the closure of the plant.

However, Lord Wilberforce did impose one important qualification on the statutory authority defence that could have offered the plaintiff a way forward. In short he stated that, in order to bring the defence into play, it would not suffice to show that the nuisance was the inevitable result of operating a refinery of the design that had been built. Rather, it would have to be shown that no refinery of whatever design could have been operated without causing the harm.⁵⁴ Given that the 1965 Act did not contain any details regarding the configuration of the main plant, Gulf would have had to justify its design choices on this basis. In fact, this shows that their Lordships' disquiet, regarding the potential availability of injunctive relief in these circumstances, was illogical because at that stage it was still conceivable that the case could have proceeded to a full trial. It would have been for the trial court to determine upon the facts whether the refinery could have been built or operated in a manner that was less disruptive to the local community. Establishing that the plant could have been better designed would have been a formidable task for the plaintiffs, although they could have made a strong argument that much of the noise and vibration could have been avoided by using water cooling. However, it will be recalled that Pembrokeshire County Council had stipulated the use of air cooling to avoid the visual intrusion of cooling towers. This would have raised interesting issues regarding whether a planning condition restricting the choice of design could be regarded as making the harm inevitable. Alternatively, could it have been argued that Gulf should have known about the impact of air cooling and brought the matter to the attention of the planning authority? Given the complexity of these issues it is not surprising to find that the parties agreed to settle out of court following the House of Lords ruling.⁵⁵

The effect of the House of Lords decision in *Allen* was to restrict severely the ability of the common law to play an effective part in controlling emissions from the plant. Of course, one might conclude that this is reasonable given that such technical matters are best left to regulators and those involved in the planning process. However, in this case the planning process failed to properly consider the impact upon the local population, and the regulator failed to control the emissions. The approach adopted by the House of the Lords meant that the local residents were unable to use the common law as a means of correcting this example of regulatory failure.

## Case law developments after *Allen v. Gulf Oil Refining Ltd*

The aspect of the *Allen* case that has received most judicial attention in the years following the decision concerns Edmund Davies LJ's assertion that, irrespective of whether a project enjoys statutory authority, it may nevertheless alter the character of the neighbourhood to such an extent that nuisance claims can no longer be brought. This theme was pursued in a number of cases concerning town and country planning law.⁵⁶ Although a planning consent may not amount to a statutory authority, it may serve to bring about a change in the character of the neighbourhood. Thus, once industrial development is permitted to sprout up in a hitherto residential area it may change the nature of the locality to the extent that such industrial land use can no longer be regarded as unreasonable.

In recent litigation, similar reasoning has been extended to the nature of environmental permits. In *Barr v. Biffa Waste Services Ltd*, local residents brought private nuisance claims arising from odours and flies stemming from the defendant's pre-treated landfill site.[57] Biffa argued that the nuisances were an unavoidable consequence of operating a site of that nature and sought to rely upon its environmental permit as justification. It argued, in the alternative, that either the permit constituted a statutory authority or the permit was conclusive evidence that its land use was reasonable. The High Court rejected the statutory authority argument, on the grounds that the permit conferred no special duties or powers on Biffa, but accepted the reasonable user argument. This extends the line of reasoning in the planning cases but arguably goes much further. As with the planning cases, the permit renders the land use reasonable and removes its tortious quality. The fact that a single permit issued to a single operator achieved this instant result indicates that environmental permits are regarded as closer to statutory authorizations than planning consents. The decision runs counter to the long-established notion that permits remove statutory obstacles to pursing a particular land use but operate without prejudice to existing common law rights.[58] In this respect it blurs the distinction between an instrument that is merely permissive and one that confers an authority. This distinction is not made clearly in English law in that there is much use of loose terminology. However, the distinction is made very clearly in German administrative law, where a permit is a very different beast from a licence. It is only the latter that is capable of conferring rights on the holder to commit what might otherwise constitute a nuisance.[59]

The fact that the permit was regarded as the 'be all and end all' in the *Biffa* case tells us much about how the courts now view the relationship between common law and statute in an environmental context. Of particular note is Coulson J's finding that private nuisance should align itself with two relevant provisions of environmental law, namely Section 79 of the Environmental Protection Act (EPA) 1990 on statutory nuisance and Section 73(6) on civil liability for damage caused by waste. As regards statutory nuisance, Coulson J noted that it is a defence for the operator to argue that he had used 'best practicable means' (BPM). It would, therefore, be odd if a local resident was in a position to rely upon a stricter standard of liability under nuisance.[60] Similar reasoning was adopted in respect of civil liability under Section 73(6).[61] Liability under Section 73(6) is triggered only where a waste management offence has been committed under Section 33 EPA 1990. The fact that Biffa had acted entirely in accordance with its permit meant that there had been no waste management offence and it followed that there could be no civil liability under Section 73(6). Coulson J argued that the statutory regime would be undermined if a common law action in nuisance succeeded despite the fact that the operator had complied with the permit.[62]

As regards the first argument, it is anathema to the common law to assert that private nuisance should be yoked to statutory nuisance. Statutory nuisance arose in the early days of public health law at a time when the UK Parliament regarded continental-style command-and-control methods of regulation with deep suspicion. By overtly borrowing concepts from the common law, the promoters of the legislation hoped to render regulation more palatable to a Parliament that instinctively recoiled from interference by the state.[63] Statutory nuisance has never, however, been regarded as an alternative to the common law or as a means of defining the boundaries of private nuisance. Statutory nuisance operates as an administrative mechanism for addressing the general inconvenience or annoyance caused to the community as a whole. Space must be left for the common law to address the individual harms that may not be remedied by the use of the local authority's powers.

Similar criticisms can be levelled against the argument that the cause of action afforded by Section 73(6) of the EPA 1990 was intended to replace the common law. Liability under the section is confined to harm stemming from waste management offences under Section 33 and is therefore limited in scope. It is not clear how allowing common law claims in respect of nuisance-type harms not covered by the Act would undermine the statutory regime. Section 73(6) is designed to provide redress in respect of specific losses that may flow from an offence under Section 33. It is not intended to provide a comprehensive response to all types of harm associated with waste management. Where Parliament intends a statutory provision on civil liability to provide a comprehensive response, it normally makes that clear. An obvious example includes Section 12(1)(b) of the Nuclear Installations Act 1965, which specifically ousts common law remedies in respect of harm caused by 'nuclear occurrences'.

Common law can provide an effective means of protecting private interests only if it remains free to conflict with what regulators and policy makers have determined to be in the public interest. If the common law is forced to shadow the approach adopted under public powers and statutory regimes, it loses its capacity to correct private losses that may stem from a failure by the decision maker to address individual concerns.[64] Where Parliament intends to remove private rights or close down common law causes of action, it should do so by express words. This is the essence of the *Allen* case.[65] The House of Lords interpreted the legislation in a manner that enabled the promoter to expunge private rights in the absence of express words to that effect in the legislation and without provision being made for compensation. Similarly, in the light of the *Biffa* case, it seems that we now have a situation in which a permit can abrogate private interests without Parliament having expressly conferred such an authority on the regulator.

## Conclusions: the common law, localized harm and devolved powers

The above case studies illustrate that nuisance has the potential to fulfil a vital role as means of compensating for the failure of the planning and regulatory systems to anticipate the localized effects of industrial facilities. Indeed the copper industry was not planned at all and was not subject to any form of specialist regulation for the bulk of its existence. By the time the oil industry moved in to Pembrokeshire, a planning and pollution control system of sorts was in place, although it proved utterly unresponsive to the types of harm that occurred. In both instances, determined litigants made valiant attempts to seek redress, by way of common law actions, regarding the losses that occurred as a result of the absence of effective regulation. The great strength of the common law resides in its ability to reflect the situation 'on the ground' and the localized interests that may be brushed aside by considerations deemed to be in the national interest, as viewed from a UK perspective. This does not mean that a Luddite model of nuisance should be promoted that endeavours to turn back the clock and stand in the way of development. However, without a robust common law there may be little incentive to minimize harm or provide compensation where losses are unavoidable.

Doctrinal developments have undermined the ability of the common law of nuisance to perform this role effectively. Of particular concern is the manner in which the character of the neighbourhood test or locality doctrine has been applied since it emerged in *St Helens Smelting v. Tipping*. As Simpson forcefully argued, it is entirely arbitrary to draw a distinction between tangible and intangible harm.[66] The harms suffered by the residents in Waterston were serious and no doubt modern medical science would have been able to identify physical health effects associated with sleep deprivation and the continual fear of accidents. Nevertheless, the harms failed to cross the material damage threshold, with the result that, even if the claimants had won outright on the statutory authority point, their efforts might have come to nought.[67] Regarding the statutory authority aspects, this constitutes the other major nuisance issue where doctrinal developments have blunted the effectiveness of nuisance. The majority of the House of Lords adopted a generous interpretation of the statute and made assumptions that were not warranted by the text of the enabling statute. Furthermore, the House of Lords may have been motivated in part by a desire to avoid a decision that could have threatened the future of the £20 million plant. As noted above, this dilemma could have been avoided by using the equitable discretion to award damages in lieu of an injunction. This in turn opens up a new debate on the discretion and the contemporary relevance of the *Shelfer* criteria, which is beyond the scope of this chapter; suffice it to say that strong arguments have been made to the effect that it is high time to re-evaluate the criteria.[68]

In short, the main problem with these doctrinal developments is that they seek to neutralize otherwise valid claims and maintain a legal fiction to the effect that there is no *real* dispute. The harms suffered by the residents of Waterston were real enough from their perspective, notwithstanding the fact that they may not have crossed the material damage threshold. Furthermore, an overly generous interpretation of the statutory authority defence trivializes serious harms and renders them an acceptable price to pay for an activity that is deemed to be in the national interest. This does not mean that the court should substitute its own analysis regarding what should be deemed to be in the national interest. The courts are notoriously bad at performing such welfare calculations and have little desire to engage in this process. This explains the tendency to point to the existence of a statutory power or authorization as evidence for the assertion that those with the appropriate expertise have already made the calculation. However, as the *Allen* case demonstrates, this often entails making very big assumptions regarding what the decision maker actually did and did not take into account. Campbell has argued that the courts should move away from such welfare calculations rather than endeavouring to perform such calculations themselves or assuming that the decision maker must have weighed up all the evidence.[69] Instead, they should adhere to a property rights-based analysis of nuisance. The job of the courts should be to ensure that a polluter is not permitted to expropriate his neighbour's right to the undisturbed use and enjoyment of his property without first attempting to reach a bargain. This is redolent of a Coasean analysis in which an injunction serves as an instruction to the parties to attempt to reach a settlement.[70] However, the Coasean analysis is often criticized on account of the assumptions it makes regarding the capacity of the parties to reach a bargain. The most ironic aspect of the *Allen* case is that the parties were well on the way to achieving a mutually acceptable solution before Gulf pulled out of negotiations in the light of new legal advice. In many respects the common law had done its job by forcing the polluter to the negotiating table. Moreover, it demonstrated that there are circumstances in which a Coasean approach might actually work in practice. However, this was all undone when it became clear that the statutory authority defence could be applied in a manner that would allow the polluter to ride roughshod over local concerns. Had a model of nuisance been applied that facilitated financial settlements, the polluter would have been forced back to the negotiating table. Of course, Parliament must remain free to restrict existing common law rights through conferring statutory powers on promoters; however, the courts should insist upon such powers being expressed in a clear and unequivocal manner and they should be narrowly construed.

We must acknowledge that planning controls have improved immeasurably since the 1960s and, if a new oil refinery were to be built today, it would have to undergo a thorough environmental impact assessment and, as a major infrastructure project, comply with the Planning Act 2008.[71] Similarly, there is no comparison between the manner in which an industrial plant is regulated today and the distinct lack of regulation of the copper industry in centuries past. Such plants are now subject to a sophisticated environmental permitting system and the exigencies of integrated pollution prevention and control.[72] However, this does not mean that there is room for complacency and the confident belief that regulatory failures leading to individual harms could not occur in future. For example, the number of wind farms in Wales looks set to increase dramatically in the coming years.⁷³ Given the need to reduce greenhouse gas emissions and given the controversy regarding nuclear energy, there are clear public interest arguments in favour of such schemes. However, although they produce clean energy, wind farms have been accused of having a deleterious effect on the immediate environment and the health of local residents. Concerns have focused on the noises produced, such as a low hum at the edge of audibility, and flicker caused by the shadows of the rotating blades. A number of cases have been brought in the USA, although most have been defeated by the argument that the alleged harms lack the physical quality necessary for an actionable nuisance.⁷⁴ Interestingly, research commissioned by the Department for Energy and Climate Change (DECC) pooh-poohs such claims in a manner redolent of the off-hand way in which the complaints raised by the residents of Waterston were dismissed.⁷⁵ However, even if research were to identify a positive link between wind farms and ill-health, it is likely that such 'personal injury claims' would be precluded from the scope of private nuisance. Perhaps the *coup de grace* on such claims would be the fact that the Planning Act 2008 expressly preserves the statutory authority defence without adding any additional gloss.⁷⁶ This means that the existing common law authorities, including of course *Allen v. Gulf Oil Refining Ltd*, would be applied if a court was called upon to interpret the defence.

From the perspective of Welsh devolution, it must be questioned whether the law of nuisance, as it currently stands, is sufficiently receptive to the localized harms that may arise from grand projects deemed to be in the national interest. It is worth noting that the draft Legislative Competence (Environment) Order for Wales facilitates legislative action on nuisances.⁷⁷ However, it is doubtful if this would facilitate any wholesale reform of common law nuisance with a view to addressing the doctrinal developments referred to above. When viewed in the light of the explanatory memorandum, it is more likely that the powers would be used to increase the scope of statutory nuisances that exist within the realm of public law.⁷⁸ Nevertheless, it is conceivable that, where a statute makes provision for damages in respect of individual loss for breach of statutory duty, the definition of harm could be broadened to encompass a wider range of nuisance-type harms.⁷⁹ Unfortunately, there is a major exclusion under the draft LCO that could prohibit many useful developments in this field. No legislation may be enacted in respect of 'energy nuisances' for which there is statutory authority.⁸⁰ This would preclude the strengthening of nuisance laws (whether in the shape of common law reform, new statutory duties or statutory nuisance) to address the novel harms associated with wind farms. As regards more traditional and established energy industries, such as oil refining, it would preclude efforts to impose new statutory duties in respect of a broader range of nuisance-type harms.

In conclusion, it seems that the 'safety net' once offered by nuisance is becoming increasingly full of holes. Perhaps the only solution is to ensure that planning decisions are taken closer to those affected on the ground.⁸¹ Given that, at least in energy policy, planning powers are still tightly controlled from London, this seems unlikely in the foreseeable future.[82]

## Addendum

It should be noted that, after the original version of this chapter had been submitted, the Court of Appeal overturned the decision of the High Court in the case of *Barr v. Biffa Waste Services Ltd* [2012] EWCA Civ 312, [2012] All ER (D) 141 (Mar). In short, the Court of Appeal held that a waste management permit has no special status that enables it to operate as conclusive proof regarding the reasonableness of the holder's activity.

## Notes

1. By the 1960s the copper-refining industry was a shadow of its former self, although production at the Haford site continued until 1981 under the management of Yorkshire Imperial Metals, part of ICI. See 'A world of Welsh copper project' (a project of the University of Glamorgan funded by the Leverhulme Trust), *http://www.welshcopper.org.uk/en/copper-guides_FAQs.htm#fade* (accessed 9 October 2012).
2. [1981] A. C. 1001.
3. (1868) L. R. 3 H. L. 330.
4. (1832) 4 B. & Ad. 30, 110 E. R. 366.
5. Stockton and Darlington Railway Act 1823 (4 Geo. 4. c. 33), s. 8. For a historical analysis of the case and the extent to which it marked a watershed in terms of the relationship between common law and statute see M. Wilde and C. Smith, 'R. v. Pease', in C. Mitchell and P. Mitchell (eds.), *Landmark Cases in the Law of Tort* (Oxford: Hart, 2010), ch. 1.
6. *Aldridge v. Great Western Railway Co.* (1841) 3 Man. & G. 514, 133 E. R. 1246; *Piggot v. Eastern Counties Railway Co.* (1846) 3 C. B. 228, 136 E. R. 92; *Vaughan v. Taff Vale Railway Co.* (1860) 5 H. & N. 679; *Jones v. Festiniog Railway Co.* (1868) L. R. 3 Q. B. 733; A. C. Pigou, *The Economics of Welfare*, 4th edn (London: Macmillan, 1932), II.II.5; R. H. Coase, 'The problem of social cost', *Journal of Law & Economics*, 3 (1960), 1–44.
7. [1930] A. C. 171.
8. See R. Frost, *Electricity in Manchester* (Manchester: Neil Richardson, 1993), pp. 41–3.
9. A copy of the programme for the official Royal opening ceremony is still held in the Pembrokeshire County Records Office (PCRO) (HDX/157/70), together with a number of other documents.
10. The proximity of the plant is brought home by aerial photographs of the plant held by the Pembrokeshire County Records Office (PCRO): HDX/1621/2. The Methodist chapel still stands resolutely on the approach to the main gate of the site.
11. The correspondence file of Haverfordwest Rural District Council on the Gulf refinery is held by the Pembrokeshire County Records Office (PCRO): HAR/SE/19/28.
12. The vibration stemmed from the fact that, as a condition of the planning consent, the plant had to be air-cooled as opposed to water-cooled. This avoided the need to build visually intrusive cooling towers but necessitated the installation of giant noisy fans; letter from Mike Howells (solicitor representing Waterston residents) to author (10 May 2010).
13. Email from Mike Howells to author (18 May 2010). There is also correspondence relating to the fire on the file maintained by Haverfordwest RDC, HAR/SE/19/28.
14. HAR/SE/19/28.

15  At this time the Alkali Inspectorate was housed by the Ministry of Housing and Local Government. HC Deb. vol. 518 col. 1793 (20 October 1953).
16  The petition itself and related correspondence are contained in a Ministry of Housing and Local Government file held by the National Archive: HLG 55/236.
17  Ibid. A briefing note to the Minister indicated that the Alkali Inspectorate was relying on the 'best practicable means' (BPM) test, established by the Alkali Acts, to secure reductions in emissions. However, there was no indication whether they had met with any success in this endeavour.
18  See Mr Bernard Braine in an adjournment debate on proposed new Agip refinery on Canvey Island: HC Deb. vol. 704 cols. 1011–17 (21 December 1964).
19  The main archival evidence for the government's views on the scheme are contained in files on the project were maintained by the Ministry of Fuel and Power [National Archives (NA) NA POWE 61/369] and the Welsh Office (NA BD 11/3924).
20  There was a seemingly heated exchange between a Mr John Daniels and the County Planning Officer, Mr J. A. Price, in which Mr Daniels drew attention to the Regent Refinery and the sky 'glowing red at night'. See a report of the meeting in the *Western Mail* (23 February 1965) a copy of which is pasted into the Ministry of Fuel and Power's file (NA POWE 61/369).
21  Ibid.
22  In any case it is doubtful whether the Inspectorate would have determined that the plant fell short of the BPM requirement. At the time there were no specific emission limits for many of the harmful compounds produced by oil refineries such as sulphur dioxide, as indicated by a short scientific article published by an Alkali Inspector in the early 1970s: L. E. Hockin, 'The British approach to the control of industrial emissions to the atmosphere', *Annals of Occupational Hygiene*, 15 (1972), 399–406. On the local authority's stance, see HAR/SE/19/28. The correspondence indicates that from the outset the local authority viewed its role as facilitating the development rather than questioning or challenging the scheme.
23  See *The Times* (London), 3 June 1972, 3.
24  Remarkably, this drastic solution was actually adopted in an American example some 30 years later. In 2002, American Electric Power (AEP) bought the town of Chesire, Ohio, lock stock and barrel following years of inconclusive litigation resulting from the sulphurous emissions. See B. Hale, 'Power giant buys town to avoid pollution lawsuits', *The Times* (London), 14 May 2002, 27. See HAR/SE/19/28 for the villagers' support.
25  It seems that Gulf reached this view having taken legal advice and there was a strong belief that the new hard-line attitude came from Gulf's head office in Pittsburgh, USA; email from Mr Mike Howells to author (18 May 2010).
26  Ibid.
27  Simply by virtue of the fact that the list of plaintiffs was in alphabetical order and Mrs Allen was at the top of the list. The solicitor, Mr Mike Howells, was given the use of an empty council house in Waterston to use as an office. Villagers were asked to complete a claim form prepared by Mr Howells; email from Mike Howells to author (18 May 2010).
28  [1980] Q. B. 156.
29  See, for example, on the railway sparks cases, above: *Aldridge v. Great Western Railway Co.*; *Piggot v. Eastern Counties Railway Co.*; *Vaughan v. Taff Vale Railway Co.*; *Jones v. Festiniog Railway Co.*
30  See *Allen* [1980] 1 Q. B. 156, 167C–168C.
31  Ibid., p. 169E–F.
32  Of course, the extent to which liability in nuisance is strict has been a matter of some debate in recent decades, especially since the House of Lords decision in *Cambridge Water v. Eastern Counties Leather* [1994] 2 A. C. 264. In short, the position is now that, where damage has already occurred, it is necessary to show that the harm was foreseeable at the material time. Such considerations are not relevant where the harm

is continuing and a remedy is sought in respect of the future loss. In the event of Lord Denning's worst-case scenario involving damage caused by an explosion it is possible that residents would have had claims under *Rylands v. Fletcher*. However, given the historic links between *Rylands* and private nuisance, emphasized by Lord Goff in *Cambridge Water*, the foreseeability requirement would have been the same.

33 See J. A. Jolowicz, 'Liability for accidents', *Cambridge Law Journal*, 26 (1968), 50–63.
34 See *Allen* [1980] Q. B. 156, 171E–H.
35 Ibid., p. 172B–D.
36 See *Hunter v. Canary Wharf* [1996] 2 W. L. R. 348 (Court of Appeal judgment); *Wheeler v. Saunders* [1996] ch. 19; *Gillingham Council v. Medway Dock Co.* [1993] Q. B. 343. The consensus that has emerged from these decisions is that major strategic planning decisions may effect a fundamental change in the character of the neighbourhood whereas permissions relating to small-scale developments would not.
37 See HAR/SE/19/28.
38 See A. W. B. Simpson, 'Victorian judges and the problem of social cost: *Tipping v St Helen's Smelting Company* (1865)', in A. W. B. Simpson (ed.), *Leading Cases in the Common Law* (Oxford: Clarendon Press, 1995), p. 190, ' "Material" here is quite ambiguous between meaning either "physical", or alternatively "non-trivial" '.
39 *Allen* [1980] Q. B. 156, 169D.
40 *Allen v. Gulf Oil Refining Ltd* [1981] A. C. 1001.
41 Ibid., p. 1012F.
42 Ibid., p. 1013B–C.
43 Ibid., p. 1014E–F.
44 Ibid., p. 1024A.
45 Ibid., p. 1016E–F.
46 Ibid., p. 1012A–D.
47 Ibid., p. 1020G.
48 Ibid., p. 1021F.
49 Ibid., p. 1021G.
50 Ibid., p. 1013B.
51 The leading case on the factors that the court should take into account when deciding whether to exercise its equitable discretion in favour of awarding damages in lieu of an injunction is *Shelfer v. City of London Electric Lighting Co.* [1895] 1 Ch. 287. Lindley LJ stated that injunctive relief should not be withheld simply on the basis that the defendant is willing to pay for the damage or should be regarded in some sense as a 'public benefactor'. It must be shown that the grant of an injunction would be oppressive to the defendant according to certain criteria. The Court of Appeal has recently affirmed the *Shelfer* approach and has also made it clear that economic hardship cannot fall within the oppression criteria; see *Watson v. Croft Promo-Sport Ltd* [2009] EWCA Civ 15, N. P. C. 15.
52 S. Tromans, 'Nuisance: prevention or payment?', *Cambridge Law Journal*, 41 (1982), 87–109.
53 Ibid., p. 108. Similar concerns were expressed by Jolowicz, who criticized the House of Lords' dogmatic acceptance of the *Shelfer* approach and the fact that it did not take the opportunity to review the decision in the light of contemporary circumstances; see J. A. Jolowicz, 'Should courts answer questions? Does statutory authority to build confer immunity from liability for use?', *Cambridge Law Journal*, 40 (1981), 226–30.
54 *Allen* [1981] A. C. 1001, 1014B.
55 Email from Mike Howells to author (18 May 2010).
56 See above: *Hunter v. Canary Wharf*; *Wheeler v. Saunders*; *Gillingham Council v. Medway Dock Co.*.
57 [2011] EWHC 1003 (TCC), [2011] 4 All E. R. 1065.

58 See Peter Cane, *Tort Law and Economic Interests* (Oxford: Clarendon Press, 1996), p. 392.
59 See Horst Schlemminger and Claus-Peter Martens, *German Environmental Law for Practitioners* (The Hague: Kluwer Law International, 2004), p. 118.
60 *Biffa*, [343]–[347].
61 Ibid.
62 Ibid., [358].
63 See N. Morag-Levine, 'Is precautionary regulation a civil law instrument? Lessons from the history of the Alkali Act', *Journal of Environmental Law*, 23 (2011), 1–43.
64 See P. Cane, 'Tort law as regulation', *Common Law World Review*, 31, 4 (2002), 305–31.
65 [1981] A. C. 1001.
66 Simpson, 'Victorian judges and the problem of social cost'.
67 The recoverability of damages in nuisance (either public or private) in nuisance is a vexed issue. The prevalent view is that personal injury claims have no place in private nuisance, which is concerned solely with the protection of private interests in land. See *obiter* comments of Lord Hoffmann in *Hunter v. Canary Wharf* [1997] A. C. 655, 707–8, and in *Transco v. Stockport M. B. C.* [2003] UKHL 61, [2004] 2 A. C. 1 at [35]. However, in *Corby Group Litigation* [2008] EWCA Civ 463, [2009] Q. B. 335, the Court of Appeal held that there is nothing in these pronouncements to suggest that the exclusion of personal injuries should be extended to public nuisance, which is not solely concerned with the protection of interests in land. As regards this issue, the House of Lords has been fond of citing Professor Newark's seminal article on 'The boundaries of nuisance': F. H. Newark, 'The boundaries of nuisance', *Law Quarterly Review*, 65 (1949), 480–90. Newark described an action for nuisance for personal injury as a 'heresy' (p. 488). Palmer mounts an interesting challenge against this now-orthodox view. In his historical analysis he argues that nuisance was inextricably connected with the protection of health. Fumes and noxious odours, the mainstay of early nuisance actions, were thought to spread disease under Miasma theory. See R. C. Palmer, 'Personal injury in private nuisance: the historical truth about actionability of "bodily security"', *Environmental Law and Management*, 21 (2009), 302–11.
68 See *Shelfer v. City of London Electric Lighting Co.*, above; Tromans, 'Nuisance'.
69 D. Campbell, 'Of Coase and corn: a (sort of) defence of private nuisance', *Modern Law Review*, 63, 2 (2000), 197–215.
70 Coase, 'The problem of social cost'.
71 Environmental impact assessments are pursuant to Council Directive (EEC) 85/337 on the assessment of the effects of certain public and private projects on the environment [1985] O. J. L. 175/40.
72 Permitting system pursuant to the Environmental Permitting (England and Wales) Regulations 2010 SI 2010/675; integrated pollution prevention and control pursuant to European Parliament and Council Directive 2008/1 (2008) O. J. L. 24/8.
73 At the time of writing the UK energy minister, Mr Charles Hendry, indicated in an interview that the number of wind turbines in Wales was likely to increase significantly; see BBC, 'More wind farms in Wales likely says minister', http://www.bbc.co.uk/news/uk-wales-16093611 (accessed 13 December 2011).
74 For analysis of the US cases see S. H. Butler, 'Headwinds to a clean energy future: nuisance suits against wind energy projects in the United States', *California Law Review*, 97 (2009), 1337–75; K. Culley, 'Has Texas nuisance law been blown away by the demand for wind power', *Baylor Law Review*, 61 (2009), 943–72.
75 See, for example, results of a report commissioned by DECC on shadow flicker, http://www.decc.gov.uk/en/content/cms/news/pn11_025/pn11_025.aspx (accessed 18 August 2011).
76 See Planning Act 2008 s. 158.
77 See Matter 6.4.

78 See Welsh Assembly Government, 'A summary of the Environment Legislative Competence Order' (2010), *http://wales.gov.uk/docs/desh/policy/100222environmentlco summaryen.pdf* (accessed 18 August 2011).
79 See, for example, Environmental Protection Act 1990 s. 73(6), which confers a cause of action on individuals who have suffered personal injury or property damage as a result of the commission of a waste management offence under s. 33.
80 Matter 6.4(a).
81 This issue is addressed in the present volume by Victoria Jenkins in Chapter 8 on sustainable communities.
82 Energy policy has not been devolved, which means that decisions are taken directly by DECC pursuant to powers conferred by Electricity Act 1989 s. 36, pursuant to which a new gas-fired power station has recently been authorized near Port Talbot; see Press Release 23 February 2011, *http://www.decc.gov.uk/en/content/cms/news/pn11_016/ pn11_016.aspx* (accessed 5 September 2012).

# Chapter 5

# Nature conservation in Wales

*Lynda M. Warren*

The legal regime for nature conservation may be about to change dramatically now that Wales has enhanced law-making powers. The *Natural Environment Framework* (NEF), a major review of environmental law and policy initiated in September 2010 by the then Minister for the Environment, Housing and Sustainable Development, raised the possibility of a restructuring of environmental bodies in Wales and a move towards natural resource management based on the ecosystem approach and designed to deliver ecosystem services.[1] If even some of the ideas being floated come to fruition, the result will be a different way of looking at biodiversity and the purpose and practice of nature conservation.

At the moment, however, Wales is not very different from the rest of the UK in the way it addresses nature conservation. This is partly because of a common heritage of legislation and policy over the last sixty years or more and partly because of the influence of European and international commitments, which take effect at the UK level. This chapter sets out the current framework for nature conservation law in Wales, covering both the substantive law and the institutional and policy frameworks, before going on to discuss the possible implications of the devolution settlement on the implementation of NEF reforms.

## The evolution of UK nature conservation law

The modern regime for the protection of sites for nature conservation purposes has its origins in the reforming policies adopted by the incoming Labour government in the aftermath of the Second World War. Species protection measures have a much longer history and have been largely shaped by legislation for the protection of birds.

The nature conservation movement had its origins in nineteenth-century concerns over the exploitation of birds, which led to the enactment of several Acts to protect different species of birds, culminating in the Wild Birds Protection Act 1880. Numerous other bird protection Acts followed, culminating in the Protection of Birds Act 1967. Meanwhile there were few measures to protect other species, and for nearly 100 years birds were the main subject of species protection legislation. Attention was broadened in the 1970s with the passage of the Conservation of Wild Creatures and Wild Plants Act 1975. This was followed in 1981 by the Wildlife and Countryside Act, which set the scene for all subsequent wildlife law and is still the main source of domestic nature conservation law.

The protection of habitats did not arise directly from measures to protect species but was a development of the land use reforms introduced in the 1940s. Countryside protection followed a different path and has a longer history. Its origins lie in the aesthetic movement of the late nineteenth century and the desire to preserve beautiful things, including the natural environment, for posterity.

The two strands of habitat protection and countryside preservation were each included in the first piece of major nature conservation law, the National Parks and Access to the Countryside Act 1949. For the first time, measures were introduced for the designation of 'protected areas'. There were two main types; nature reserves, which were designed to protect the scientific interest of sites, and national parks, which were designed to protect aesthetic values and provide a recreational facility for the public. These differences of objective are well illustrated by reference to the purposes of each protected area as stated in the Act as originally worded:

> 'nature reserve' means land managed for the purpose –
> (a) of providing, under suitable conditions and control, special opportunities for the study of, and research into, matters relating to the fauna and flora of Great Britain and the physical conditions in which they live, and for the study of geological and physiographical features of special interest in the area, or
> (b) of preserving flora, fauna or geological or physiographic features of special interest in the area,
> or for both of those purposes.
>
> (Section 15)

> ['national parks'] are those extensive tracts of country in England and Wales as to which it appears to the [National Parks] Commission that by reason of –
> (a) their natural beauty, and
> (b) the opportunities they afford for open-air recreation, having regard both to their character and to their position in relation to centres of population,
> it is especially desirable that the necessary measures shall be taken for the purposes [of preserving and enhancing their natural beauty and of promoting their enjoyment by the public].
>
> (Section 5)

The legal framework for nature conservation in the UK has traditionally shown closer links with land use planning than with environmental law on pollution control. The reason for this can be traced back to the deliberations leading to the National Parks etc. Act, which forged the link between planning and conservation. The Act was passed just two years after the introduction of major planning reforms in the Town and Country Planning Act 1947. Both pieces of legislation were shaped by the recommendations of influential committees.[2] The result is that the scope of nature conservation law has largely been determined by the need to consider scientific aspects of nature. It is a body of law to do with species, habitats, geology and landforms. The public interface with nature, in terms of scientific study and education, is also encompassed, but broader public involvement through recreation has been dealt with separately under a body of countryside law. More recently, the latter has drawn closer to the rural development agenda, thereby emphasizing the socio-economic aspects of countryside law and policy. When the new wave of pollution laws was being promulgated from the 1960s onwards, the focus was on public health and site inspections, with emissions standards and discharges qualities forming the basis for controls. The relationship with planning was left to planning guidance.[3]

Note that even at this early date there is already a difference in geographical coverage. Nature Reserves could be created in Great Britain, i.e. England, Scotland and Wales, whereas National Parks were restricted to England and Wales. Northern Ireland was not covered by the Act at all. The reasons for these differences lie in part in the deliberations of the specialist committees set up to advise the government on the desirability of establishing these new protected areas. The advisory committee for Scotland advised against National Parks because it was felt that they were not needed.[4]

The 1949 Act also provided for the creation of what was to become the most important site protection mechanism for nature conservation in the United Kingdom, the Site of Special Scientific Interest or SSSI.[5] Section 23 imposed a duty on the newly created Nature Conservancy to notify the local planning authority that land in its area was, in the opinion of the Conservancy, of special interest by reason of its flora, fauna, or geological or physiographical features. The idea behind this measure was to alert planners to the presence of features of scientific interest that they might not otherwise be aware of so that their existence could be taken into account by planning authorities when making decisions on development proposals. This measure attracted very little attention during the passage of the Act through Parliament and certainly was not regarded as in any way controversial. This was presumably because the designation was seen as nothing more than a factual statement about the quality of the land; there was no duty on the local planning authority to act upon the information provided. Since then, the SSSI has been strengthened through a series of incremental legal changes. The link to the planning regime remains, however, and arguably has shaped policies for nature conservation ever since. In the immediate post-war years, which is when the National Parks etc. Act was passed, no one realized the extent of the land use changes that would result from the intensification of farming. Despite its name, the town and country planning regime has more to do with urban development than with land use in the countryside. For the most part, agriculture is either excluded from planning control or deemed to be permitted development and this has limited the effectiveness of nature conservation policies. The link with planning has even had important consequences for conservation in the marine environment, where SSSIs have been held not to apply because there is no planning jurisdiction.[6]

The National Parks etc. Act 1949 set the scene for regimes of site protection based on nature conservation and the protection of the countryside, and these evolved as two separate strands of law and policy, each with its own institutional arrangements. Table 5.1 lists the main legislative milestones in this evolution. The two policy threads of nature conservation and countryside have come together through the creation of combined agencies but integration of the law has not followed. Instead, modern concepts such as biodiversity and sustainable development have largely been bolted on to existing legal frameworks.

The European Community introduced its first conservation legislation in 1979 in the form of the Birds Directive. The need to implement this directive in the UK provided a strong imperative for the next major piece of domestic nature conservation legislation, the Wildlife and Countryside Act 1981. Amongst other things, this Act revolutionized the use of the SSSI designation and transformed it into the cornerstone of conservation policy. With few exceptions, all subsequent protected area mechanisms have been based on the protection provided through designation as an SSSI. Further changes to the SSSI have been made to increase the protection through the introduction of powers and duties that enable the SSSI to be used as the basis for land management regimes designed to deliver conservation outcomes.[7] The main change to species protection law has been the addition of a duty on ministers to publish a list of species and habitats of 'principal importance for the purpose of conserving biodiversity'. This was originally contained in s. 74 of the Countryside and Rights of Way Act 2000 but can now be found in ss. 41 and 42 of the Natural Environment and Rural Communities Act 2006. Nature conservation legislation enacted following devolution has reflected the changes in governance to a greater or lesser degree, as can be seen from the most recent statutes shown in Table 5.1. It is significant, in this respect, that the duty to publish biodiversity lists is directed separately to Welsh and English ministers.

## The impact of European nature conservation law

The greatest influence on nature conservation law in the UK over recent years has undoubtedly been the obligation to implement the Birds and Habitats Directives.

TABLE 5.1 History of nature conservation legislation

| Date | Instrument | Comment |
|---|---|---|
| 1949 | National Parks and Access to the Countryside Act | Covers nature conservation and countryside protection. Creates National Parks, Areas of Outstanding Natural Beauty, Nature Reserves, SSSIs and the National Parks Commission |
| 1954 | Protection of Birds Act | Lays foundation for all subsequent species protection |
| 1967 | Countryside (Scotland) Act | Establishes Countryside Commission Scotland |
| 1968 | Countryside Act | Replaces National Parks Commission with Countryside Commission |
| 1972 | Nature Conservancy Council Act | Replaces Nature Conservancy with Nature Conservancy Council |
| 1975 | Conservation of Wild Creatures and Wild Plants Act | Extends species protection measures to other species |
| 1981 | Wildlife and Countryside Act | Implements EU Birds Directive and Bern Convention. Introduces comprehensive species protection measures. Reforms SSSIs. Creates Marine Nature Reserves |
| 1990 | Environmental Protection Act | Replaces Nature Conservancy Council with English Nature, the Countryside Council for Wales and the Joint Nature Conservation Committee |
| 1992 | Natural Heritage (Scotland) Act | Replaces Nature Conservancy Council with Scottish Natural Heritage |
| 2000 | Countryside and Rights of Way Act | Reforms SSSI regime in England and Wales. Provides for Biodiversity Lists |
| 2000 | National Parks (Scotland) Act | Provides for the creation of National Parks and Marine National Parks in Scotland |
| 2004 | Nature Conservation (Scotland) Act | Amends SSSI provisions |
| 2006 | Natural Environment and Rural Communities Act | Merges English Nature and the Countryside Agency to create Natural England. Provides for Biodiversity Lists |
| 2009 | Marine and Coastal Access Act | Creates Marine Conservation Zones |
| 2010 | Marine (Scotland) Act | Creates Marine Protected Areas |
| 2011 | Wildlife and Natural Environment (Scotland) Act | Amends species protection measures and amends SSSIs |

While this obligation is applied at a Member State level, it also has an impact at the sub-national level; the devolved administrations are held accountable for its implementation by the UK government and, on occasion, by the European Commission itself.

The Birds Directive covers the protection, management and control of bird species and lays down rules for their exploitation. Article 2 requires Member States to take measures to maintain the populations of bird species at a level commensurate with ecological, scientific and cultural requirements, taking account of economic and recreational requirements. The duty applies to all species of birds that are naturally occurring in the wild state. The main measures prescribed for meeting the objectives of Article 2 are forms of habitat protection.[8] Some species are singled out for special protection measures because they are considered to be rare or endangered.[9] For these species, the directive requires Member States to create Special Protection Areas (SPAs). In addition to the habitat protection measures, Member States are required to establish a general system of protection for the birds themselves.

The need to implement the Birds Directive was one of the reasons for the enactment of the Wildlife and Countryside Act 1981. The habitat protection measures were delivered through a strengthened SSSI system, which proved to be one of the most controversial parts of the Act. Implementation of the species protection measures was less contentious. Part I of the Act contains protection measures for bird species. These were modelled on the existing measures in the Birds Acts, which were themselves a model for the European legislation.

The Habitats Directive extends the concept of wildlife protection from birds to other animals and plants. Like the Birds Directive, it provides for the protection of species and their habitats, but the details are somewhat different. Its aim is to contribute towards ensuring biodiversity through the conservation of natural habitats and wild fauna and flora. The measure of success is whether or not the features of interest are at a favourable conservation status. The definition of favourable conservation status is not straightforward but, in essence, conservation status is deemed to be favourable when the natural range and coverage of a natural habitat is stable or increasing and the natural range of a species is not reducing.[10]

In terms of habitat, it is one of the aims of the directive to establish a European network of protected areas, known as Natura 2000. The network is to comprise SPAs classified under the Birds Directive and Special Areas of Conservation (SACs) designated under the Habitats Directive. Designation of SACs is not simply a matter for the individual States; instead Member States submit proposals to the European Commission, which then makes the final decisions on which need to be designated. The directive lists the plant and animal species and habitat types for which SACs must be designated, and the final selection of sites is made on the basis of a number of detailed criteria.

The requirements for the protection of SACs are set out in Article 6. Article 6(1) states the basic requirement for Member States to establish the necessary conservation measures, including the use of appropriate management plans where necessary. Article 6(2) sets the standard for protection. It requires Member States to

> take appropriate steps to avoid, in [SACs], the deterioration of natural habitats and the habitats of species as well as disturbance of the species for which the areas have been designated, in so far as such disturbance could be significant in relation to the objectives of [the] Directive.

Article 6(3) sets out the procedures to be followed whenever there are plans that might affect an SAC. It states that:

> any plan or project not directly concerned with or necessary to the management of the site but likely to have a significant effect thereon, either individually or in combination with other plans or projects, shall be subject to appropriate assessment of its implications for the site in view of the site's conservation objectives. In the light of the conclusions of the assessment of the implications for the site . . . , the competent national authorities shall agree to the plan or project only after having ascertained that it will not adversely affect the integrity of the site concerned and, if appropriate, after having obtained the opinion of the general public.

If the assessment does indicate that there will be adverse effects, the plan or project may still proceed if it must be carried out 'for imperative reasons of overriding public interest, including those of a social or economic nature'.[11] It will be necessary, however, for the Member State to take compensatory measures to ensure the overall coherence of Natura 2000. If the site contains a priority natural habitat and/or species, the relevant considerations are largely restricted to those relating to human health and safety. Although the provisions for the designation of SPAs and SACs remain separate, the provisions of Article 6 of the Habitats Directive apply to SPAs as well as SACs.[12]

The species protection measures in the Habitats Directive have proved less troublesome than those on site protection. They bear considerable similarity to those set out for birds in the Birds Directive. Thus, Articles 12 and 13 require Member States to establish a system of strict protection for animals and plants. Again, there are provisions for derogation provided there is no satisfactory alternative and the derogation is not detrimental to the maintenance of the populations of species at a favourable conservation status. The main difference from the Birds Directive is that the measures apply only to listed species.

## The influence of international wildlife law

The UK is party to a number of multilateral environmental agreements operating on both a regional and a global scale, several of which require or encourage contracting parties to designate protected areas for a variety of purposes. The UK has not found it necessary to pass domestic legislation to implement these agreements, and sites are protected using existing measures, notably those relating to SSSIs. One consequence of this approach is that there is a tendency for multiple badging of sites, whereby a single site may serve to implement UK commitments under a number of different international agreements.[13] The greatest impact of international legal requirements has been in three areas: the need to implement the Berne Convention, which led to the enactment of the Wildlife and Countryside Act 1981; obligations under the Convention for the Protection of the Marine Environment of the North East Atlantic (OSPAR Convention) for the creation of marine protected areas; and the 2010 biodiversity target set under the Convention on Biological Diversity.

The Berne Convention on the Conservation of European Wildlife and Natural Habitats 1979 was implemented in Great Britain by the Wildlife and Countryside Act 1981.[14] It provided the first real commitment to protect species and habitats and, because most of its provisions were mandatory, it was enforceable. This Convention, which comes under the auspices of the Council of Europe, is significant now mainly because it was strongly influential in the development of the EC Habitats Directive.

Annex V of the OSPAR Convention is concerned with the protection of marine ecosystems and biodiversity.[15] A recommendation made in 2003 urged contracting parties to create an ecologically coherent network of Marine Protected Areas in the north east Atlantic by 2010. This echoed a commitment made at the World Sustainable Development Summit in 2002 to create a representative network of marine protected areas by 2012. As stated in the UK Marine Policy Statement, the creation of such a network is central to the policies of the UK government and the devolved administrations, although, as is discussed below, it is difficult to see how it is going to be achieved.[16]

In 2002, the Conference of the Parties to the Convention on Biological Diversity set a target to achieve a significant reduction in the current rate of biodiversity loss at global, regional and national levels by 2010.[17] The target was endorsed at the World Summit on Sustainable Development in 2005 and incorporated in the Millennium Development Goals.[18] In 2001, the EU set a more ambitious target to halt the decline of biodiversity by 2010 and restore habitats and natural systems.[19] The failure to meet the 2010 biodiversity targets was the trigger for the new approach to natural resource management in Wales.

## Current legal provisions for site protection

As explained above, the conservation of specific sites is based on the notification of SSSIs and the designation of National and Local Nature Reserves. Despite a long history of criticism of the SSSI, s. 28 of the Wildlife and Countryside Act remained largely unchanged until the need to comply with the Habitats Directive prompted a more general overview of site safeguard.[20] This review led to the Countryside and Rights of Way Act 2000, which made radical changes to the SSSI regime in England and Wales, largely removing the element of voluntary compliance on the part of landowners, which had dogged implementation in the past. Meanwhile, the Conservation (Natural Habitats, etc.) Regulations 1994 presented an amended SSSI regime to apply to sites proposed for designation as Special Areas of Conservation under the Habitats Directive.[21]

The process of SSSI notification and protection is basically the same in England and Wales. Sites are notified to landholders and others on the basis of their scientific interest. Notification documents include a list of potentially damaging operations (PDOs) and a Management Statement indicating a management vision for the site. Once a site has been notified, the landholder cannot carry out the PDOs without the prior agreement of the Countryside Council for Wales (CCW). However, landholders may be eligible for financial assistance under management agreements designed to meet the objectives of the management statement. If the management of the site is not satisfactory, CCW can issue a Management Scheme, spelling out what needs to be done. If the landholder refuses to take heed of this scheme, he or she may be served with a Management Notice requiring action to be taken. The presence of an SSSI also has implications for other public bodies in the way they exercise their functions with respect to designated land, and it is also possible for CCW to make byelaws for the protection of SSSIs.

The Conservation (Natural Habitats, etc.) Regulations 1994 strengthened the 1981 SSSI regime with respect to European sites. One significant difference is the inclusion of provisions for a Special Nature Conservation Order to be made to prevent operations being carried out where they are considered likely to have a detrimental effect. The Order comes into immediate effect and, although it only lasts for nine months, can be extended by the Secretary of State if necessary. To date, no orders have been made in Wales. Compulsory purchase is also available as a last resort. The Regulations also include rules for the determination of the acceptability of plans and projects that might affect a European site, based on Article 6 of the Directive. These rules act retrospectively to a limited extent in that there is a requirement for consenting authorities to review consents already given.

The protection of marine habitats and species has proved controversial and difficult to place on a legal footing. The Marine Nature Reserve, introduced in the Wildlife and Countryside Act 1981, has been replaced under the Marine and Coastal Access Act 2009 by the Marine Conservation Zone, which is the only site protection mechanism for marine habitats of national importance. Protection for marine species and habitats is provided for in the Birds and Habitats Directives, as is reflected in the implementing instruments.

## Species protection

As noted above, there is no blanket protection of all individual species of wildlife. Instead, protection is restricted to those species deemed special, because they are particularly rare or because they migrate, for example. There is a strong subjective element to be seen in the lists of species to be protected, which are heavily biased towards vertebrates and higher plants.

Part I of the Wildlife and Countryside Act makes it an offence intentionally or recklessly to kill, injure or take any wild bird; to take, damage, destroy or otherwise interfere with the nest of any bird while under construction or in use; to obstruct or prevent any wild bird from using its nest; or to take or destroy an egg of any wild bird. Higher penalties apply if the bird concerned is listed under Schedule 1 to the Act. It is also an offence intentionally or recklessly to disturb a wild bird listed under Schedule 1 while it is building its nest or is in, on or near to a nest containing eggs or young; or to disturb dependent young of a Schedule 1 species of bird. There are a number of exceptions to Section 1. Bird species listed under Part I of Schedule 2 may be killed or taken outside their close season.

Following devolution, the species lists are no longer the same across Great Britain, and other small differences to the wording of the Act have been introduced. At the moment the differences are between Scotland on the one hand and England and Wales on the other, but, with the advent of additional law-making powers for Wales, there is no reason why Wales should not have its own list. These are likely to reflect the status of species in the different countries. For example, in Scotland, the capercaillie (*Tetrao urogallis*) has been afforded extra protection by adding it to Schedule 1 Part 1, whereas in England and Wales it remains on Schedule 2 Part I. Similarly, the white-tailed eagle (*Haliaetus albicilla*) is given extra protection by virtue of two new Schedules to the 1981 Act introduced by Scottish legislation.[22]

Part I provisions for other species of animals are similar to those for birds, with one important exception. Only those species listed in the Act are protected; for other species there is no direct species conservation law, although protection may be provided through habitat protection measures and under animal welfare legislation. In addition, a few species are also covered by their own individual statutes. The list of animals protected is regularly revised through a process known as the quinquennial review, although the five-year time period is not always adhered to. For plants, the highest level of protection is reserved for listed species. As with animals, the list is subject to regular review. It is an offence intentionally to pick, uproot or destroy any wild plant of a listed species. For other wild plants, it is not an offence to pick them but they cannot be legally uprooted without permission of the landowner. The statutory reviews of the schedules are undertaken by the Joint Nature Conservation Committee, which then advises ministers. Powers for making the orders to amend the schedules have been devolved.

The list of species protected under the Habitats Directive is more extensive than that under the Act but there are considerable overlaps. Further species protection is provided under the Natural Environment and Rural Communities Act 2006, which imposes separate duties on ministers in England and Wales to publish a list of species and habitats of principal importance and to take reasonable steps to further their conservation and encourage others to do the same. As with the 1981 Act, the lists are to be kept under review.

## The impact of devolution

For the most part, prior to devolution, primary and secondary nature conservation legislation applied in Great Britain and similar measures were introduced in Northern Ireland after a short time lag. Thus the SSSI provisions of the 1949 and 1981 Act applied to England, Scotland and Wales, as did the 1994 Conservation Regulations. The first indication of a divergence of ways came with the break-up of the Nature Conservancy Council in the early 1990s. Institutional arrangements for the delivery of nature conservation in Great Britain were devolved in 1990, long before national devolution took place. Until then, the Nature Conservancy Council was the official body responsible for nature conservation in Great Britain. The Countryside Commission was responsible for recreational aspects of countryside policy in England and Wales and the Countryside Commission Scotland exercised similar powers in Scotland. Part VII of the Environmental Protection Act 1990 set up separate statutory nature conservation bodies for England and Wales but did not change the functions. Following the devolution of responsibilities under the Environmental Protection Act 1990, nature conservation and countryside functions were merged in Wales. Similar changes were made in Scotland by the Natural Heritage (Scotland) Act 1991, which created Scottish Natural Heritage. Unlike the Environment Act, however, this Act did introduce some changes to functions. Section 1(1) of the Act requires it to have regard to the desirability of securing that anything done in relation to the natural heritage of Scotland is undertaken in a sustainable manner.[23] The Act also introduced some changes to the administrative arrangements for SSSIs, including the establishment of an advisory committee. With the creation of the Scottish Parliament, Scotland has gone ahead with its own legislative programme. The National Parks (Scotland) Act 2000 makes provisions for the creation of national parks in Scotland, and the Nature Conservation (Scotland) Act 2004 makes changes to the SSSI legislation comparable, but not identical, to those introduced in England and Wales under the Countryside and Rights of Way Act 2000. The Marine (Scotland)

Act 2010 provides for a Scottish approach to the designations of marine protected areas for a variety of purposes including nature conservation. Most recently, the species protection provisions of the Wildlife and Countryside Act and various game Acts have been revised in the Wildlife and Natural Environment (Scotland) Act 2011. With enhanced legislative powers now available in Wales, it is possible that further divergence between the UK countries may follow.

The Environmental Protection Act 1990 made changes to the institutional arrangement in England by creating a new body, English Nature, but did not merge it with the Countryside Commission. Responsibilities for nature conservation and countryside remained separate, strongly suggesting that the change to combined agencies elsewhere was one of administrative convenience rather than being firmly based on any change in policy. The Countryside Commission subsequently merged with the Rural Development Commission to form the Countryside Agency. This move reflects a shift in perception of the countryside, from a backdrop for conservation to being part of a larger rural agenda in which public enjoyment and recreation become linked to tourism and jobs. In 2006, a further change was made by bringing together English Nature with the landscape, access and recreation part of the Countryside Agency and the environmental land management part of the Rural Development Service to create a new body, Natural England. Meanwhile, the creation of the Environment Agency and the Scottish Environment Protection Agency under the Environment Act 1995 further emphasized the different approach being taken in Scotland. Although the Environment Agency is properly called the Environment Agency for England and Wales, the Welsh operation was always seen as somewhat different. With the establishment of the National Assembly for Wales and new ministerial responsibilities, the distinction became stronger. Environment Agency Wales, although still part of the Environment Agency, is also answerable to the Welsh Government. To the extent that the Agency has responsibility for freshwater fisheries and has several other conservation functions, the development of a distinctive Welsh character for the Environment Agency Wales is of relevance to nature conservation in this country.

Local democracy also has an important role to play in nature conservation, most notably in relation to land use planning. Planning is largely a devolved matter, and different planning regimes operate in each of the four administrations and each administration issues its own planning guidance. The nature conservation value of a site is one of the factors that local planning authorities have to consider when formulating development plans and deciding on planning applications.[24]

The demise of a nature conservation body for Great Britain in 1990 led to concerns that this would result in a loss of national perspective. It was also unclear how international matters would be dealt with in future and, in particular, how the separate country agencies would work together to meet the requirements of European legislation. The government's solution was to create a committee of the country agencies, the Joint Nature Conservation Committee (JNCC), with responsibility for delivering 'special functions' including the establishment of common standards and the provision of advice on nature conservation in Great Britain as a whole and overseas.[25] With the advent of devolution, the importance of a body with a national perspective has increased and the JNCC has been reconstituted with additional independent members appointed by the government.[26]

The full potential impact of devolution on the institutional arrangements for nature conservation became apparent as the UK's Labour government worked to fulfil its 2005 election manifesto pledge to enact a Marine Bill, which, *inter alia*, would address some of the perceived deficiencies in marine conservation law. The delivery of marine spatial planning in UK waters was one of the key aims of the government's marine policy. However, because responsibility for planning and conservation has been devolved and the devolved powers extend at least to the territorial sea adjacent to each administration, the Westminster Parliament could not legislate for the creation of new marine protected areas without the agreement of the devolved administrations. The result is that, while the Marine and Coastal Access Act 2009 does provide for the creation of Marine Conservation Zones (MCZs) and goes so far as to require the Welsh Government to designate them in order to contribute to a UK network of marine protected areas, it cannot dictate how the MCZ provisions are to be used. As is discussed below, Wales has chosen to adopt a different approach from that applied in English and offshore waters.

## Marine conservation: a Welsh perspective

The Marine and Coastal Access Act 2009 is the most recent statute concerned with nature conservation in Wales and provides a useful case study for considering the impact of devolution on conservation. The Act provides for the creation of MCZs, one purpose of which is to form part of a network contributing to conservation in the UK marine area, i.e. the waters around the UK out to 200 nautical miles. The UK marine area is divided into country regions, however, and these regions are sub-divided into inshore and offshore regions. The respective limits of UK and devolved powers vary with the different regions and with the different functions under the Act. For MCZs, the UK government has powers of designation for English inshore waters and offshore waters with the exception of the Scottish offshore region; Wales can designate MCZs only in its inshore region and Scotland has powers of designation for offshore regions. There are no powers to make MCZs in Scottish or Northern Irish inshore waters; these are covered, or expected to be covered, by devolved measures.

The UK government, working with Natural England and the JNCC, has endorsed a stakeholder-led approach for the identification of potential MCZs. Wales has taken a very different approach.[27] Some 70 per cent of Welsh territorial waters is already under some form of protective designation and it was decided to use the additional powers provided under the Act to designate a small number of highly protected MCZs, which would, in effect, amount to no-take zones. Potential sites are being identified by an expert group and the wider stakeholder community has not yet been invited to provide comments. Because Welsh powers of designation only extend to the limit of 12 nautical miles, this presents the somewhat anomalous situation in which offshore waters have been considered by stakeholder-led work and inshore waters have not. There is no legal hierarchy to require the designating authorities to work together to select sites that are most suitable for the ecologically coherent network aspired to in the UK Marine Policy Statement despite the fact that the creation of a network of sites is given as a key reason for designating MCZs in the first place.[28]

## The Natural Environmental Framework: *A Living Wales*

The failure to meet the 2010 biodiversity targets led to policy decisions at Westminster and in Wales to undertake major reviews of biodiversity policy in order to address the situation. In England, the Secretary of State commissioned a review of protected areas, the report from which informed the 2011 White Paper on the environment.[29] In January 2010, Jane Davidson, the then Minister for Environment, Sustainability and Housing, made a statement on biodiversity to the Welsh Cabinet.[30] A report commissioned for the National Assembly for Wales provided further details of the progress made towards halting biodiversity loss, which made it clear that the 2010 targets would not be met.[31] The failure led the minister to begin to develop a new approach – the Natural Environment Framework (NEF) – to enable more integrated management of the environment.[32] Work on the new framework is addressing a number of issues of direct relevance to nature conservation in Wales including the need for a stronger evidence base for ecosystems, a realistic reflection of the values of ecosystems and their services, updating of regulatory and management approaches to deliver the new approach, redesigning partnership mechanisms between different sectors of society and refreshing institutional arrangements. It is too soon, yet, to see what these changes are likely to mean for nature conservation but there are already some key pointers. One of the most significant developments arising from the NEF is the decision by John Griffiths, the Environment Minister, to accept the business case for a single environment body to be created through the merger of the Countryside Council for Wales, the Environment Agency Wales and the Forestry Commission Wales.[33] If all goes to plan, the new body will be vested on 1 April 2013.

Evidence provided to the workstream looking at regulatory and management approaches has shown broad satisfaction with the existing legal framework, although a number of proposals for relatively minor amendments have been made. Most of the concerns have been on the limitations of the legislation to deliver wider environmental benefits and on the failure of the authorities to adopt a flexible joined-up approach to regulation. Important as these comments are, the responses are perhaps more significant in what was not said rather than what was. The bulk of the evidence on nature conservation and biodiversity in responses to the NEF consultation has stuck to ways of improving on the existing regimes and there has been little evidence of questioning whether the framework is fundamentally capable of protecting biodiversity as part of the natural environmental resources of Wales.[34]

The NEF is a Welsh Government manifesto commitment. At the time of writing, a Green Paper on the environment was expected to be launched at the end of January 2012, to be followed with a White Paper. The First Minister has included an environment Bill in the legislative programme for this Assembly.[35] The proposed Bill is intended to enhance environmental protection and deliver ecological gains, while easing the regulatory burden. Taking a most extreme view, this could mean a completely new way of looking at nature conservation. Instead of the present regime, in which nature conservation is regarded as a sectoral interest competing with other sectoral interests, a natural resource plan could elevate the importance of biodiversity (and other environmental resources) to become paramount considerations.

## The future of nature conservation in Wales: some concluding comments

The legal regime for nature conservation has served well. Incremental changes introduced by amendment over the years have succeeded in bringing the scientific aspect of nature conservation closer to public enjoyment aspects so that the contribution of biodiversity to social, environmental and economic well-being is at least partly integrated. The increased importance attaching to biodiversity in the European context has also been accommodated without fundamentally changing the British approach to nature conservation. However, it may be that the extent of patching and mending old laws and policies has reached its limit and that there is now a need for a fundamental restructuring of our approach. To a great extent this will be limited by the constraints applied by European directives but the EU may also change its stance. Certainly the international approach to nature conservation seems to be more attuned to placing biodiversity in a setting of sustainable development in which management and regulation take an ecosystems approach and that recognizes the importance of ecosystem services as part of a sustainable future.

The key requirement for change is the need to look for desirable outcomes rather than simply box-ticking compliance with individual bits and pieces of legislation. This will require a more flexible approach to the interpretation and implementation of legislation. A review of the way in which article 6 of the Habitats Directive is currently interpreted might be a useful start, as evidence from the NEF consultation suggests that the implementation of this article is highly bureaucratic and time-consuming and does not necessarily lead to satisfactory outcomes.[36] The UK Government has announced a review of the implementation of the Habitats and Birds Directives in England with the aim of reducing the burden on business while maintaining the integrity of the purpose of the directives.[37] It is likely that this announcement will have resonated with the Welsh Government, which will no doubt be interested in the outcome.

In terms of legal changes, there may be a need to review the range of protected area mechanisms to see if these can be simplified and made to work in a more flexible manner that goes further than current legislation allows. *Making Space for Nature* suggested as much for England and there is no reason why the same conclusions would not apply in Wales. Species protection measures also need to be revisited, not least the range of species that we currently chose to protect. The Law Commission has included wildlife legislation in its programme of law reform, and this exercise may provide a good opportunity not only to update and refresh the legal framework but also to propose specific measures for Wales.[38] The Welsh Government will be working with the Law Commission on this review. Depending on the outcome of the initial scoping study, the Law Commission aims to produce a draft bill by mid-2014. If the goal in future is to be the protection of ecosystems then there may no longer be any justification for giving extra-special protection for birds, for example, while at the same time virtually ignoring some animal and plant groups altogether, regardless of their relative importance to ecosystem functioning.

There will continue to be an issue with the extent of devolved powers. Devolution is still a relatively new concept for the UK, and there remain a number of anomalies (not least the confusion engendered by having a Westminster Parliament and administration that are acting both for England and for the UK as a whole). Of course, ecosystems do not respect national boundaries, and the smaller the administrative units the more boundaries there are. It is already apparent that the UK will find it challenging to meet its international obligations under the OSPAR Convention to create an ecological coherent network of marine protected areas by 2012 because there are no powers to bring the devolved administrations together to define what such a network should consist of. Regardless of how well the current and future Welsh administrations protect Welsh nature in a Welsh context, there will be a need to work with the other parts of the UK, and this will require a more mature approach to cooperative working than appears to exist at present.

## Addendum

Several of the initiatives referred to in this chapter have been taken forward subsequently. *Sustaining a Living Wales*, a Green Paper on the NEF proposals, was launched in 30 January 2012, closely followed by *Natural Resource Wales*, a Green Paper on the establishment of a single environment body. *Marine Conservation Zones (MCZs): Potential Site Options for Welsh Waters* was issued in April 2012. Finally, the review of the Habitats and Birds Directive reported in March 2012 and made some recommendations for improving the process of implementation.

## Notes

1 The Natural Environment Framework was announced in the consultation document *A Living Wales: A New Framework for Our Environment, Our Countryside and Our Seas*, issued on 15 September 2010. It is available at *http://wales.gov.uk/consultations/ environmentandcountryside/eshlivingwaleseons/?lang=en* (accessed 8 May 2012).
2 For a detailed account of the origins of the National Parks etc. Act and the role of these committees, see J. Sheail, 'The National Parks and Access to the Countryside Act of 1949: its origins and significance', in T. C. Smout (ed.), *Nature, Landscape and People since the Second World War* (Tuckwell Press: East Linton, 2001).
3 Note that this relationship is not always a straightforward one. Although *Gateshead Metropolitan Borough Council v. Secretary of State for the Environment* [1995] Env. L. R. 37 found no problem with leaving potential pollution control issues to the regulator to decide after planning permission has been granted, it is not always possible to ignore pollution aspects during planning considerations, especially if a statutory environmental assessment is required.
4 *National Parks and the Conservation of Nature in Scotland* (Cmd. 7235, 1947).
5 The Area of Special Scientific Interest (ASSI) designation in Northern Ireland is equivalent to the SSSI, which applies in Great Britain.
6 The argument is that, because an SSSI has to be notified to the planning authority, there cannot be an SSSI notification if there is no planning authority to notify. This interpretation has not been challenged in the courts but, even if it were found to be incorrect, there would still be little appetite to apply a designation based on regulating the way owners and occupiers use their land to a marine situation where private landownership is not an issue. For further details see L. M. Warren, 'Law and policy for marine protected areas', in C. P. Rodgers (ed.), *Nature Conservation and Countryside Law* (Cardiff: University of Wales Press, 1996).
7 The Countryside and Rights of Way Act 2000 made substantial amendments to s. 28 of the Wildlife and Countryside Act 1981, including powers for the statutory nature conservation bodies to formulate management schemes for SSSIs and enforce them through management notices served on the owner or occupier of the land in question.
8 Article 3 requires Member States to preserve, maintain or re-establish a sufficient diversity of habitat for all species through, *inter alia*, the creation of protected areas.
9 Annex 1 lists 175 species requiring special protection, and the provisions also apply to migratory species, with special attention being made to the protection of wetland habitats.
10 For details see Article 1(e) in relation to habitats and Article 1(i) in relation to species.
11 Article 6(4).
12 Article 7.
13 The Dyfi Estuary provides a good Welsh example. The estuary and the surrounding area has been designated as a Biosphere Reserve and land within it carries the following additional designations: SSSI, National Nature Reserve, marine SAC, SPA, Ramsar site and National Park.
14 UKTS 56 (1982), Cmnd. 8738.
15 32 ILM (1993) 1072.

16 Published by Defra on behalf of the UK Government and the Devolved Administrations in March 2011; available at *http://wales.gov.uk/topics/environmentcountryside/consmanagement/marinefisheries/planning/?lang=en* (accessed 8 May 2012).
17 31 ILM (1992) 818; Decision VI/26 of COP6. For details see *http://www.cbd.int/decision/cop/?id=7200* (accessed 8 May 2012).
18 For details of Summit, see *http://www.un.org/jsummit/html/documents/summit_docs/2309_planfinal.htm* (accessed 8 May 2012). For details of the Millennium Development Goals, see *http://www.un.org/millenniumgoals/bkgd.shtml* (accessed 8 May 2012).
19 *http://ec.europa.eu/environment/nature/biodiversity/comm2006/index_en.htm* (accessed 8 May 2012).
20 See K. V. Last, 'Habitat protection: has the Wildlife and Countryside Act 1981 made a difference?', *Journal of Environmental Law*, 11 (1999), 15–34.
21 SI 1994/2716. The Regulations have been largely replaced by the Conservation of Habitats and Species Regulations 2010 (SI 2010/490), which apply to both England and Wales.
22 Nature Conservation (Scotland) Act 2004 s. 50 and Schedule 6.
23 'Natural heritage' is defined as including the flora and fauna of Scotland, its geological and physiographical features, and its natural beauty and amenity; s. 1(3).
24 Technical Advice Note (TAN) 5, *Nature Conservation and Planning* (2009), advises local authorities on how to take account of biodiversity interests when applying the generic *Planning Policy Wales*. Both are available at *http://wales.gov.uk/topics/planning/policy/tans/?lang=en* (accessed 8 May 2012). In England, advice is contained in Government Circular 06/05 *Biodiversity and Geological Conservation: Statutory Obligations and Their Impact within the Planning System* and Planning Policy Statement 9 *Biodiversity and Geological Conservation*; available at *http://www.communities.gov.uk/planningandbuilding/planningsystem/planningpolicy/planningpolicystatements/pps9/* (accessed 8 May 2012).
25 This was set up under s. 156 of the Environmental Protection Act 1990.
26 The JNCC was reconstituted as a company limited by guarantee under Schedule 3 of the Natural Environment and Rural Communities Act 2006.
27 Further information on MCZs in Wales is available at *http://wales.gov.uk/topics/environmentcountryside/consmanagement/marinefisheries/conservation/protected/conservationzones/?lang=en* (accessed 8 May 2012).
28 The UK Marine Policy Statement sets out statutory policy as agreed by all the UK administrations. It can be downloaded at *http://wales.gov.uk/topics/environmentcountryside/consmanagement/marinefisheries/planning/?lang=en* (accessed 8 May 2012). Section 123 of the Act requires the designation of MCZs in order to contribute to the achievement of a network contributing to the conservation or improvement of the marine environment in the UK marine area.
29 *Making Space for Nature: A Review of England's Wildlife Sites and Ecological Network*, Report to Defra, September 2010; *The Natural Choice: Securing the Value of Nature*, Cm 8082, June 2011.
30 Cabinet Written Statement, 18 January 2010.
31 *http://www.assemblywales.org/10-054.pdf* (accessed 8 May 2012).
32 Full details of the NEF are available at *http://wales.gov.uk/topics/environmentcountryside/consmanagement/nef/?lang=en* (accessed 8 May 2012).
33 Further details of the decision and of the business case supporting it are available at *http://wales.gov.uk/topics/environmentcountryside/consmanagement/seb/?lang=en* (accessed 8 May 2012).
34 The responses are available to download at *http://wales.gov.uk/consultations/environmentandcountryside/eshlivingwalescons/?lang=en* (accessed 8 May 2012).
35 The text of the First Minister's announcement is available in the Record of Proceedings at *http://www.assemblywales.org/bus-home/bus-chamber-fourth-assembly-rop.htm*

*?act=dis&id=219617&ds=7%2F2011#vot* (accessed 8 May 2012). A fuller account of the proposed environment Bill can be found in *The Welsh Government's Legislative Programme 2011–2016* Paper No. 11/048, which is available at *http://www.assembly-wales.org/11-048.pdf* (accessed 8 May 2012).

36 See *http://wales.gov.uk/consultations/environmentandcountryside/eshlivingwalescons/?lang=en*, above.

37 The announcement was made by the Chancellor in his Autumn Statement to Parliament on 29 November 2011; available at *http://www.hm-treasury.gov.uk/as2011)_index.htm* (accessed 8 May 2012).

38 *Eleventh Programme of Law Reform*, paras 2.83–2.88; available at *http://lawcommission.justice.gov.uk/docs/lc330_eleventh_programme.pdf* (accessed 8 May 2012).

## Chapter 6

# Badgers, bovine tuberculosis and the role of science in the formulation of Welsh environmental and agricultural policy

*Patrick Bishop*

To claim that environmental law and environmental policy is heavily, even primarily, science based is too trite an assertion by far.[1] The influence of scientific discourse on the environmental movement is unsurprising; it was scientists who first demonstrated the now almost axiomatic link between unregulated human activity and environmental degradation.[2] Indeed, it has been suggested that contemporary environmental law should move away from a pluralistic notion of legitimacy to one based primarily on science.[3] However, while one cannot deny the importance of science in the context of environmental law and the formulation of environmental policy, a science-led approach is not unproblematic. It is often the case that, implicitly, those who assert that science-led or evidence-based environmental policy is to be lauded subscribe, to a greater or lesser extent, to the notion that science is able to provide an answer to any policy question. Experience teaches us that is not the case; as Ravetz has opined: 'it [science] now faces a crisis of confidence, of legitimacy and ultimately of power.'[4] Scientific evidence is seldom incontestable and, particularly where a scientific study is carried out specifically to inform policy, the results are often, if not invariably, open to interpretation.[5] This chapter will primarily draw upon the Welsh Government's plans to eradicate bovine tuberculosis (hereafter bTB), as a means of analysing the role and influence of science in the formulation of environmental and agricultural policy. In this context, the most pertinent (and controversial) question is the extent to which the culling of badgers (*Meles meles*) is able to make a significant contribution to the reduction and eventual eradication of bTB. The central objective is an exploration of the extent to which science is able to constrain political choice. From a narrow perspective, science is clearly able to restrict policy formulation in the technical sense that science reveals the parameters of what is possible. This chapter will focus on the broader issue of the influence of science on policy design, particularly in the context of policy makers who openly subscribe to a science-led approach. A discussion of the nature and scale of the problem of bTB will be followed by an evaluation of the scientific evidence in relation to the efficacy of badger culling. The proceeding sections will consider the varied roles of science in informing decision making and the formulation of policy prior to an analysis of the Welsh Government's use of scientific evidence in the context of bTB.

## Bovine tuberculosis: the nature and scale of the problem

Bovine tuberculosis, caused by the bacterium *Mycobacterium bovis* (*M. bovis*), has been a persistent problem in UK cattle farming for a considerable time. The disease first gained the attention of the public and policy makers in the late nineteenth century, with widespread concern over the dangers to human health from consuming infected meat.[6] In 1934, the Gowland Hopkins Report recognized that infected milk, and not meat, was the dominant source of human infection.[7] Since then the widespread use of pasteurization has led to the virtual eradication of bTB in humans.[8] Thus, bTB in a contemporary context is predominantly viewed as an animal health problem. Given the costs associated with state-funded compensation for compulsorily slaughtered infected animals (considered below), successive governments have sought to mandate measures with the overall aim of bTB eradication.

The debate about whether badger culling is able to assist in the eradication of bTB is complex and multi-dimensional; the Welsh Assembly's initial decision to authorize culling has led to the pro-cull and pro-badger factions adopting rather entrenched positions.[9] However, there is a loose consensus on both sides of the debate that bTB requires government attention. Thus, it is the efficacy of badger culling, not whether bTB is a significant problem, that is principally at issue. The eradication of bTB, described by the Welsh Assembly Government (as it was then titled) as 'one of the biggest threats to Cattle farming in Wales', is an issue of extensive socio-economic importance.[10] In 2009, in excess of 11,500 bTB-infected cattle were slaughtered and, since 2000, approximately £120 million has been spent on the payment of compensation to Welsh farmers following the compulsory slaughter of infected animals.[11] It is a relatively safe assumption that the true economic cost of bTB extends beyond the publicly funded compensation system. An approximate figure for the cost of the average confirmed herd breakdown is £30,000; of this total figure, £20,000 falls to the state (predominantly in the form of compensation and the cost of testing) and the remainder is borne by the farmer/cattle owner (costs associated with herd movement restrictions, loss of breeding lines etc.).[12] As illustrated by a recent survey conducted by the Farm Crisis Network, in addition to the economic costs associated with bTB, the consequences of a confirmed herd breakdown and the resulting destruction of infected animals will often entail a human cost for farmers and their families in terms of concern, anxiety and, in some cases, physical illness exacerbated by stress.[13]

The preceding discussion has attempted to summarize what may be termed the mainstream view that bTB is a serious problem that necessitates state intervention. However, the economic and social costs highlighted above flow directly from the Welsh Government's adherence to a test and slaughter policy. The desirability and efficacy of this policy has not gone unquestioned. Given that bTB no longer represents a serious threat to public health (on the assumption that widespread pasteurization of milk continues), Torgerson and Torgerson have argued that, in the absence of any evidence that the current bTB control mechanisms are economically effective in terms of improvements in animal health/welfare and industry profitability/viability, the current programme represents a 'clear example of misallocation of public resources.'[14] Thus, it is argued the current bTB control programme should be abandoned until such time that evidence of a positive cost–benefit ratio exists. The abandonment of the current bTB control policy would unquestionably have ramifications for the UK cattle industry on the basis that EU law prohibits the live export of cattle that have tested positive for bTB.[15] Torgerson and Torgerson are rather sanguine in relation to the damage to international trade that would flow from the abandonment of a bTB eradication programme, on the basis that the cost of the policy exceeds the value of live exports from the UK.[16] Moreover, it is noted that only 1.4 per cent of the UK cattle population is exported each year.[17] While it is generally accepted that the economic value of live cattle exports is relatively modest, it should be noted that such statistics should be analysed in light of the bovine spongiform encephalopathy (BSE) crisis, which totally devastated UK cattle exports.[18] However, even if live export levels returned to pre-BSE crisis levels, it would remain difficult to discern a noticeable positive cost–benefit ratio. In the year immediately preceding the BSE crisis (1995), live cattle exports were worth approximately £70 million to the UK economy.[19] During 2009 in England alone, the cost of the test and slaughter policy to the tax payer was £63 million.[20] As previously noted, from 2000, the policy incurred costs of £120 million in Wales. Thus, even if live export levels fully recovered, it is safe to assume that the costs associated with the current bTB eradication programme would continue to outweigh any benefits in terms of international trade. However, the formulation of a bTB eradication plan is an EU-imposed obligation.[21] Thus, a laissez-faire approach is unlikely to be considered a viable option for the foreseeable future. Indeed, the Independent Scientific Group on Cattle TB has accepted the basic premise of the foregoing discussion:

> [T]he economic cost of cattle TB is a voluntary cost associated with the standard methods of reacting to or looking for breakdowns, rather than the cost the disease itself would impose on livestock production. Nor is it clear that the inherent benefits of dealing with the threat of TB in this way exceed the costs incurred – but this question is not posed because the routine test and slaughter policy is now treated as the baseline situation.[22]

While it continues to be widely accepted that bTB requires state intervention, policy makers will continue to search for the most efficacious solution, which in turn raises the question of the role of badger culling in any bTB eradication programme.

## The efficacy of badger culling: the scientific evidence

Despite the explicit reference to 'bovine' in bTB, the disease is not limited to cattle and it is widely accepted that a reservoir of *M. bovis* exists in wildlife, including badgers.[23] The suspected link between badgers and bTB was first made in 1971, and since then the efficacy of badger culling has been a widely debated issue.[24] It is a cruel irony that the link between bTB and badgers roughly coincided with moves to provide statutory protection.[25] While a consensus emerged against the cruel and inhuman practice of badger baiting, the discovery of bTB-infected badgers created a new and arguably greater threat to one of the UK's most charismatic wild species.

From 1973 to 1997, badger culling was extensively utilized in areas with a high incidence of bTB in cattle; in tandem with this approach, a number of scientific studies were carried out with the aim of investigating a possible link between badgers and the infection of cattle with bTB.[26] Despite this a conclusive link between badgers and bTB in cattle remained elusive, as Enticott has noted:

> Critically, there remained no 'proof' that badgers passed TB to cattle. Rather MAFF's approach sought to problematise proof and causality as a function of statistical observation between evidence of TB and absence of badgers, rather than establishing how the disease was spread.[27]

The statistician's mantra that 'correlation does not imply causation' is particularly apt in this context.[28] In response to growing concern over the government's approach to bTB, an independent scientific review was commissioned under the chairmanship of John Krebs. The resulting report concluded that 'Most of this evidence is indirect, consisting of correlations rather than demonstrations of cause and effect.'[29] It was therefore recommended, *inter alia*, that an expert group should be convened to conduct a randomized culling trial to test the effectiveness of different strategies and to provide unambiguous evidence of the role of badgers in the spread of bTB.

In response to the recommendations of the Krebs report, the UK government assembled an Independent Scientific Group (hereafter 'ISG') to oversee a long-term randomized experiment to test the effectiveness of badger culling as a means of controlling bTB.[30] The randomized badger-culling trial (hereafter RBCT) spanned a period of nine years (1998–2007) at a cost of approximately £50 million. A close analysis of the methodology employed is beyond the scope of this chapter (and the expertise of the author) and the detailed statistical data produced may be incomprehensible to anyone without scientific training. Nevertheless, the conclusion provided in the final report of the ISG is as simple as it is stark: 'After careful consideration of all the RBCT and other data presented in this report, including an economic assessment, we conclude that badger culling cannot meaningfully contribute to the future control of cattle TB in Britain.'[31] In terms of other options for controlling bTB, the ISG supported further research on the use of cattle- and badger-based vaccination but noted that, given the legal and practical obstacles to the use of vaccination, it should be considered only as a longer-term option.[32] Thus, the overall conclusion of the ISG was that the main 'tool' in the control and eradication of bTB should be improved cattle-based control measures including, *inter alia*, more thorough controls on cattle movements, quarantine of purchased cattle and shorter testing intervals.[33]

## The varied roles of science in informing decision making

As previously noted, environmental law and policy is heavily influenced by science; to claim that a legal instrument or policy approach is influenced and guided by science provides an aura of respectability. This is unsurprising; no sensible policy maker would openly subscribe to the formulation of policy based on superstition, conjecture or even anecdote. In sum, for decision makers, a science-led approach represents motherhood and apple pie. However, science and objectivity cannot always be equated; academic literature is replete with assertions that science is a value-laden, socially constructed concept.[34] Moreover, Doremus has referred to the 'truism that environmental policy choices must always be made in the face of significant uncertainties.'[35] Despite the commonly held view that science is seldom able to provide definitive, conclusive and indisputable conclusions, policy makers remain wedded, at least ostensibly, to the desirability of adopting a science-led approach to the formulation of policy.

As a matter of linguistic convenience one may talk of 'science', but a more appropriate term is 'sciences'; the extent to which one may make a claim of conclusiveness (or lack thereof) varies with the scientific discipline in question. It is possible to construct a hypothetical spectrum of science, with 'hard' science and 'soft' science situated at opposite ends. Although the dividing line between 'hard' and 'soft' sciences is therefore somewhat blurred, the latter is arguably of greatest relevance to environmental law and policy. In the context of environmental policy informed by science, inconclusiveness and contestability are unavoidable, a position succinctly summed up by Ravetz thus: 'All too often, we must make hard policy decisions where our only scientific inputs are irremediably soft.'[36] Stated in a more nuanced manner, the sciences that are of most significance to environmental law may be situated towards the 'soft' end of the spectrum: 'ecology and the related biological sciences will never reach the precision and elegance of physics and mathematics.'[37] To make such a claim in no way denigrates such disciplines, as Babich has noted: 'it takes nothing away from the respect due to scientists working in the field to note that toxicology and epidemiology are still young, fundamentally "soft" sciences.'[38]

While one may talk in generalized terms of the nature of science and its apparent limitations as a clear guide to the formulation of environmental policy, it is possible to construct a taxonomy that encompasses the full range of scientific methods. To this end a number of commentators have attempted to distinguish what may be termed traditional science (the archetypal white-coat-clad 'boffin' engaged in experimentation simply for the acquisition of knowledge and furtherance of understanding) and science conducted specifically to guide and inform policy. A number of terminological innovations seek to illustrate the point: 'normal' and 'post-normal' science; 'sound' and 'regulatory' science; and 'science policy'. Whichever nomenclature is used, such distinctions share common themes; science conducted for the express purpose of informing regulatory policy is often characterized by time and resource constraints and/or the absence of peer review.[40] Further, particularly in the area of risk-based standards (e.g. devising a regulatory scheme designed to reduce human exposure to carcinogens), scientific conclusions will often involve a significant element of extrapolation: from high to low dosage levels, from animals to humans, from short-term to long-term exposure.[41]

The obvious question that flows from the preceding discussion is the extent to which the science conducted for the purpose of determining the efficacy of badger culling as a tool of bTB eradication policy falls into the category of regulatory science. The distinction between traditional and regulatory science is not always easy to draw in a clear-cut manner; thus, the response to such a question is complex. In a narrow sense, the RBCT represents regulatory science on the basis that the experiment was specifically commissioned to inform government policy on bTB. Nevertheless, the RBCT certainly lacks many of the characteristics associated with regulatory science. First, a study spanning nine years and with a budget of £50 million cannot sensibly be classified as an experiment subject to time and resource constraints. Second, in addition to a comprehensive final report, the findings of the RBCT were routinely published in reputable, peer-reviewed journals on an ongoing basis. In terms of the issue of external peer review, a note of caution is necessary: peer review cannot automatically be construed as the *sine qua non* of scientific rigour, as Doremus has noted:

> No peer reviewer can know how hard the scientists under review actually worked to practice objectivity and scepticism. The best reviewers can do is to evaluate whether the judgements made fall within the broad range of professionally accepted ideas.[42]

External peer-review may not represent a panacea but open and transparent scientific discourse may usually be relied upon to reveal a patent lack of objectivity.[43] Third, the nature of the RBCT was such that there was no necessity to engage in the extensive extrapolation one associates with science designed to inform risk-based regulation. While any non-scientist, comparatively ignorant of the rigours of the scientific method, should be reluctant to pronounce judgement on the reliability of a scientific endeavour, it seems that one might reasonably conclude that the RBCT may be classified as sound science. Although no doubt cognizant of the dangers of exceeding the boundaries of their area of expertise, the Court of Appeal in *Badger Trust v. The Welsh Ministers* reached a similar conclusion. Smith LJ noted that the RBCT appeared 'to have been well conducted and to have provided reliable information.'[44]

One conclusion that might be gleaned from the foregoing discussion is that any decision to authorize badger culling in Wales is not supported by the scientific evidence and thus any claim of science led policy rings hollow. Yet such a conclusion, however tempting, is bordering on simplistic for the following reason. The results of RBCT did actually demonstrate a reduction in the incidence of bTB. The consultation document produced prior to the enactment of Tuberculosis Eradication (Wales) Order 2009, which authorized the culling of badgers (subsequently quashed by the Court of Appeal in *Badger Trust v. The Welsh Ministers*), relied heavily on an article published by Jenkins *et al*. in the *International Journal of Infectious Diseases*, providing an analysis of the data produced during the RBCT conducted by the ISG.[45] The article focused on the use of proactive culling and the potential effects on the incidence of bTB during the post-cull period. Within the trial zone, a 30.2 per cent reduction in bTB was recorded, with an increase in the incidence of bTB outside the culling area of 12.5 per cent (thought to be attributable to the perturbation effect).[46] The advice provided to the Welsh Minister by the Chief Veterinary Officer for Wales concluded that Jenkins *et al*. estimated that twelve herd breakdowns, out of a potential 130, were prevented by the proactive cull, thus providing an overall 9 per cent reduction in herd breakdowns.[47]

While the scientific evidence highlighted above would have clearly influenced the decision-making process, it did not provide a definitive answer to the question of whether to instigate a badger cull. This is perhaps unsurprising; the view that science cannot address policy questions is commonplace:

Most of the conflicts over natural resource management boil down to disagreements about values and priorities. Unless scientific information reveals that all competing goals can be achieved, it will not solve these underlying conflicts.[48]

Thus, the RBCT was able to provide data that demonstrated a reduction in herd breakdowns in areas subject to proactive culling, but this alone does not answer the policy question of whether culling should be used as a means of tackling bTB. This question is situated at the interface between science, law and policy and the next section views this from the statutory basis chosen for the purposes of the proposed cull.

## Legal analysis of badger-culling policy decisions

The Welsh Assembly's first move towards the utilization of badger culling as a method of bTB control came with the enactment of the Tuberculosis Eradication (Wales) Order 2009.[49] Following the Court of Appeal's decision to quash the order, and a further consultation exercise, the Welsh Assembly passed the Badger (Control Area) (Wales) Order 2011, which authorized the destruction of wild of badgers within an area of Wales referred to as the Intensive Action Pilot Area (IAPA).[50] In both instances the Welsh Minister acted pursuant to a power granted by the Animal Health Act 1981. In particular, Section 21 provides that the National Assembly for Wales may issue an order authorizing the destruction of wild animals provided that the two-stage test contained in Section 21(2) is satisfied, namely:

(a) that there exists among the wild members of one or more species in the area a disease to which this section applies which has been or is being transmitted from members of that or those species to animals of any kind in the area, and
(b) that destruction of wild members of that or those species in that area is necessary in order to eliminate, or substantially reduce the incidence of, that disease in animals of any kind in the area.[51]

Section 21 does not explicitly require the discretion (as evidenced by the word 'may') to be exercised in cognizance of scientific evidence. However, such a requirement may be readily implied. To this end, the questions whether a disease exists among wild animals, whether it is being transmitted to other animals and whether the destruction of wild animals will lead to the elimination or substantial reduction of a disease can be answered only with significant scientific input, a position which has been judicially recognized:

> I do not think that it is disputed that the section 21 consideration of whether the destruction of members of a wild species is necessary to eliminate or

reduce the incidence of a disease in animals must be based on scientific evidence. Hunch and anecdote would obviously not be sufficient; nor would impermissible extrapolation.[52]

Thus, whether or not to cull badgers involves the juxtaposition of scientific, legal and policy questions; in particular, the available scientific evidence and Section 21 of the Animal Health Act 1981 restrict the range of policy options available. This position accords with Tarlock's claim that science is able to constrain political choice.[53] In essence, the relevant minister is not granted unfettered discretion to order the destruction of wild animals; the power is triggered only where the requirements provided by Section 21 are met and, as affirmed by the Court of Appeal, whether the threshold is passed is a question that necessitates the use of scientific evidence. To this end, the power to review administrative action vested in the courts creates what Angelo has described as a 'gatekeeper role'.[54] The Court of Appeal in the *Badger Trust* case effectively fulfilled such a role; although hesitant to provide a test based on a minimum percentage reduction, a majority of the court (Smith and Stanley Burnton LJJ) concluded that a 9 per cent reduction could not be considered substantial for the purposes of Section 21.[55] The majority view would seem to rule out a lawful badger cull, at least on the current available scientific evidence. However, the Court's interpretation of 'substantial reduction' does not sound the death knell for any proposed badger cull when one considers that the Court unanimously concluded that the minster had erred in drafting the order to encompass the whole of Wales when the advice received related only to the IAPA. Section 21 specifically refers to a substantial reduction 'in that area', i.e. the area to which the order relates. Given this, it seems to some extent that geographically limiting the order to the IAPA permits the minister to ignore or at least downplay the significance of any increases in the rate of bTB that might occur outside the IAPA, arguably producing a reduction in bTB that crosses the 'substantial' threshold.[56] Therefore, it is possible, although perhaps unlikely, that, on account of increases in a disease outside the area to which an order relates, the culling of wild animals would result in no net reduction in disease or even a net increase. Without stating it in such stark terms, the Court implicitly acknowledged such a possibility:

> It falls to be considered when she considers whether to exercise her discretion to make the order. She may conclude that the increase in the incidence of the disease outside the specified area would be so great as to obviate the benefits of a reduction in the incidence of the disease within the area, so that the order should not be made.[57]

Notwithstanding the Court's implicit concern that 'salami slicing' is a possibility that might represent an abuse of the statutory language, it is unsurprising that the second order [Badger (Control Area) (Wales) Order 2011] is limited to the IAPA.

## The 'gatekeeper' role of law and science

The decision of the Court of Appeal in the *Badger Trust* case is an illustration of the extent to which the law (Animal Health Act 1981, Section 21), in tandem with an implicit requirement to support administration action by reference to scientific evidence, is able to define and confine the parameters of available environmental policy options. The position is summed up by Rosneau:

> Politicians cannot exercise control over environmental outcomes without resource to scientific findings. They may claim that findings are not clear-cut or remain subject to contradictory interpretations, but they are nonetheless dependent on what the practice of science uncovers . . . criteria of proof are at the heart of environmental politics . . . the outcomes of environmental issues depend as much on the persuasiveness of the evidence as on various criteria of power.[58]

However, the extent to which law and science are able to fulfil a gatekeeper role effectively is limited by a number of factors. First, the legal source of administrative action does not always create an explicit or implicit requirement to bolster decisions by reference to available science, let alone insist on supportive scientific evidence as a condition precedent of administrative action. Therefore the extent to which legal instruments may attempt to ensure that policy formulation is supported by scientific discourse is contingent. Second, and more significantly, the very nature of science is problematic in this context. At the risk of labouring a point already made, there is 'a widespread misconception . . . that science can provide objective, perfectly rational, decisions.'[59] Scientific evidence is seldom binary, providing a clear course of action for environmental policy makers, but to some extent the future of bTB eradication policy is binary: to instigate a badger cull or not. Thus, the often inconclusive and contestable nature of science severely limits the extent to which science can actually constrain the political choices that influence the selection of environmental policy options.

Finally, from a legal perspective, science is able to confine policy formulation only to the extent that the courts are able and willing to strike down administrative action through judicial review. Even in the USA, where a 'best available science mandate' is a relatively common feature of decision making on the part of environmental protection agencies, the courts have adopted a rather deferential approach when reviewing scientific judgements.[60] This is unsurprising; a more interventionist approach when questioning the rigour of scientific evidence would clearly take the judiciary beyond its legitimate realm of expertise. To revert once more from the general to the specific, it is interesting to note that, in the *Badger Trust* case, the science that demonstrated a reduction in the incidence of bTB was not questioned; the issue was framed as whether such a reduction could be construed as 'substantial' or not. Even so, science was able to constrain political choice on the basis that, if the evidence had revealed no reduction in herd breakdowns, the use of Section 21 to order the destruction of badgers would have been doomed to failure *ab initio*. The innate nature of scientific evidence and discourse is such that one has to accept contestability and inconclusiveness; however, the way government responds to such evidence is something that can be subjected to criticism.

## The Welsh Government's use (and abuse?) of science

Rather sardonically, it has been stated that 'every lawyer knows what "good science" is: the science that supports his or her case.'[61] The Welsh Assembly Government's selective use of science in relation to bTB seems to suggest that one might also tenably claim that the same is true of policy makers. It has been noted that those unwillingly subject to regulation have often deliberately attempted to propagate uncertainty in relation to the science that supports such regulation: 'The manufacture of doubt has become so commonplace that it is now unusual for the science behind an environmental regulation to remain unchallenged.'[62] Equally, a government minded to adopt a laissez-faire approach to environmental regulation may seek to challenge and undermine scientific discourse that supports the case for state intervention.[63] In a similar fashion, it is arguable that the UK government, with the acquiescence of the Welsh Assembly Government, has sought to selectively utilize or 'cherry pick' the conclusions drawn from the RBCT.

Following the unequivocal conclusion of the ISG that 'badger culling cannot meaningfully contribute to the future control of cattle TB in Britain', the UK government's chief scientific officer, Sir David King, was commissioned to lead a group of scientists with a view to conducting a review of the evidence produced by the ISG.[64] The conclusion of the King Report was similarly unequivocal: 'In our view a programme for the removal of badgers could make a significant contribution to the control of cattle TB where there is a high incidence of TB in cattle, provided removal takes place alongside an effective programme of cattle controls.'[65] At first sight, the fact that two groups of respected scientists could reach such opposing conclusions based on a single body of data may seem surprising. However, in a response authored by former members of the ISG the divergence of opinion was explained, *inter alia*, on the basis of differing terms of reference. The ISG was charged with the task of presenting 'Ministers with a range of scientifically-based policy options which will be technically, environmentally, socially and economically acceptable', whereas King was asked to make comment on scientific issues, a brief which did not 'extend to economic or other practical issues.'[66] It is certainly the case that economic considerations, particularly operational efficiency and cost–benefit analysis, had influenced the recommendations of the ISG. In summary it was concluded that: 'if a proactive culling strategy along the lines of the RBCT were to be adopted it would cost over £1 million for every £27,000 saved in breakdowns, clearly economically indefensible.'[67] Furthermore, the calculations did not take into account the economic contingent value of any badgers killed in the culling operation.[68] One view of the influence of economic and practical considerations on the conclusions of the ISG is that a group of epidemiologists, statisticians and veterinary scientists had proceeded beyond their realm of expertise, as Pouyat has noted: 'the challenge occurs when scientists are forced to make decisions that go beyond the statistical outcomes of their research results, as is often the case in the making of public policy.'[69] Such a perspective is premised on the desirability of separating science and policy and/or value judgements, i.e. scientists conduct experiments and produce and interpret the resulting statistics whereas policy development is the role of government and other state agencies.[70] In the area of regulatory science, such separation is rarely completely achievable; in the case of the ISG, the terms of reference specifically required the consideration of non-scientific issues and to some extent the membership of the ISG reflected this by the inclusion of an eminent agricultural economist with a specialist interest in the economic analysis of livestock disease (Professor John McInerney).

The foregoing discussion is an illustration of the often overbearing influence that determining the parameters of the question will have on the scope for reaching conclusions. In relation to natural resource management, Doremus and Tarlock have noted:

> There can be a strong feedback loop; once management judgements are made, they can strongly influence the collection and interpretation of scientific data, which in turn can tend to entrench the original management decisions.[71]

The terms of reference may be drawn in such a manner in order to further reinforce such a feedback loop: 'the framing of the problem is not purely technical, but has its own policy dimension.'[72] The ISG concluded that proactive culling did actually lead to modest reductions in the incidence of bTB within the trial area but that the costs associated with culling would greatly outweigh the benefits of fewer herd breakdowns. Thus it might have reasonably been predicted that preventing King from embarking on a consideration of economic and other practical considerations would lead to a different conclusion from that reached by the ISG.

The King report certainly proved controversial among members of the scientific community. In an editorial published in the journal *Nature*, it was concluded: 'the mishandling of the issue by David King, the UK government's chief scientific adviser, is an example to governments of how not deal with such advice, once it has been solicited and received.'[73] The editorial proceeds to suggest implicitly that King was motivated by political considerations: 'King's motives remain unknown but his actions are likely to encourage speculation that his report was written to please the farmers.'[74] The trenchant criticism of the UK's chief scientific officer is particularly significant given the viewpoint that: 'Ordinarily, disagreements in the scientific literature are fairly impersonal and bland; scientists ... do not accuse each other of stepping outside the scientist's role.'[75] Further, while we cannot determine King's motivation with any degree of certainty, one may certainly make the general point that, when scientists are directly or indirectly motivated by political considerations, this has the potential to undermine confidence in science itself, as Edley has opined: 'When a political choice is disguised as "science", the ostensibly technical reasoning may appear arbitrary or flawed.'[76]

If the advice of the ISG was indeed 'mishandled' then one cannot directly apportion blame to the Welsh Government, on the basis that the review of the evidence was commissioned by Defra. However, in a witness statement prepared in relation to the *Badger Trust* case, the Chief Veterinary Officer to the Welsh Assembly Government, Christianne Glossop, similarly attempted to cast doubt on the findings of the ISG. It was noted that 'the RBCT sought to test the effect of badger culling alongside the then existing policy for control of tuberculosis in cattle: it did not attempt to impose additional cattle control measures such as an increased cattle testing regime.'[77] It was also hypothesized that is was 'highly possible' that but for the cessation of cattle testing during the foot and mouth outbreak (2001–2), the benefits of culling recorded by the RBCT would have been greater.[78] While the Glossop statement falls short of directly challenging the conclusions of the ISG, one of the possible effects of such speculation is to subtly undermine both the methodology and conclusions of the ISG.

Any policy maker who subscribes to the formulation of science-led policy is afforded the luxury of choice when determining the 'science' it plans to follow. The nature of scientific discourse is such that our understanding of natural phenomena is open to challenge; accepted theories may be challenged and refined by further experimentation or differing hypotheses. Policy makers are able to take advantage of the fact that science is constantly evolving and/or open to contrary interpretations. In any particular area, the scientific community may hold a number of opposing views, none of which can be conclusively proven to be correct or incorrect. In summary, scientific evidence is malleable and therefore the policy that follows such science is equally malleable. Inherent in the concept of science-led policy is the notion that science is capable of leading the way. Science certainly is capable of doing this but in a number of different directions simultaneously. Thus, given the luxury of choice in its selection of science, the Welsh Government was able to utilize the available evidence is a selective manner. For example, the consultation paper published prior to the 2010 order relied heavily on the 2008 Jenkins *et al.* paper, which highlighted a reduction in the incidence of bTB of 30.2 per cent within the trial area. However, following the quashing of the order, the new consultation exercise document made no reference to a further study by Jenkins *et al.*, which concluded: 'Beneficial effects inside culled areas were greatest shortly after culling ended, but then declined over time and were no longer detectable four years after the last annual cull.'[79]

## Conclusion

In conclusion, this chapter has primarily sought to investigate the claim that science is able to constrain political choice and that the outcome of environmental conflicts is dictated, to a greater or lesser extent, by the persuasiveness of the evidence. It has done so by offering an analysis of the use and influence of science in the formulation of bTB policy in Wales. In a narrow sense, this policy is reliant on the support of science as a condition for any moves to authorize badger culling. The relevant provisions of the Animal Health Act 1981, as interpreted by the Court of Appeal in the *Badger Trust* case, require a scientific mandate in order to demonstrate that the destruction of badgers will lead to a 'substantial reduction' in bTB. Thus, in so far as any proposed cull requires a statutory basis, scientific evidence does indeed limit the choice of policy options. However, in a broader sense the role of science as 'gatekeeper' is limited to a considerable extent by the inherent nature of scientific discourse. For scientists, the continual process of test and challenge is a hallmark of scientific rigour, but this process has the potential to engender doubt and inconclusiveness, which in turn endows policy makers with considerable latitude. Thus, unless a true consensus can be reached that science points in a particular direction, broad claims for the assumed benefits of 'science-led policy' need to be viewed with considerable caution.

In its manifesto published prior to the 2011 National Assembly election, the Labour party pledged to take a science-led approach to evaluate the best way of tackling bTB.[80] Following the election, it was announced that a committee of experts would conduct a further review of the scientific evidence and any culling of badgers within the IAPA would be postponed pending the publication of the review.[81] Thus, another viewpoint will be added to the multitude of scientific opinions already expressed. A charitable interpretation of such a process of review is that policy makers seek to ensure that the science on which they base their decisions is as robust as possible. Even if this were the case, such an approach is not unproblematic; the possibility of 'paralysis by analysis' is one potential drawback.[82] An alternative interpretation is that policy makers are able to challenge any scientific evidence that does not accord with their predetermined political preferences. Such a contention is not new; academic literature on law and science is replete with assertions to the effect that the technical and often esoteric nature of scientific evidence is able to act as a veil that effectively operates to hide judgements that are essentially political in nature.[83] Such a state of affairs has considerable ramifications for the transparency of the policy-making process and the accountability of policy makers.[84]

Whether the Welsh Government opts to instigate a cull of badgers or not, the resulting policy can reasonably be claimed to be science led. If the proposed cull is abandoned, then the Welsh Government can point to the conclusions of the ISG and the 2010 Jenkins *et al.* paper as 'proof' that badger culling is not an efficacious solution to bTB. Equally, if it is revealed that the planned cull is to proceed, there is ample evidence to support such an approach; the King report is the most obvious example along with the 2008 Jenkins *et al.* paper. Further, even the RBCT revealed that proactive culling did indeed lead to reductions in the incidence of bTB. Thus, we have a perfect illustration of the limitations of science as a constraint on the political choice of policy options. Adherence to a science-led approach therefore represents somewhat of a low-risk option for policy makers; in the context of bTB, a pro-cull approach is highly unlikely to be questioned by the farming industry, which remains firmly wedded to the belief that badger culling should be utilized.[85] For the public at large, even those who would instinctively favour badger protection, the claim that science supports badger culling may lead to resigned acceptance that the policy is unavoidable. While most of the electorate may lack the time, inclination or expertise to challenge any claim of purportedly science-led policy, the same cannot be said of the pro-badger lobby. Thus, the ability of science to limit policy options is arguably enhanced where a vocal and well-organized opposition to the proposed policy exists, a group that is able to scrutinize the available evidence fully. Even then the view of such a lobby may be easily dismissed as based on sentiment rather than an objective assessment of the evidence. Notwithstanding the deferential attitude of the Courts to administrative discretion in cases of uncertainty, the legality of any future policy involving badger culling is ultimately an issue of statutory interpretation. Thus, despite the technical limitations of lawyers, this issue could once again be brought before the Courts.

## Addendum

Since the initial completion of this chapter, the findings of the expert panel, commissioned by the Welsh Government to conduct a review of the scientific evidence, were announced by the Minister for Environment and Sustainable Development.[86] The published review represents a rather dry assessment of the evidence base and, perhaps conscious of appropriate role boundaries, desists from highlighting a preferred policy option. It is acknowledged that:

> [W]hile a bTB Eradication Programme should be informed by the scientific and other evidence base, the precise measures adopted will be a political judgement based on an evaluation of a range of factors including the interests of the different stakeholders.[87]

The Welsh Government's response was the publication of a Strategic Framework for Bovine TB Eradication in Wales, the headline policy of which is the abandonment of proposed badger culling in favour of a programme of badger vaccination.[88] The nature of scientific evidence is such that the cessation of plans to instigate badger culling can justifiably be claimed to be a science-led change of policy; but, as the foregoing analysis has sought to illustrate, a decision to continue with such a policy would also have been supported by scientific evidence. Given the Welsh Government's new-found enthusiasm for badger vaccination, it is likely that the focus of public discourse will now shift to a debate on the efficacy of badger vaccination.

## Notes

1. H. Doremus and D. Tarlock, 'Science, judgement, and controversy in natural resource regulation', *Public Land and Resources Law Review*, 26 (2005), 1–2; S. Funtowicz, I. Shepherd, D. Wilkinson and J. Ravetz, 'Science and governance in the European Union: a contribution to the debate', *Science and Public Policy*, 27 (2000), 327–36.
2. For example, A. Leopold, *A Sand County Almanac* (Oxford: Oxford University Press, 1949); R. Carson, *Silent Spring* (Boston, MA: Houghton Mifflin, 1962).
3. D. Tarlock, 'Environmental law: ethics or science?', *Duke Environmental Law and Policy Forum*, 7 (1996), 193–5.
4. J. Ravetz, 'The post-normal science of precaution', *Futures*, 36 (2004), 347–57, p. 348.
5. For further discussion on the limitations of 'regulatory science' see n. 40 and adjacent text.
6. See generally A. Proud, 'Some lessons from the history of the eradication of bovine tuberculosis in Great Britain', *Government Veterinary Journal*, 16, 1 (2006), 11–18.
7. Economic Advisory Committee, *Report of the Committee on Cattle Diseases* (Cmd. 4591, HMSO, 1934).
8. The Health Protection Agency reported just thirty-nine cases of *M. bovis* infection in the UK in 2005 and some of these originated with other humans. For the purposes of comparison, over 2,500 deaths per year were attributed to bTB during the 1930s. J. Evans, E. Smith, A. Banerjee and R. Smith, 'Cluster of human tuberculosis caused by *Mycobacterium bovis*: evidence for person to person transmission in the UK', *The Lancet*, 369 (2007), 1270–6.
9. The terms 'pro-cull' and 'pro-badger' are used loosely but certain figurehead organizations are associated with each side of the debate: the National Farmers Union Cymru (*http://www.nfu-cymru.org.uk*) has led the calls for badger culling, which in turn has been vociferously resisted by the Badger Trust (*http://www.badger.org.uk*).
10. *Bovine TB Eradication Programme: Consultation on Badger Control in the Intensive Action Area* (Welsh Assembly Government Consultation Document, 20 September 2010), p. 1.
11. Ibid. The power to order the slaughter of cattle is provided by the Animal Health Act 1981, s. 32(1), which provides:

    The Minister may, if he thinks fit, cause to be slaughtered any animal which –
    (a) is affected or suspected of being affected with any disease to which this section applies; or
    (b) has been exposed to the infection of any such disease.

    The definition of 'disease' for the purposes of the Act was extended to include bTB by virtue of the Tuberculosis (Wales) Order 2010/1379, art. 6.

12 Breakdown is when cattle are proven to be infected with bTB, e.g. by post-mortem examination. Defra, *Bovine Tuberculosis: The Government's Approach to Tackling the Disease and Consultation on a Badger Control Policy* (London: Defra, 2010), p. 40.
13 Farming Crisis Network, *Stress and Loss: A Report on the Impact of Bovine TB on Farming Families* (Northampton: Farming Crisis Network, 2009), p. 5
14 P. Torgerson and D. Torgerson, 'Public health and bovine tuberculosis: what's all the fuss about?', *Trends in Microbiology*, 18 (2010), 67–72, p. 69. The view that TB no longer represents a serious threat to human health has been questioned; N. Smith and R. Clifton-Hadley, 'Bovine TB: don't get rid of the cat because the mice have gone', *Nature*, 456 (2008), 700, argue that a test-and-cull policy and abattoir surveillance prevents bTB from advancing to its more infectious stages. Thus, removing animals at an early stage and controlling the prevalence of the disease in the national herd is therefore likely to reduce the probability of transmission to humans. In summary, it is contended that abandoning the current bTB control programme would be analogous to removing the cat because you no longer see any mice.
15 EU Directive 64/432/EEC on animal health problems affecting intra-Community trade in bovine animals and swine. Art. 3(1) provides that each Member State shall ensure that only those bovine animals that fulfil the general conditions laid down in the directive are sent from its territory to that of another Member State. Such conditions include:

> Art.3(2)(a): Bovine animals covered by this Directive must show no clinical sign of disease on the day of loading;
>
> and
>
> Art.3(6)(b): Bovine animals for slaughter, if over four months old, must in addition, if they do not come from an officially tuberculosis-free bovine herd, have reacted negatively to an intradermal tuberculin test.

By virtue of annex A, a bovine animal is considered to be tuberculosis-free if it shows neither clinical signs of tuberculosis nor a reaction to an intradermal tuberculin test carried out not more than thirty days before loading.
16 Torgerson and Torgerson, 'Public health and bovine tuberculosis', 69.
17 Ibid.
18 S. Gordon, 'Bovine TB: stopping disease control would block all live exports', *Nature*, 456 (2008), 700.
19 N. Atkinson, 'The impact of BSE on the UK economy', paper presented to the First Symposium on Animal and Human TSEs, Buenos Aires, 11 August 1999, *http://www.veterinaria.org/revistas/vetenfinf/bse/14Atkinson.html* (accessed 12 July 2011).
20 Defra, *Bovine Tuberculosis*, p. 4.
21 Council Directive 77/391/EEC introducing Community measures for the eradication of brucellosis, tuberculosis and leucosis in cattle, art. 3(1), provides: 'Member States in which the cattle populations are infected with bovine tuberculosis shall draw up plans for accelerating the eradication of this disease in their national territories.'
22 *Bovine TB: The Scientific Evidence* (Final Report of the Independent Scientific Group on Cattle TB, 2007), p. 154
23 The Welsh Badger Found Dead Survey tested 459 dead badgers between 26 October 2005 and 31 May 2006; fifty-five badgers tested positive for *M. bovis*. See 'Survey of *Mycobacterium bovis* infection in badgers found dead in Wales' (29 January 2007, Veterinary Laboratories Agency), available at *http://wales.gov.uk/topics/environmentcountryside/ahw/disease/bovinetuberculosis/researchandevidence/badgerfounddeadsurvey/?lang=en* (accessed 8 July 2011).
24 R. Muirhead, J. Gallagher and K. Burn, 'Tuberculosis in wild badgers in Gloucestershire: epidemiology', *Veterinary Record*, 95 (1974), 552–5.
25 Badgers Act 1973.

26 Badgers have been the subject of qualified protection since the Badgers Act 1973; s. 1 provided the general offence of taking, injuring or killing badgers. However, s. 7 provided a defence where the killing etc. was necessary for the 'purpose of preventing the spread of disease'. A similar approach is adopted by the Protection of Badgers Act 1992; by virtue of s. 10(2)(a), the appropriate minister may grant a licence to kill badgers for the purpose of preventing the spread of disease. Thus, the 1973 Act provided a defendant with an *ex post* defence to be utilized before a court. In contrast, the 1992 Act provides *ex ante* authorization for conduct that would otherwise constitute an offence. For a summary of the scientific findings of the various studies, see Independent Scientific Group on Cattle TB, *Bovine TB*, pp. 27–34.

27 G. Enticott, 'Calculating nature: the case of badgers, bovine tuberculosis and cattle', *Journal of Rural Studies*, 17 (2001), 149–64, p. 155.

28 See generally J. Aldrich, 'Correlations genuine and spurious in Pearson and Yule', *Statistical Science*, 10, 4 (1990), 364–76.

29 J. Krebs, R. Anderson, T. Clutton-Brock, I. Morrison, D. Young, C. Donnelly, S. Frost and R. Woodroffe, *Bovine Tuberculosis in Cattle and Badgers* (London: MAFF Publications, PB3423, 1997), para. 6.

30 The RBCT took place in thirty 100-km$^2$ areas of England, grouped into ten sets of three areas, termed 'triplets'. In each triplet, one area was subject to repeated culling (proactive culling); one area received culling in response to bTB outbreaks in cattle (reactive culling); and the third area received no culling (survey only).

31 Independent Scientific Group on Cattle TB, *Bovine TB*, p. 14.

32 Ibid., p. 26. EU Directive 78/52/EEC establishing the Community criteria for national plans for the accelerated eradication of brucellosis, tuberculosis and enzootic leukosis in cattle, art.13(b)(ii): prohibition on vaccinating cattle against bTB. The legality of vaccinating badgers would depend on the chosen method of vaccination; the deposit of vaccine-laden food in areas populated by badgers would be entirely lawful. Trapping badgers for the purpose of directly administering a vaccine would prima facie contravene the Protection of Badgers Act 1992. However, such an approach could be legitimized by the grant of a licence pursuant to s. 10(2)(a). See further M. Chambers *et al.*, 'Bacillus Calmette–Guérin vaccination reduces the severity and progression of tuberculosis in badgers', *Proceedings of the Royal Society B*, 1953 (2010), 1–8 (concluding that vaccination of captive badgers reduced the progression, severity and excretion of *M. bovis*). Following the grant of Limited Market Authorisation (March 2010), injectable Bacille Calmette Guérin badger vaccine (BadgerBCG) has been in use in the Defra-funded Badger Vaccine Deployment Project (BVDP) in the Stroud area of Gloucestershire since July 2010. A primary aim of the project is to provide training for lay vaccinators who can then be licensed to trap and vaccinate badgers commercially outside the project area. See further http://www.fera.defra.gov.uk/wildlife/ecologyManagement/bvdp/index.cfm (accessed 12 July 2012).

33 Independent Scientific Group on Cattle TB, *Bovine TB*, p. 21. The extent to which cattle movements can contribute to the spread of animal disease is illustrated by the 2001 foot and mouth epidemic. See D. Campbell and R. Lee, 'Carnage by computer: the blackboard economies of the 2001 foot and mouth epidemic', *Social and Legal Studies*, 12, 4 (2003), 425–59.

34 B. Latour and S. Woolgar, *Laboratory Life: The Social Construction of Scientific Facts* (London: Sage, 1979); M. Callon, 'Some elements of a new sociology of translation', in J. Law (ed.), *Power Action and Belief: A New Sociology of Knowledge* (London: Routledge, 1986); J. Law, *Organising Modernity* (Oxford: Blackwell, 1994). Cf. H. Lacey, *Is Science Value Free? Values and Scientific Understanding* (London: Routledge, 2004).

35 H. Doremus, 'Scientific and political integrity in environmental policy', *Texas Law Review*, 87 (2008), 1601–53, p. 1620.

36 J. Ravetz, 'What is post-normal science', *Futures*, 31 (1999), 647–53, p 649.

37 Doremus and Tarlock, 'Science, judgement, and controversy in natural resource regulation', 18.
38 A. Babich, 'Too much science in environmental law', *Columbia Journal of Environmental Law*, 28 (2003), 119–75.
39 Ravetz, 'What is post-normal science'; J. Jones, 'Regulatory design for scientific uncertainty: acknowledging the diversity of approaches in environmental regulation and public administration', *Journal of Environmental Law*, 19, 3 (2007), 347–65; S. Funtowicz, I. Shepherd, D. Wilkinson and J. Ravetz, 'Science and governance in the European Union: a contribution to the debate', *Science and Public Policy*, 27 (2000), 327–36.
40 Funtowicz *et al.*, 'Science and governance in the European Union', 333.
41 Babich, 'Too much science in environmental law', 124–5; O. Houck, 'Tales from a troubled marriage: science and law in environmental policy', *Science*, 302 (2003), 1926–9.
42 Doremus, 'Scientific and political integrity in environmental policy', 1652.
43 '[S]ubmission to the scrutiny of the scientific community is a component of "good science," in part because it increases the likelihood that substantive flaws in methodology will be detected'; Blackmun J in *Daubert v. Merrell Dow Pharmaceuticals* 509 U. S. 579 (1993), p. 593 (US Supreme Court).
44 [2010] EWCA Civ 807, [77].
45 SI 2009/21614; H. Jenkins, R. Woodroffe and C. Donnelly, 'The effects of annual widespread badger culls on cattle tuberculosis following the cessation of culling', *International Journal of Infectious Diseases*, 12 (2008), 457–65. (Woodroffe and Donnelly were members of the ISG.)
46 The perturbation effect may be defined as: '[S]ubstantial disruption to the social organization and behaviour patterns of individuals in a population ... This may be accompanied by an increase in the frequency of movements of individuals between social groups'. See S. Carter, R. Delahay, G. Smith, D. Macdonald, P. Riordan, T. Etherington, E. Pimley, N. Walker and C. Cheeseman, 'Culling-induced social perturbation in Eurasian badgers *Meles meles* and the management of TB in cattle: an analysis of a critical problem in applied ecology', *Proceedings of the Royal Society B*, 274 (2007), 2769–70.
47 Cited in the *Badger Trust* case, [35].
48 Doremus and Tarlock, 'Science, judgement, and controversy in natural resource regulation', 6.
49 SI 2009/21614.
50 SI 2011/693. The IAPA is primarily located in north Pembrokeshire, but includes small parts of Ceredigion and Carmarthenshire. A detailed map is available at *http://wales.gov.uk/docs/drah/publications/110304annex2en.pdf* (accessed 6 August 2011).
51 The functions of the appropriate minister under the Act were transferred to the National Assembly for Wales by virtue of the National Assembly for Wales (Transfer of Functions) Order 1999 SI 1999/672, art. 2, sch. 1. The Animal Health Act 1981, as originally enacted, did not list TB as a disease for the purposes of the statute. The Tuberculosis (Wales) Order 2010/1379, art. 6, extends the definition of the term 'disease' contained in s. 88 of the Act to include TB.
52 Per Smith LJ in the *Badger Trust* case, [77].
53 Tarlock, 'Environmental law', 197.
54 M. Angelo, 'Harnessing the power of science in environmental law: why we should, why we don't, and how we can', *Texas Law Review*, 86 (2008), 1527–73, p 1532.
55 *Badger Trust* case, [83] and [107].
56 Ibid., [85] and [85].
57 Ibid., per Stanley-Burnton LJ, [108]; a similar view was taken by Smith LJ [85].
58 J. Rosneau, 'Environmental challenges in a global context', in S. Kamieniecki (ed.), *Environmental Politics in the International Arena: Movements, Parties, Organizations and Policy* (Albany: State University of New York Press, 1993), p. 258.

59 Doremus and Tarlock, 'Science, judgement, and controversy in natural resource regulation', 17.
60 Doremus, 'Scientific and political integrity in environmental policy', 1631.
61 Houck, 'Tales from a troubled marriage', 1928.
62 D. Micheals and C. Monforton, 'Scientific evidence in the regulatory system: manufacturing uncertainty and the demise of the formal regulatory system', *Journal of Law and Policy*, 17 (2005), 17–35.
63 H. Doremus, 'Science plays defense: natural resource management in the Bush administration', *Ecology Law Quarterly*, 32 (2005), 249–305. See also 'White House adviser linked to cuts in climate-change report', *Nature*, 30 October 2007 (discussing the allegation that the chief science adviser to President George W. Bush had 'watered down' congressional testimony on the health effects of global warming).
64 Independent Scientific Group on Cattle TB, *Bovine TB*, p. 14.
65 D. King, *Bovine Tuberculosis in Cattle and Badgers: A Report by the Chief Scientific Adviser* (submitted to the Secretary of State, Defra, on 30 July 2007), para. 51. Available at http://www.bis.gov.uk/assets/biscore/corporate/migratedD/ec_group/44-07-S_I_on (accessed 18 July 2011).
66 F. Bourne, C. Donnelly, D. Cox, G. Gettinby, J. McInerney, W. Morrison and R. Woodroffe, *Response to 'Tuberculosis in Cattle and Badgers: A Report by the Chief Scientific Adviser'*, available at http://archive.defra.gov.uk/foodfarm/farmanimal/diseases/atoz/tb/isg/documents/isg-responsetosirdking.pdf (accessed 10 July 2011).
67 Independent Scientific Group on Cattle TB, *Bovine TB*, p. 159.
68 Economists are able to create a 'price' for environmental benefits, e.g. protection of badgers, by utilizing a process called contingent valuation, which is essentially a form of opinion poll; researchers ask a cross-section of the population how much they would be willing to pay to preserve a wild species or other environmental benefit. See generally F. Ackerman and L. Heinzerling, 'Pricing the priceless: cost-benefit analysis of environmental protection', *University of Pennsylvania Law Review*, 150 (2002), 1553–84. See also R. Bennett and K. Willis, 'The value of badger populations and control of tuberculosis in cattle in England and Wales: a note', *Journal of Agricultural Economics*, 58, 1 (2007), 152–6 (concluding that people did not like the idea of a policy that intentionally killed large numbers of badgers and were relatively highly willing to pay not to have such a policy).
69 R. Pouyat, 'Science and environmental policy: making them compatible', *Bioscience*, 49, 4 (1999), 281–2.
70 Doremus, 'Scientific and political integrity in environmental policy', refers to such separation as 'role boundaries' (1640) and further contends that 'education on the distinction between scientific and value judgements and on the extent to which they might be faced with intertwined judgements' (1649–50) is an important aspect of reinforcing political and scientific integrity. The potential problem of blurred role boundaries is not unique to environmental policy; see also P. Wald, 'Analysts and policymakers: a confusion of roles', *Stanford Law and Policy Review*, 17 (2006), 241–74 (highlighting the confused parameters of the roles of intelligence analysts and policy makers).
71 Doremus and Tarlock, 'Science, judgement, and controversy in natural resource regulation', 12.
72 Funtowicz *et al.*, 'Science and governance in the European Union: a contribution to the debate', 333.
73 'In for the cull: a government that asks for independent scientific advice had best be ready to take it', *Nature*, 450, 1 November 2007, 1–2.
74 Ibid., 2.
75 Doremus, 'Scientific and political integrity in environmental policy', 1619.
76 C. Edley, 'The governance crisis, legal theory, and political ideology', *Duke Law Journal*, 3 (1991), 561–77. The charge of political influence was strenuously refuted by King in a letter published in a later edition of *Nature*, 450, 15 November 2007, 346.

77 Witness Statement of Professor Christianne Glossop, 5 March 2010, para. 48, *http://www.pembrokeshireagainstthecull.org.uk/Glossop_Statement.pdf* (accessed 12 July 2011).
78 Ibid., para. 49.
79 H. Jenkins, R. Woodroffe and C. Donnelly, 'The duration and effects of repeated widespread badger culling on cattle tuberculosis following the cessation of culling', *Plos One*, 5 (2010), 1–7, p 5.
80 Labour Party, *Welsh Labour Manifesto 2011*, p. 88.
81 'Review of scientific evidence base for the eradication of bovine TB in Wales', *http://wales.gov.uk/topics/environmentcountryside/ahw/disease/bovinetuberculosis/?lang=en* (accessed 10 July 2011).
82 Jones, 'Regulatory design for scientific uncertainty', 356.
83 Doremus and Tarlock, 'Science, judgement, and controversy in natural resource regulation', 20; Houck, 'Tales from a troubled marriage', 1928; N. de Sadeleer, *Environmental Principles: From Political Slogans to Legal Rules* (Oxford: Oxford University Press, 2002), p. 177; Enticott, 'Calculating nature', 152.
84 Doremus, 'Scientific and political integrity in environmental policy', 1629; Doremus and Tarlock, 'Science, judgement, and controversy in natural resource regulation', 20; W. Wagner, 'The "bad science" fiction: reclaiming the debate over the role of science in public health and environmental regulation', *Law and Contemporary Problems*, 66 (2003), 63–76; Edley, 'The governance crisis, legal theory, and political ideology', 576.
85 The Farming Crisis Network survey discovered that 81 per cent of respondents thought that TB should be tackled in badgers (p. 8); see also Enticott, 'Calculating nature', 157.
86 John Griffiths AM, Minister for Environment and Sustainable Development, 'Oral statement: a programme for eradicating bovine tuberculosis in Wales', 20 March 2012, *http://www.assemblywales.org/bus-home/bus-chamber-fourth-assembly-rop.htm?act=d is&id=231873&ds=3%2F2012#tb* (accessed 3 April 2012).
87 *Report of the TB Science Review Group*, November 2011, 5.
88 *http://wales.gov.uk/docs/drah/publications/120320tbstrategicframeworken.pdf* (accessed 12 April 2012).

# Chapter 7

# The Food Strategy for Wales: a soft law instrument?

*Robert Lee*

---

The Food Strategy for Wales (hereafter 'Strategy' or 'Food Strategy') was published in 2010 'to identify and address the issues around food (in Wales) including how best to balance the need for increased food production with the need to protect our environment for the immediate and the longer term future.'[1] The author of the present chapter was part of a team undertaking all of the research and preparatory work leading to the consultation exercise on the draft food strategy.[2] The team approached the work employing a range of research methods, which are referred to below, the intention being to undertake an assessment of strategic needs. However, with the Strategy now published and in place, an intriguing question occurred: what is the status of the Strategy that we helped to create? In particular, has the research activity produced a document that might now be considered 'soft law'?

The significance of this question lies in the flexible nature of soft law, which is considered below, and its employment by a devolved administration. In particular it suggests that the presence of recognized devolved government may make room for policy innovation without recourse to, or in the absence of, formal legal powers. On this analysis, devolution produces the underpinning legitimacy for soft law instruments quite apart from any other transfer of legal competence. Another question then arises, namely what space is there for the deployment of soft law instruments given the domination of hard, multi-level rules in arena such as trade law, competition and finance, all of which are highly significant in relation to food production and supply? To address these issues, after reviewing the nature of soft law itself, this chapter analyses the potential of the Food Strategy to constitute soft law by reference to its nature, content and purpose.

## Core elements of soft law

The notion of soft law emanates from and is perhaps best understood in the context of international law, where Fitzmaurice has pointed out that it may refer to either the form of law or its effect. In other words it might seek to lay down norms but not in any source that is recognized as international *law*, or it may take the form of an international law instrument, such as a treaty, but could hardly be considered enforceable or binding because of its vague, normative context.[3] This chapter considers the first of these categories: instruments that are not conventionally recognized as hard law but that in some way seek to regulate conduct or encourage self-regulation. There is a huge diversity of such instruments, which may take the form of communications, declarations, codes of conduct etc.

In the context of European Community Law, Senden has suggested that these soft law instruments exhibit three 'core elements'.[4] These are: that the instrument is concerned with rules of conduct or commitments; that it is accepted as having no binding force as such; but that it aims to have a practical effect on behaviour. Senden suggests that, although the diversity of such instruments makes it impossible to lay down clear criteria for soft law in terms of nature, function, legal effect and the like, core features of soft law can be ascertained by examining the instrument itself, its contents and the intention of its drafters. One category of soft law identified by Senden is that of *steering instruments*, which are said to establish or give further effect to Community objectives and policy. Senden's analysis provides the tools for this chapter, which examines the Welsh Food Strategy by reference to its nature (the instrument itself), contents and purpose (the intention behind it) in steering food policy in Wales.

It might be said then that, in the EU context, a soft law instrument is likely to have the endorsement of a community institution, such as the Commission, but that in terms of its adoption it lacks the formality demanded by Treaty provisions on law making. Given this, it may be difficult for the Commission, or indeed the Court, to demand compliance with its provisions or otherwise enforce it. Yet, while its provisions lack legally binding force, in practice they may be followed to establish clear patterns of conduct which practically may be very little different from legal compliance. At the same time, not every policy instrument promulgated by the European Commission would be considered soft law, as there are many which would be widely accepted as merely informative or explanatory in nature.

A good example of this type of soft law instrument in the context of European environmental law might be the environmental action programmes dating back to the Dublin Summit of 1972. In the absence of any specific reference to environment in the Treaty of Rome, these programmes helped to drive forward programmes of pollution control, environmental improvement, conservation of natural resources and principles of environmental sustainability. In the absence of a more explicit environmental mandate in the founding Treaty, they helped also to legitimize European Commission activity in this area, though the first five at least were explicitly non-binding.[5] There are now many other, such soft law provisions in EU environmental law such as the Commission Communication on Sustainable Development or documents such as enforcement or environmental strategies.[6]

Etherington has suggested that the polycentric nature of environmental issues demands a more flexible approach to accommodate the interests of a wide range of parties so that flexible rules and policies enshrined within a soft law framework may be utilized.[7] Pointing to Fuller, the concept of polycentricity is said to refer to a complex network of relationships with multiple points of interaction and many ripple effects of decision making.[8] In such territory, 'open textured' instruments leaving room for policy and public interest arguments may serve us better than hard law. Commentators on food supply chains frequently remark on their complexity, which presents a challenge in asserting the public interest in food supply.[9] Bell and McGillivray in their discussion of tertiary rules and guidance in environmental law point to a number of functions, one of which is a statement of policy or practice.[10] Such statements are significant because they are recorded and signify a general level of consent to a policy. Although they are intentionally vague on issues of how such policies might be pursued, there is no doubting that soft law instruments can have normative significance.[11]

There can be little doubt of the broad shift to soft law instruments in areas which might in the past have been subject to hard law and command-and-control types of approach. This is a theme pursued by the present author and one of the editors elsewhere but can be seen in relation to the contaminated land regime in England and Wales in which primary legislation is underpinned not only by regulations but by a plethora of forms of hard and soft law guidance.[12] To take another example, the planning process in Wales has taken on a distinct identity through technical advice notes (TANs) sitting below the legislative framework.

This suggests some doubts about the efficacy of such hard law approaches, which might be seen as more remedial rather than constructive or preventative or might be regarded as resource-intensive in terms of policing compliance. A soft law appeal to conformity in conduct might be seen to be more flexible or corporatist, though it may come at the price of a loss of certainty of compliance. In the EU context such approaches might be thought more in line with ideas of subsidiarity, proportionality and, free from the straitjacket of hard law drafting, more transparent in approach. In the context of a devolved administration, the soft law approach may make an appeal for cooperation in the national interest and, in the context of a Strategy that to a large extent concerns private enterprise, might promote collaborative governance models that hold greater allure and exert more influence than more formal regulation. One might add that, if the common rationale for regulatory intervention is market failure, a food strategy concerns market operations which are not necessarily failing but which government would seek to promote. Soft law would seem to constitute a more appropriate approach in such circumstances.

## The nature of the Food Strategy

In examining the first element of the criteria suggested by Senden, it is suggested that the nature of the instrument is analysed. In fact, as an early part of the work on the Welsh Strategy, the team conducted a review of many other strategies related to food or food production.[13] The review was particularly keen to locate regions similar to Wales, both structurally and with similar dynamics in its agricultural and food sector. Not all strategies were regional; some were national and some urban.[14] All nine English regions had food strategies, typically produced in 2006 or 2007, whereas Scotland's food strategy was published in June 2009. However, the form and content of other strategies was highly informative almost irrespective of the geographical base. In a documentary analysis of 45 food strategies from around the world, including Europe, Australia, North, Latin and South America, the review adopted certain measures in terms of how comprehensive and well integrated these appeared and of how clearly options were articulated and objectives and timescales set. It is important to note that there was no impact assessment of these strategies or attempt to gauge their success. In most cases the novelty of the strategies alone would have made this an impossible task; indeed one of the remarkable traits of food strategies is their emergence under contemporary pressures.

While the better-devised food strategies set a range of objectives for the food system, there was very often an identifiable focus to the strategy as a whole. A common theme was rural and agricultural development. For example, a strategy might seek to bridge a widening urban/rural division. For example, the British Columbian strategy emphasizes the preservation of family farming units through rural/urban linkages and increasing local food production.[15] Unsurprisingly, many of the food strategies from the English regions, being sponsored by Regional Development Agencies, accentuate food production as a significant contribution to economic development.[16] Some strategies rehearse initiatives for local food sectors and food sourcing, including issues of food procurement.[17] Other strategies have less emphasis on economic development but stress a wider range of interests including environmental and ecological protection or public health and nutrition.[18]

The review of food strategies also prompted consideration of the components of those strategies found to be most compelling. The first such component is that strategies should deliver a vision of what may be achieved. In some strategies a simple goal may carry this vision. For example, the Oakland strategy sets out to improve food literacy and the idea that Oakland consumers will exercise food-related choices in favour of public health and sustainability.[19] Presenting a vision was no easy matter; originally it was thought that this would appear at the conclusion of the Welsh Food Strategy. However, once the idea occurred of presenting the vision as a reflection at the end of the ten-year strategy (in 2020) of how food cultures in Wales had changed in ten years, it became clear that this should go at the front of the strategy and that the detail of how this vision would be delivered would proceed from that initial vision. The concept of a vision is much softer than notions of targets or goals. In fact the Strategy is short of both milestones towards the 2020 vision and indicators of progress. This was made known to both the Food and Drink Partnership and the Welsh Assembly Government with a strong recommendation that these should be placed alongside the Strategy but their formulation was not part of the brief in preparing the Strategy and it was felt that their inclusion in the document itself would detract from the direct messages which it conveyed.[20] Nonetheless, the absence of these mechanisms renders the Strategy much softer in tone.

If the task of a strategy is to lead change then not only did the nature of that change have to be articulated but stakeholders had to be drawn in and cultures harnessed to deliver change. A useful example of this is to be found in the strategy for the South East of England, *Farming for the Future*, which offers examples of 'champions' of change in different farming sectors.[21] A final component was that of integration. It was clear that the food system intersects with a wide range of other issues on the sustainability agenda, ranging from social sustainability issues connected with nutrition (such as school meals) to issues of environmental sustainability (such as food waste). The difficulties attaching to the task of integrating many policy areas led to an organizing theme for the development of the strategy: building connections and capacities. This is considered below under content, but it is relevant here in discerning the nature of the Welsh Strategy rather than food strategies in general.

This notion of connectivity and capacity gave the Strategy a strong focus on sustainable development, which is described as its foundation through 'the provision of safe, affordable, healthy food, and on a food system that produces positive social benefits whilst imposing the lowest possible environmental impacts.'[22] The emphasis in this sentence on externalities, both positive and negative, is worth noting. One common task of regulation is the internalization of social costs, so that by placing this task at the heart of the Strategy, in the section outlining its goals, there may be some suggestion that the Strategy is seeking to fulfil a traditional function of hard law through a soft law instrument.[23] If, as is often mooted in international law literature, soft law has a tendency to harden over time, these soft law approaches may herald later, more formal regulation.[24]

The Welsh food sector must be sustainable but that cannot remain the only goal. The quotation from the Strategy in the previous paragraph correctly suggests strong concerns with environmental and social sustainability. However, in order to sustain itself the Welsh food sector must also be competitive. This ability to compete is best measured by the profitability of food enterprises in Wales as opposed to a high dependence on subsidy. The sector must move away from its present fragile state and develop resilience to the periodic shocks that threaten the stability of the food system. These four qualities of sustainability, profitability, competitiveness and resilience seemed key to any future strategy for the Welsh food sector. Indeed these became the goals for which the Strategy should aim. Progress towards these goals could be seen as an indicator of the progress of the Strategy itself. Some of these goals, such as profitability and competitiveness, might seem more of a task for the private sector, whereas there is an obvious public interest in issues such as sustainability and resilience. This public/private hybrid nature of the Strategy goes a long way towards illuminating its very soft law approach since its interests spread beyond the public realm.

## The content of the Food Strategy

The second tool of analysis for soft law suggested by Senden is to review the content of the potential soft law instrument.[25] As indicated above, the Strategy sets out the vision and the goals but, in order to deliver these, at the heart of the document is the attempt, first, to articulate the necessary restructuring of the food sector and, second, to construct drivers to deliver this change. These two elements of the Strategy can now be considered.

### *Building connections and capacities*

Implicit in what is said above about the nature of the Strategy is that it should be based on a more proactive and systemic approach. The theme of 'Building Connections and Capacities' would be at the centre of the strategy. This would hope to draw on efforts already made to reinvigorate Welsh food culture and to continue this process through engaging private, public and civic stakeholders in realizing the potential of the Welsh food sector.[26] The success of the Strategy would be measured by reference to the traction given to the goals, articulated earlier, of profitability, competitiveness, resilience and sustainability. Delivering these goals would mean integrating policy sectors related to food and negotiating the links and the tensions between these other policy areas, many of which already had their own strategies. On the other hand these other policy areas, such as health, transportation, tourism, conservation and waste, could all be drivers towards the delivery of the Strategy over a ten-year period. In addition, these same drivers present a range of demands and opportunities, outside the public policy realm, within Wales and globally, which could be crucial in achieving goals such as profitability.

Strategy-led change had to deliver, therefore, the future profitability, competitiveness, resilience and sustainability of the Welsh food sector. The goals are interlinked. Greater competitiveness relied on concepts of sustainable production and resource efficiency. This would help drive profitability and build resilience into the system. Each goal would to some degree build upon the institutional, collaborative and relational capacities already well developed in Wales. The move would be towards an internationally well-recognized and -regarded provider of foods of the highest standard and provenance by building on domestic quality standards and the celebration of food.

In order to do this, it becomes necessary to locate areas in which capacity or connections should be assembled. The first of these was that of producing, processing and marketing local and locality-branded foods from Wales. This requires an outward-looking approach based on domestic strength. In terms of connections, it suggests fostering local and regional initiatives while looking to engage with in external markets. Indications of provenance become instrumental in advancing a distinctive Welsh brand, particularly in relation to export markets, in which Welsh producers may find it difficult to compete in terms of cost of production unless the quality and sustainability of Welsh food is well recognized.

However, this approach is more than a mere suggestion to develop and promote local food products; the connection here would be between regional production and processing and a local resource base with identifiable Welsh links. Similarly this initiative is wider than the mere branding or labelling of goods as Welsh, but it is about reaching markets (farmers' or organic markets, public purchasing, corporate retail outlets) where goods can be differentiated by reference to origin. This is not merely about niche or specialist foodstuffs; lower-value foods and ingredients can also be marketed on this basis. Indeed, it is important that all food sectors contribute to the distinctive nature of Welsh food, not simply by reference to quality but also by other attributes such as reliability or eco-efficiency.

This will mean that factors such as eco-efficiency are clearly articulated as part of the marketing of the products of a Welsh food system. The message is one of quality by virtue of sustainable methods of production. In this way Welsh food becomes synonymous with certain values such as the sustainable management of resources, care for the countryside and landscape, and best farm practices as a functioning food system within a low-carbon economy. The promotion of these values is an all-Wales task, with urban centres acting as a conduit for an interconnected rural Wales. Specific activities are suggested in the Strategy, beginning with local markets and other forms of local consumer supply but also including catering supply chains both within the private and the public sector. Public sector purchasing, by refocusing on qualities that speak to this agenda, such as fresh and organic produce, can promote economic and environmental sustainability while improving public service delivery.[27]

One reason why careful and planned public and private sourcing of food is vital arises from the need to support producers at a time of decline and at a time when traditional Common Agricultural Policy subsidies are under pressure and review.[28] Purchasing decisions and supply chain collaboration can offer legitimate forms of business support. This suggests a collaborative, entrepreneurial culture with a priority of sustaining rural Welsh communities and their social and economic life. While the food industry in Wales must become more competitive, there is ample room for cooperation between producers networking jointly, for example to market products or increase capacity.[29] The reconnection is not simply through supply chains but through a bridging of urban and rural divisions so that the urban population of Wales is ready to enjoy the benefits of Welsh food products. In our review of strategic options, we do not make distinctions between producers of different size or sector. Instead we wrote:

> These principles should explicitly *encompass* all sections of the agri-food supply chain (from producers to consumers) and all established and emerging production and value-adding sectors (from red meat and dairy, to horticulture, aquaculture and coastal fisheries). The approach must emphasize the *multi-functionality* of farming, of food production and processing, and of the countryside, and look to enhance the economic, social and biological *diversity* of the Welsh rural resource base.[30]

The approach envisaged, then, is one of emphasizing multi-functionality and diversity within Welsh-provenance foods but to move towards more harmonized and efficient product and service development based on identified best practice. Just as the consumer base is multifarious both inside and outside the UK, so too the Welsh food system must have the capacity to respond to diverse demand.

The idea of Welsh-provenance foods is largely one that would be pursued by the private sector and as such might be seen to be a little removed from a soft law approach.[31] However, food provenance labelling is already carefully controlled in the EU. The origin of foods, such as beef, honey, olive oil and fresh fruit and vegetables, is regulated through labelling but in April 2011, at the request of the European Parliament, the Council of Ministers agreed to extend this to swine, sheep, goat and poultry meat. The Parliament has indicated that it wishes to go further, by indicating the provenance of all meat and poultry, milk and dairy products and other single-ingredient products.[32] However, in addition to maximising such mandatory labelling requirements, advantage can be taken of the EU scheme for Protected Food Names by reference to either Protected Geographical Indication or, as is the case for Welsh lamb, Protected Designation Origin schemes. The promotion of provenance in the Strategy through exploiting food-labelling law, although it depends on the activity of food producers themselves, again seems an entirely apposite task for soft law.

One final area in which better connections are needed is across sectors and policy areas within Wales. Food education, both inside and outside schools, and food events that might deliver better food literacy, such as food festivals, have a big part to play. Education and training must also deliver the skills base required to fulfil the visions of the Strategy. Tourism presents unique opportunities in Wales, through particular activities such as fishing or walking, but more generally because of the opportunity to market food with a distinct territorial connection. Specific emphasis can be put on freshness and locality; tourist locations (such as Welsh castles) can provide on-site points of sale. Tourist routes can be planned to incorporate leisure activity based on food and drink.

As outlined above, there are many other cross-cutting policy areas such as health or rural development. The approach of the Strategy was to foster greater integration and concerted action across such sectors. We suggested that:

> To ensure that WAG policies, as well as local authority and public sector policies, make a credible and consistent food policy statement, public policy should be subjected to more 'food-proofing'. This would help to overcome the debilitating lack of food policy integration in the public sector, where currently only the main sponsoring departments of WAG have an explicit food policy statement.[33]

The area of integration, in particular, is noteworthy in terms of the soft law analysis. It is likely that no new powers are necessary to make the sorts of connections between policy areas envisaged in the Strategy. Thus improvements to transport infrastructure could legitimately take into account the needs of food supply chains or those charged with promoting tourism could centre some of this endeavour on the attractions of Welsh food.[34] However, if government departments and quangos in Wales are to engage with this then they need some form of instruction to do so. The element of steering here is probably stronger in integrating public functions than it is in making other connections such as networking or consortial activity between producers.[35] Nonetheless, the endorsement of the Strategy by the Welsh Assembly Government, which is considered below, mandates departments of government to participate in the promotion of the interests of the Welsh food sector, which certainly seems an appropriate soft law task.

## Drivers to reconnection

Having chosen the theme of building connections and capacity, the next task was to attempt to identify activities that might take us in the direction outlined in the previous section. These we labelled drivers. The policy integration considered above, while a reform in its own right, might also be seen as a driver to change. For example, in the education arena, higher education institutions in Wales could stimulate good practice and innovation through research and development, skills training and the dissemination of know-how. There are many other examples of clear correlations between objectives for food and other policy goals. To take one example, the push in the waste strategy to become a 'zero waste' nation could have strong ties into food policy with an emphasis on waste minimization, packaging reductions, better business responsibility for waste production and a strong emphasis on waste composting.[36] Similar ties might be made with the public health agenda and that on rural and urban regeneration. In terms of environmental policy, this could focus on the development of more sustainable practices and ecological efficiencies through resource management. In other words, as with the waste strategy, there are other soft law instruments with which the Food Strategy intersects, and it is the ordering of these various soft law initiatives that will drive change.

Another driver that arises immediately from the emphasis on local and locality-branded food might be an active exercise in revaluing these qualities in such a way that a premium is placed upon them. This might seem an overly ambitious attempt to influence market choice, but the task appears easier because of the limited and entrenched, embedded supply chains for many Welsh agri-food products. Our fear was that these supply chains may be devaluing the primary and local processing end towards the top of the chain. In turn this would devalue the nutritional quality of Welsh products in the eyes of the consumer. The hope of the strategy is that consumer expectations of Welsh food could be better managed.[37] Revision of public and private food procurement could help produce new collaborative relationships to promote and sustain Welsh food and fish. Local producers, local resources, local environments and local consumers must all play a part in a 'local' food system. However, that system cannot afford to be parochial, since it looks to reach new and expanded markets. This was part of the appeal of providence indicators successfully established for Welsh red meat. There is room for more food niches and clusters within other food sectors in Wales.

To some extent the aim is to make available to stakeholders a narrative to enunciate the benefits of Welsh food as part of a wider initiative of engendering and embedding a food culture through instrumental activity such as farmers' markets, food awards, champions, and media and other events.[38] This calls for a good degree of entrepreneurial activity not merely on the part of established businesses but also from start-up companies, community groups and social enterprises. These marketing types of initiative may seem far removed from the interests of soft law, but this is not true everywhere. For the public sector's part, it can create entrepreneurial opportunity through the sustainable management of demand in its role as a major procurer of food and related services, while stimulating demand through better food education and food planning.[39] Public and private initiatives could help build capacity within the food supply system and to improve the infrastructure of the food system such as abattoirs where there is clear evidence of vulnerability.[40] The closure of abattoirs is in no small part the result of external, hard law, regulation, so here we see some soft law attempts to redress the balance.[41]

## The purpose of the Food Strategy

The final soft law indicator, suggested by Senden, is the intention of the drafters of the instrument. This is a little awkward in the present context, since the drafting was largely by the BRASS team. Changes to the draft strategy were few. Work was to a tender issued by through the Food and Drink Partnership and the status of the Strategy itself was not a matter of any great reflection in the completion of the work. Nonetheless, it is possible to review the purpose of the Strategy by reference to both the context in which it was produced and the procedural elements of its production. These are examined in turn.

### The context of the food strategy

It is most interesting to reflect on why a Food Strategy was thought necessary and perhaps why there has been a recent proliferation of such strategies, not simply in the UK but elsewhere. For over twenty years from the mid-1980s the British experience was that food prices fell in real terms as food supply chains delivered bulk-quality foods at a reasonable price. In such circumstances it is perhaps unsurprising, though nonetheless mistaken, that there was relatively little strategic government thinking about food. So what has changed? One palpable change is the return to inflationary food pricing since 2008, with grocery prices rising by 5 per cent in 2011.[42] However, this price rise itself reflects rising input costs such as energy, fertilizers and transportation and is indicative of resource pressures in food production. In addition, priorities for the agri-food sector are beginning to shift under pressures of carbon reduction and other factors in the environmental sustainability agenda, such as concerns about food waste or embedded water in food products. Talk of food security is no longer restricted to the developing world as the developed world readjusts to once again regarding food as a public good and refocuses on the externalities attaching to food production and processing. The social sustainability agenda is also engaged, as indicated by consumer demand for information regarding the health and nutritional benefits of food and about its provenance. Moreover there is much greater consciousness of the linkages between food production and rural development, in which issues of landscape, ecology and amenity come into play.

In relation to the economic sustainability of the agri-food sector in Wales, many of the background factors considered in the previous paragraph imply change in the business model. It was known at the time of considering the strategy that Wales faces a marked decline in the number of actors, whether farmers or processors, in the Welsh food sector and that sustainable infrastructure is increasingly difficult to maintain.[43] This is true also for the research and development base for agriculture in Wales, potentially inhibiting innovation. Meanwhile, competition, whether from other regions of the UK or from global trade, is as fierce as ever and is more directed than before with a strong focus on both branding and quality. The challenge is one of responding to these competitive forces and to changing consumer demands at a time of austerity in which public expenditure cuts might have the effect of increasing policy fragmentation across the public good agenda for food.

Wales is in an ever more competitive relationship not only with other regions in the UK but also in Europe given that, in traded value terms, the share of food imports increased from 62 per cent to 69 per cent between 1993 and 2006.[44] The competition is not merely about trade in Europe, though branded local goods have been a long-standing feature of European food trade.[45] In effect, regions also compete to provide food-related tourism, amenity and a range of food-related entrepreneurship which can attract investment in production and spending through consumption.

There are indications, then, of a growing interest in UK food security, as evidenced by a plethora of recent government reports on the issue.[46] It has been suggested that the long-standing focus of food law has been on food safety rather than wider issues of food security. Work with Chatham House has mooted the possible shortfalls of many inputs into food (such as oil, fertilizers, water and soils), which may make food an ever more precious commodity in global terms.[47] In this context there is such a strong national interest that one might expect a devolved administration in Wales to contribute to the progress of UK food security. Issues such as resource pressure and escalating food inflation help entrench the soft law status of the Strategy because it begins to address matters at the heart of the Welsh economy.

## Procedural elements of the Food Strategy

Because the Food Strategy was overseen by the Food and Drink Partnership, which contains stakeholders, including producers, and because our earlier Chatham House work included empirical work with food suppliers, including workshops in Wales, there had been inputs from producers from Wales and beyond in the devising of the Strategy which went out to consultation. The consultation on the draft Food Strategy took place between 6 July 2010 and 28 September 2010. Over 600 consultees were contacted directly and the consultation was also publicized on the Welsh Assembly Government internet site, and through various regional newspapers.[48] In addition, a series of public consultation meetings were held in north, mid, south west and south east Wales, and a number of presentations were also made to relevant stakeholder and Food & Drink Advisory Partnership groups. There were a series of regional business-focused seminars, as well as one-to-one round table discussions with key stakeholders. The comments from these events were captured and made available.[49] A total of 102 formal responses were received.

According to the Summary of Responses:

> A significant proportion of respondents supported and shared the vision set out for food in Wales over the next 10 years and expressed strong support for the cross cutting approach adopted within the strategy. There was broad agreement that food should be a more central element in the wider economic and social agenda and respondents welcomed the proposed focus on links between health, education, tourism, and producer/consumer interaction.[50]

This demonstrates not only buy-in to the Strategy but a willingness of the private sector 'to work in partnership with government and other organisations to contribute further to support these aims.'[51] It seems, then, that the Strategy achieves the broad aim of steering the food sector to closer cooperation and it is suggested that the soft law status of the Strategy is best placed to achieve this. The consultation exercise itself is indicative of a soft law instrument, as there is a clear acknowledgement of the need for agreement and endorsement and a strong desire to promulgate the draft widely among stakeholders.

All the responses to the consultation were considered in the revisions made to produce the final Strategy, and the Welsh Assembly Government agreed there was a need to develop a robust and transparent evidence base, indicators of progress, and a strategy renewal and evaluation process. There was a commitment to shorter-scale delivery plans. Interestingly, the Strategy states that the delivery plans may involve legal reforms, such as mandating a certain portion of local food in the purchasing behaviour of institutional buyers, but it then goes on to endorse the soft law approach by stating that:

> Not every change needs to be a legal one. 'Softer' approaches, including statements of good practice, voluntary codes, better education, and public/private partnering, may prove much more effective mechanisms for delivery. This approach may be particularly effective where the goal is to integrate different policy areas. The Strategy supports a much more creative use of these 'soft' approaches within the implementation plans.[52]

In addition to this revealing statement, there are two issues here. The first is that the Strategy binds the government to further activity. Moreover, there is a raft of other documents which are dependent on the Strategy and which will take their place as part of its wider regime. These features of the Strategy seem redolent of law, albeit soft law.

There are other indicators of the formal status of the Strategy; for example, it is the subject of an equality and diversity review.[53] To launch the consultation on the draft Strategy, there was a plenary debate in the Welsh Assembly on 6 July 2010, which is rather more than much secondary legislation ever achieves.[54] It was formally launched by the Rural Affairs Minister on 10 December 2010 and described as 'an ambitious step change [which] sets a radical direction for industry and

Government.' This again suggests an acceptance that the purpose of the Strategy is to engender change. Procedurally, then, there are many elements of the introduction of the Strategy that appear similar to that which one would expect for legislation; this bolsters the status of the Strategy as soft law.

## Conclusion

It seems, then, that the Food Strategy, almost unwittingly, creates soft law. It hardly seems to be the case that this soft law approach was made necessary by a lack of formal hard law powers. Quite apart from delegated powers in the food area and the possibility of Legislative Competence Orders, by the launch in December 2010 a favourable vote seemed likely in a March 2011 referendum to extend the law-making powers of the National Assembly in line with Part 4 of the Government of Wales Act 2006.[55] It is much more the case that the collaborative public/private enterprise envisaged by the Strategy to invigorate the food sector is better suited to the soft law approach. It advocates an approach to the governance of the food sector that extends well beyond government. It fits well at a local level within the multi-level governance of the food sector.

The Strategy does not tie the Welsh Government to the meeting of particular targets, but, even if it did so, there would be severe doubts about whether such targets would be enforceable or subject to judicial scrutiny, certainly where the meeting of the targets may depend on the deployment of resources.[56] Moreover, enforceability clearly separates out hard from soft law if the latter is to be non-binding. On the other hand, the commitments made by the Welsh Government, to deliver the vision, to integrate the functions of government in relation to food or to build other elements to support the Strategy, all carry clear political accountability.

So the difficulty is not so much in distinguishing the Strategy from hard law, because there are countless reasons, not least to do with legal formality, why it cannot claim such status; the problem lies in attaching the label 'law' after the word 'soft'. This chapter has tried to illustrate that the Strategy does do some of the work of a legal instrument. The nature, content and purpose of the Strategy all indicate change along a particular pathway. That direction, which is broadly one of sustainable development, envisaged economically, socially and environmentally, has been the subject of wide consultation and endorsement. This is a radical change from the expectation of ever-cheaper bulk food to one which pays attention to the environmental, health and social impacts of the food system and pressing problems of the security of national food supply. For a document with such ambition, the claim of the status of law, however soft, hardly seems inflated.

## Notes

1 Welsh Assembly Government, *Food for Wales, Food from Wales 2010–2020* (Cardiff: WAG, 2010), p. 10.
2 The team was from the ESRC Centre for Business Relationships, Accountability, Sustainability and Society at Cardiff University, hereafter BRASS. In the introduction to the Food Strategy, Hayden Edwards, Chair of the Food and Drink Partnership, which oversaw the work, writes: 'The draft strategy was delivered according to specification and to the set time. As chair of the partnership I am grateful for the outstanding work done by BRASS' (p. 3). I, too, am grateful to my colleagues for this work, on which this paper draws heavily.
3 Malgosia A. Fitzmaurice, 'International protection of the environment', in *Collected Courses of The Hague Academy of International Law*, 293 (Leiden: Martinus Nijhoff Publishers, 2001), 22–7.
4 L. Senden, *Soft Law in the European Community* (Oxford: Hart, 2004), p. 112.
5 The Sixth Action Programme did claim to be mandatory in the sense that EU institutions and member states should strive to achieve its goals, though no sanctions attach to failure to do so.
6 European Commission, *Common Implementation Strategy for the Water Framework Directive* (2000/60/EC); European Commission, *Our Life Insurance, Our Natural Capital: An EU Biodiversity Strategy to 2020*, COM (2011) 244 final.
7 L. Etherington, '"Mandatory guidance" for dealing with contaminated land: paradox or pragmatism?', *Statute Law Review*, 23 (2002), 203–26.
8 L. Fuller, 'The forms and limits of adjudication', *Harvard Law Review*, 92, 2 (1978), 353–409.
9 T. Marsden, J. Banks and G. Bristow, 'Food supply chain approaches: exploring their role in rural development', *Sociologia Ruralis*, 40 (2000), 424–38; M. A. Bourlakis and P. W. H. Weightman, *Food Supply Chain Management* (Oxford: Blackwell Publishing, 2004).
10 S. Bell and D. McGillivray, *Environmental Law*, 7th edn (Oxford: Oxford University Press, 2008), p. 87.
11 P. Birnie, A. Boyle and C. Redgewell, *International Law and the Environment*, 3rd edn (Oxford: Oxford University Press, 2009), p. 34.
12 R. Lee and M. Stallworthy, 'From the criminal to the consensual: the shifting mechanisms of environmental regulation', in J. Coggon, A. Kessel and A. Viens (eds.), *Criminal Law, Philosophy and Public Health* (Cambridge: Cambridge University Press, forthcoming); Etherington, 'Mandatory guidance', n. 9.
13 BRASS, *Food and Drink Strategy for Wales, Work Package 1c: Best Practice Review* (unpublished, 2009).
14 For example Germany, Denmark and Venezuela; Oakland, Bristol and London.
15 Ministry of Agriculture and Lands, *The British Columbia Agricultural Plan: Growing a Healthy Future for B. C. Families*, http://www.box.net/shared/kb824f59h8 (accessed 18 May 2012).
16 See, for example, Government Office for the North West, *Facing the Future: A Delivery Plan for Sustainable Farming and Food in the North West of England*, http://www.box.net/shared/jf25yje03r (accessed 18 May 2012).
17 A good example would be Sustain and Energy for Sustainability, *Newquay Growth Area Food Strategy* (2007), http://www.box.net/shared/5013lvhoik (accessed 18 May 2012), which seeks to support a vibrant food economy; to celebrate and promote Cornish food culture; and to strengthen the foundations of local food security. See also Scottish Government, *Recipe for Success: Scotland's National Food and Drink Policy* (June 2009), http://www.box.net/shared/bog42m7n9k (accessed 18 May 2012).
18 Brighton and Hove Food Partnership, *Spade to Spoon: Making the Connections* (2006), http://www.box.net/shared/dkf3pq5dhk (accessed 18 May 2012). See the German

initiative for healthy diet and more exercise, Deutschlands Initiative für gesunde Ernährung und mehr Bewegung, *http://www.bmelv.de/SharedDocs/Downloads/Broschueren/AktionsplanINFORM.html* (accessed 18 May 2012).
19. Oakland Mayor's Office of Sustainability and University of California, Berkeley, Department of City and Regional Planning, *A Food Systems Assessment for Oakland, CA: Towards a Sustainable Food Plan* (Oakland, CA: Oakland Mayor's Office, 2006), *http://www.box.net/shared/l9gv6y5ckz* (accessed 18 May 2012).
20. See note 2 above for the Partnership's role. As this chapter considers events in 2010, 'Welsh Assembly Government' is preferred to the more recent 'Welsh Government'.
21. DEFRA, Southeast of England Development Agency and Government Office for the South East, *Farming for the Future* (Guildford: SERDA, 2008), *http://www.box.net/shared/f5ygtt9j9t* (accessed 18 May 2012).
22. Food Strategy, p. 23.
23. See the Introduction to D. Campbell and R. Lee, *Environmental Law and Economics* (Farnham: Ashgate, 2007).
24. C. Chinkin, 'The challenge of soft law: development and change in international law', *International and Comparative Law Quarterly*, 38 (1989), 850–66.
25. Fitzmaurice, 'International protection of the environment'.
26. Welsh food culture is already rich; see, for example, the Cardiff International Food and Drink Festival, the Abergavenny Food Festival and the Anglesey Oyster and Welsh Produce Festival, *http://www.wales.com/EN/Default.aspx?n1=2&n2=26&n3=63&n4=224* (accessed 18 May 2012).
27. K. Morgan, *The Public Plate* (Brass Working Paper 43, 2007).
28. See BRASS, *Food and Drink Strategy for Wales: Work Package 1a, Food Sector Data* (unpublished, 2010).
29. One good example of this is Cheeses From Wales, a Limited co-operative set up by Welsh cheese makers to provide a method of collectively selling and promoting a wide selection of cheeses, all of which are made in Wales; see *http://www.cheesesfromwales.co.uk/members.htm#join* (accessed 18 May 2012).
30. BRASS, *Food and Drink Strategy for Wales: Work Package 2, Strategic Options – Discussion Paper* (unpublished, 2010), pp. 6–7.
31. In this connection see the work of my colleagues: K. Morgan, T. Marsden and J. Murdoch, *Worlds of Food: Place, Power, and Provenance in the Food Chain* (Oxford: Oxford University Press, 2006).
32. See European Parliament Press release of 19 April 2011, *http://www.europarl.europa.eu/en/pressroom/content/20110418IPR18101/html/Food-labelling-Environment-Committee-sets-out-clearer-rules* (accessed 18 May 2012).
33. BRASS, *Food and Drink Strategy for Wales: Work Package 2, Strategic Options – Discussion Paper*, p. 7.
34. It is possible for the policy of a public body to be quashed because of irrelevant considerations – see *R. v. ILEA ex parte Westminster City Council* [1948] 1 KB 223 – but the case law tends to suggest that such considerations are often tainted by political motivation (as in the case cited) rather than being legitimate attempts to coordinate policy.
35. See Senden, *Soft Law in the European Community*, and the discussion above.
36. Welsh Assembly Government, *Towards Zero Waste – One Wales: One Planet* (Cardiff: WAG, June 2010).
37. There was an available precedent for this in the work of Hybu Cig Cymru – Meat Promotion Wales (HCC), which is the industry-led organization responsible for the development, promotion and marketing of Welsh red meat. The HCC, in its attempt to convey the qualities of Welsh red meat to consumers at home and further afield, had sought European Commission designations of Welsh Lamb and Welsh Beef as products of Protected Geographical Indication (PGI), a status highly valued and recognized throughout mainland Europe. Welsh Lamb and Welsh Beef were awarded PGI status in recognition of the quality of the product and its special regional significance, providing

consumer assurance that only lamb and beef that have been born and reared in Wales can be marketed as Welsh.

38  Since 2002 there has been an annual True Taste Food and Drink Award to recognize innovation and quality: *http://www.walesthetruetaste.co.uk/theawards/;jsessionid=D0 7vTL6dngxsnCcTSnthpVy44gyhhykmrRgfKZpMqBjXc32JQ5mp!-425304898?lang=en* (accessed 18 May 2012).

39  See, for example, K. Morgan and R. Sonnino, 'Empowering consumers: the creative procurement of school meals in Italy and the UK', *International Journal of Consumer Studies*, 31 (2007), 19–25.

40  S. Dube, 'Small abattoirs at risk from FSA costs blow', *Western Mail*, 16 November 2010.

41  R. Schofield and J. Shaoul, 'Food safety regulations and the conflict of interest: the case of meat safety and *E. coli* 0157', *Public Administration*, 78 (2000), 531–54.

42  J. Tasker, 'Renewed call to tackle food inflation', *Farmers Weekly*, 22 July 2011, citing a survey by Which, *The Rising Cost of Food* (London: Which, July 2011).

43  The contribution of agriculture to the Welsh economy fell by 69 per cent during 1999–2008; see Table 1.3, NUTS1 GVA (1989–2009) Data at *http://www.statistics.gov. uk/statbase/Product.asp?vlnk=14650* (accessed 18 May 2012).

44  The non-UK countries constituting what became the EU25 in 2004 have accounted for a high and increasing share of UK food imports since the 1990s, up from 53 per cent in 1993 (unprocessed value) to 57 per cent in 2006, but this is higher in traded value terms because the UK tends to import higher-valued food products; see Department for Food, Environment and Rural Affairs, *UK Food Security Assessment* (London: Defra, 2009, updated 2010).

45  One of the earliest cases on EU law in the British courts concerns the label of 'champagne perry' attached to Babycham, which French champagne producers sought to restrain; see *Bulmer Ltd v. J. Bollinger SA* [1974] 2 All ER 1226.

46  Environment, Food and Rural Affairs Committee, *Securing Food Supplies up to 2050: The Challenges for the UK* (Fourth Report of Session 2008–09, HC 213, 21 July 2009); Defra, *UK Food Security Assessment* (London: Defra, 2010); Cabinet Office Strategy Unit, *Food Matters: Towards a Strategy for the Twenty First Century* (London: Cabinet Office, 2008); Sustainable Development Commission, *Food Security and Sustainability: The Perfect Fit* (SDC Position Paper, July 2009); Foresight, *The Future of Food and Farming* (London: Government Office for Science, 2011).

47  S. Ambler-Edwards, K. Bailey, A. Kiff, T. Lang, R. Lee, T. Marsden, D. Simons and H. Tibbs, *Food Futures, Rethinking UK Strategy* (London: Chatham House, 2009).

48  Also through *Gwlad* (the Welsh Assembly Governments' monthly rural affairs magazine); see *http://wales.gov.uk/docs/drah/publications/100810gwlad98en.pdf* (accessed 18 May 2012).

49  Welsh Assembly Government, *Food for Wales, Food from Wales 2010–2020: Summary of Responses to the Welsh Assembly Government Consultation on the Food Strategy for Wales* (Cardiff: WAG, 2010).

50  Ibid., p. 3.

51  Ibid., p. 4.

52  Food Strategy, p. 71.

53  Available at *http://wales.gov.uk/topics/equality/inclusivepolicy/impactassessments/ foodstrat/?lang=en* (accessed 18 May 2012).

54  Reference at *http://www.assemblywales.org/bus-home/bus-chamber/bus-chamber-third-assembly-agendas.htm?act=dis&id=189156&ds=7/2010* (accessed 18 May 2012).

55  See, for example, Transfer of Functions (Agriculture and Food) Order 1999/3141, the Transfer of Functions (Agriculture and Fisheries and Food) Order 2000/1812 and the Red Meat Industry (Wales) Measure 2010 seeking to develop and promote the Welsh red meat industry.

56  *Help the Aged and Friends of the Earth v. Secretary of State for Business Enterprise and Regulatory Reform* [2010] Env L. R. 11.

# Chapter 8

# Sustainable communities in Wales: developing a new governance approach to local sustainable development in Wales's most deprived areas

*Victoria Jenkins*

### Introduction

Sustainable development is a global challenge but it will be founded upon changes in the behaviour of all actors in society, ranging from multi-national corporations to individuals at work and in their homes. Of particular significance is ensuring environmentally sustainable behaviour among the poorest people in society, who are rarely preoccupied by global environmental problems, but for whom the quality of the local environment is a key concern. In developing countries the main consideration is ensuring that the local environment can support the basic needs of its people.[1] In developed societies there is also increasing recognition that measures to improve local environmental quality can contribute to greater social sustainability.[2] It is also possible that building capacity among local communities to address problems within their immediate environment can engender a wider sense of environmental citizenship.[3] Global–local connectivity will, therefore, be highly significant in the transition to sustainable development; and thus this is a goal which can be achieved only by adopting a multi-level governance approach.[4]

The framework for international action on sustainable development is provided by the Agenda 21 action plan, which supports an integrated approach to environment and development concerns.[5] It also includes explicit recognition of the need to address issues of poverty in the transition to sustainable development, and states that deprivation is best addressed by empowering people to take action to change their individual circumstances by working together with others in the locality as a community.[6] Historically, community regeneration work in the UK has failed to properly consider the wider agenda for environmental protection or the need for public participation.[7] More recently however, the national strategy for sustainable development has been cognizant of the links between social and environmental justice; and there have been attempts to provide a more decentralized and participatory approach to community regeneration which accords with new governance thinking in the UK.[8] New governance is not easily defined, but its 'broad spirit' recognizes

> that a shift is taking place in the role of the national state, which has moved substantially away from top-down command and control regulation to a much more decentralised and consensual approach which seeks to coordinate at multiple levels, and is distinctively polycentric.[9]

This chapter will explore the development of such an approach in pursuing sustainability among the most deprived communities in Wales. This focuses on the participation of local communities in regeneration initiatives through the Welsh Government's flagship programme for social justice, Communities First. The Welsh Government also, however, calls upon local government to provide leadership in coordinating this work with that of community and town councils and the voluntary sector. In developing a model of new governance for sustainable communities in Wales, as in any other context, there are four key issues to be considered: first, the need to operate within the frameworks of governance at global and national level; second, ensuring cooperation and coordination among local actors; third, accountability among non-state actors involved in the process; and, finally, providing effective mechanisms for the participation of local citizens. However, in the particular context of sustainable development, perhaps the most significant concern is how this new governance approach will reflect the integration of social and environmental considerations.

## Sustainable development and community empowerment: a multi-level governance approach

Agenda 21 has been translated into national action for sustainable development through the creation of dedicated strategies. The most recent UK strategy, *Securing the Future*, was published by the Labour government in 2005. The priorities at this time were considered to be sustainable consumption and production, climate change, natural resource protection and sustainable communities. The focus was clearly on maintaining development within the limits of environmental resources and providing regulatory approaches to achieve this. The current coalition government has yet to publish a comprehensive strategy for sustainable development, but has provided a vision statement which mirrors these priorities, with two important differences. First, the emphasis is on valuing environmental goods and services within a model of economic growth rather than regulating to ensure development is maintained within environmental limits. Second, and of particular significance to this chapter, is a change in emphasis from providing sustainable communities to ensuring fairness and improving wellbeing.[10] This has resulted in a very different approach from the previous Labour government to the issue of community empowerment for sustainable development, which, *inter alia*, is directed to all citizens, not just those that are less well off. In Wales, however, where there are high levels of poverty and social deprivation, the Welsh Government continues to support the previous UK Labour government's vision of sustainable communities.[11]

The Welsh Government has a statutory duty to create its own sustainable development scheme to support the priorities in the UK.[12] In doing so, the current Welsh Sustainable Development Scheme *One Wales: One Planet* pays particular attention to the development of sustainable communities.[13] The Welsh Sustainable Development Scheme describes sustainable communities as 'safe, sustainable, attractive communities in which people live and work, have access to services and enjoy good health and can play their full roles as citizens.'[14] The UK Labour government's strategy for sustainable development emphasized the links between social and environmental justice; thus, improving local environmental quality was at the heart of its campaign for sustainable communities:

> Dirty and dangerous places encourage graffiti, vandalism and anti-social behaviour, which in turn undermine public confidence in them and lead people to avoid them. An unattractive and threatening local environment encourages people to use their cars for short journeys and to move to a better area if they can. It can discourage investment and lead to abandonment and dereliction.[15]

This approach is reflected in the reference to 'attractive communities' in the Welsh definition of sustainable communities; and one of the key themes of the sustainable development scheme is to 'support the people and communities of Wales to take responsibility for the quality of their local environment so that they can contribute towards a clean, safe and tidy Wales'.[16] Improving local environmental quality is, of course, only one step in adopting an integrated approach to social and environmental issues for local communities. Indeed, environmentalists may prefer to highlight the links between greater social sustainability and environmental stewardship at both the local and global levels.[17] Nevertheless, empowering communities to look after their local environment may be seen as a necessary stepping stone in this regard.

Agenda 21 highlights the significance of community in addressing the concerns of deprived peoples for sustainable development, and it advocates devolving authority, accountability and resources for combating poverty to the most appropriate level.[18] The coalition government is pursuing an agenda for community empowerment for sustainable development through its flagship policy initiative, the Big Society:

> Government can set a framework for sustainable development at national level, but many changes need to happen through the Big Society at a local level, ensuring our communities work more closely together, using local insight, energy and knowledge to develop solutions tailored to local circumstances . . . More empowered communities and a society where people are more involved in social action such as volunteering should lead to increased well-being, stronger communities and stronger social ties.[19]

However, the former Welsh Government 'made it clear that they had no plans to undertake any Big Society initiatives, stating that putting people and communities at the heart of public services was already at the core of their programme for public service improvement.'[20] Thus, as outlined below, few of the new legal powers associated with the initiative will apply in Wales. This has resulted in very different approaches to community empowerment for sustainable development in England and Wales.

## Community and sustainable development: differing approaches to community empowerment in England and Wales

Community is undoubtedly a contested notion, but the idea of community has been 'related to the search for belonging in the insecure conditions of modernity'.[21] The search for community among the urban poor has been the holy grail of urban sociology for many years, recognizing the complexities of communities of both place and interest.[22] However, the community development movement in the UK has focused on identifying spatial communities within the city, usually referred to as neighbourhoods, that may form a cohesive unit with which to engage in anti-poverty measures. This is considered to be particularly difficult given that the city can be viewed as the antithesis of traditional rural communities. However, the search for community, whether in pursuit of a lost tradition or something as yet unknown, is in itself a somewhat utopian idea. Nevertheless, the place of community in society, and its significance for the relationship between society and state, has a political importance of more immediate concern. This is once again a subject fraught with complexity; but as a starting point communitarians would emphasize the community as opposed to the individual in civic life. In particular, 'the civic tradition within communitarianism has made social capital and participation in public life central to community'.[23] Conversely, a lack of participation in public life has been associated with the destruction of social cohesion.[24]

Civic communitarianism can be used to support very different notions of participation in society, from the empowerment of the poor to take part in decision making by local government to the wholesale devolution of power to local people to provide services previously considered to be the responsibility of the state.[25] It is clear that the Big Society supports the devolution of power directly to communities. With its emphasis on well-being as well as fairness, the Big Society is also an initiative for all communities rather than focusing specifically on those that are suffering from deprivation.

The new framework of powers to support the Big Society is provided by the Localism Act 2011. Communities in England will have the right to take part in neighbourhood planning, to bid to carry out local authority services and to hold local referendums on council tax.[26] In some instances, these rights are given to parish councils or existing local community organisations; but in other situations, or in the absence of such a council or established group, a number of individuals may come together to exercise these rights on behalf of the community. For example, neighbourhood-planning powers can be exercised by a neighbourhood forum whose membership includes a minimum of 21 individuals who either live or work in the neighbourhood area concerned or are elected members of a local authority whose area falls in the neighbourhood.[27] This raises difficult questions about the representation and accountability of these groups given their significant powers in shaping the development and administration of local services.

Only the community right to buy will apply in Wales as well as England.[28] This provides local authorities with a duty to maintain a list of land in its area that is land of community value.[29] Once land is listed, its owner cannot dispose of it without notifying the local authority, which is subsequently responsible for establishing whether there are any community interest groups that have an interest in making a bid for the land.[30] The notion of a community interest group in relation to these powers will be strictly under the control of the Welsh Government;[31] and given the centrality of the neighbourhood approach to sustainable communities in Wales, as outlined below, it may well focus on the role of community and town councils (as the equivalent of parish councils in England) and the voluntary sector rather than a groups of individuals representing the community.

It is clear that the Welsh Government has rejected the model of civic communitarianism exemplified by the Big Society initiative in England and, as a devolved government, has been free to develop a distinctive approach. It will nevertheless need to provide some means of participation of local communities and organizations and ensure accountability in the process. In fact, the Welsh Government supports a local community/neighbourhood approach to sustainable communities, in which local people will be represented by Communities First Partnerships, voluntary/third sector organizations, community and town councils, and local government operations.[32]

## The major actors in the new governance framework for sustainable communities in Wales: representation, participation and accountability

Since 2001, the agenda for social justice in Wales has been furthered by the Welsh Government's Communities First programme as the focus for community regeneration work. However, Wales also has a strong voluntary sector, whose role has gained increasing recognition in tandem with wider developments in the UK under the Labour government. Furthermore, more recently the role of community and town councils has been highlighted as significant in providing services to, and working with, local communities. Finally, local government may also be involved in specific measures to work with local communities in regeneration. These actors provide very different means of ensuring community empowerment for sustainable development.

### Communities First[33]

Communities First is the Welsh Government's flagship programme 'to improve the living conditions and prospects of people in the most disadvantaged communities across Wales.'[34] The programme is most well known for the geographically defined areas that are supported, but also provides for thematic communities of interest.[35] A key principle of the programme is that local people should be involved in the process, which is delivered through Communities First Partnerships (CFPs). Partnership working has long been advocated as a means of ensuring a participatory approach to local governance, but not without criticism of the way that these often operate in practice.[36] In an attempt to address these concerns the Welsh Government has adopted the unique approach of ensuring that all partnerships operate on a 'three-thirds' basis, with equal representation of the local community, statutory and voluntary/business sectors.[37] There is evidence that the CFPs have indeed been successful in engaging local people in developing priorities for action, but these partnerships are not however, responsible for the activity and funding that will ultimately achieve the necessary change in their area and must ensure that their work influences that of other public bodies.[38] Significantly, therefore, there is also evidence that these partnerships have struggled to influence the activities of key policy actors.[39]

At first sight, the Communities First initiative would appear to have little to do with environmental issues. However, despite its clear emphasis on social justice, there has been some attempt to widen the aims of the programme through the Communities First Vision Framework.[40] The guidance on this framework includes, for example, a number of headings on environment such as, addressing climate change and distinctive biodiversity. Indeed, in 2009, the Wales Audit Office reported more outcomes in terms of environment than jobs and business, community safety or child poverty.[41] This raised concerns, however, about the breadth of the programme and its success in contributing to the alleviation of core issues associated with social deprivation in Wales, particularly child poverty.[42] As a result, the Welsh Government has stated that, from April 2012, the Communities First programme will have a much clearer emphasis on tackling poverty, replacing the vision framework with three strategic outcomes based on economic prosperity, education/skills and health; and, although work on environmental issues may take place, it will need to show how it impacts on these.[43] This outcomes-driven approach will not, however, take account of the significance of an integrated approach to social and environmental concerns or the more intangible benefits of improving local environmental quality.

One example might help to illuminate this point at this juncture. One of the Community First areas that has been identified in South West Wales is Graig Felen, a community central to the Clydach area in the Swansea Valley. As part of a wider initiative supported by Objective 1 funding from the European Union, a new Community Centre for Clydach was created in close proximity to Graig Felen, which clearly provides, in no small measure, social support for this area. The siting of the centre is also, however, entirely significant. Clydach, like many other areas in Wales, is paradoxically a deprived area according to statistics of deprivation, but one that benefits from a geographical location rich in natural beauty.[44] In this context, the Community Centre at issue is placed alongside the river, where the water falls literally through the geographical heart of the community. The siting of the centre has therefore been significant in bringing the people closer to, and making them more appreciative of, their natural environment. The extent of this cannot be measured by an objective indicator but is nevertheless grasped by the community – even if unknowingly.[45]

## The voluntary sector

The voluntary sector has long supported the work of government in the UK, and can be considered to have the potential to provide for community empowerment if and where government itself fails.[46] On coming to power in 1997, the Labour government was keen to highlight the significance of the voluntary sector in the UK, and hastened to create a compact outlining the parameters of the voluntary–statutory relationship.[47] Subsequently, in Wales, the initial agreement for devolution in the Government of Wales Act 1998 included a specific duty for the Welsh Assembly to promote this sector.[48] Thus the Welsh Government must create a scheme which recognizes the independence of the sector whilst also promoting their shared values, including sustainable development.[49] Furthermore, County

Voluntary Councils (CVCs) operate at local authority level to provide advice and information to local voluntary and community groups.[50]

There are over 31,000 voluntary, community and not-for-profit organizations in Wales, the vast majority of which are local organizations, involved largely in social issues such as sports, health, youth or arts.[51] However, there are also some notable organizations in the environmental field, such as Groundwork.[52] The voluntary sector may thus have a significant role to play in the governance of sustainable communities; but historically there is some evidence that local authorities in Wales have failed to recognize the work of voluntary organizations in contributing to local sustainability.[53] The voluntary sector is often referred to as a homogenous entity but in reality voluntary organizations take many different forms. It can include any of the following:

> spontaneous grassroots groups designed to help members do things together, philanthropic organisations that are designed to help others, service providing organisations in numerous industries ... that are financed by consumers or governments, as well as special interest groups that are set up to influence government behaviour rather than to do things directly themselves.[54]

Thus accountability is a complex issue for this sector, but one that has received little attention to date in developing a framework of new governance for sustainable communities.[55] This may be, as outlined below, the result of a clear emphasis in Wales on the role of the public sector in this regard.

## Community and town councils in Wales

The Welsh Government considers community and town councils in Wales to have an 'important citizen-focused role to play, not just in promoting strong communications and focusing on very local quality of life (or liveability) issues, but also in service delivery.'[56] This is, however, somewhat at odds with the history of these councils, which have been of little concern to mainstream local governance structures. A level of community government has existed in Wales since the Local Government Act of 1894 but the origins of community and town councils today lie in the Local Government Act 1972, which created a 'pattern of incomplete geographical coverage that continues to persist'.[57] In 2010, there were 735 such councils in Wales serving populations between fewer than 200 and more than 45,000 people.[58] These councils have operated under the powers of the National Assembly for Wales since the Government of Wales Act 1998.[59] A community council can be created by order of a local authority following a majority poll of a community meeting at which 150 or 10 per cent of the local government electors are present.[60] This suggests an attention to community that is not present in drawing local authority boundaries.[61]

Historically, by its own admission, Welsh Government has had little information or understanding of these institutions. However, in 2002, a study was carried out into the functions and future potential of these councils, followed by a second survey in 2010.[62] This research found that, although community and town councils should have a democratic mandate as an elected body, 'in practice only a minority of community and town councils have required contested ballots to elect their members in recent years and many have struggled to attract candidates.'[63] In 2002, it was also found that:

> One of the great strengths of community and town councils is that they are closer to local people than any other tier of government. Yet in practice, the quality and openness of interaction with the public by local level councils can vary significantly.[64]

Most councils as a minimum deal with signs, notice and information boards, seats and shelters. However, some, usually larger, councils, may also have a role in activities such as crime prevention and community transport.[65] In 2002, there was significant interest from larger councils in providing more services:

> Many local-level councils have argued that they are more able than principal councils to be responsive to local needs and accountable to the community and that enhancement of their role in service delivery would promote a sense of community ownership of services, facilities and amenities and act as stimulus for greater participation by local residents as community and town councillors.[66]

However, local authorities voiced concerns about economies of scale and strategic coordination, and only 16 per cent of community and town councils have a service level agreement with their local authorities today.[67]

A number of amendments were made to the role and functions of these bodies by the Local Government Measure 2011, which aimed to:

> develop and strengthen the role of community councils in Wales, enabling them to deliver a wider range of services and actions locally as well as to increase the effectiveness of their representational role and their ability to work in partnership with other bodies.[68]

## *Local government measures for community development*

Local government has a long tradition of providing services at the community level. However, local authorities have also been involved in work specifically to support community regeneration. Local authorities in Wales are a key partner in Community First partnerships and have also been involved in other initiatives such as regional collaborative communities programmes and the creation of development trusts.

## The role of local government in the new governance framework for sustainable communities in Wales: cooperation, coordination and leadership

In Wales, local government is considered to have a central role in developing the new governance framework sustainable communities. The significance of local government in the transition to sustainable development was also recognized in Agenda 21, owing to their powers over local infrastructure and local environmental policies and regulations, and because, 'as the level of governance closest to the people, they play a vital role in educating, mobilizing and responding to the public to promote sustainable development.'[69] In Wales, however, local authorities have been tasked with not just involving the public in local action on sustainability but joining up activities of other local actors. Joining up is difficult within government, but working in partnership with other sectors involves even greater complexity.[70] This is not just an issue that has relevance for the role of local authorities in regeneration, but resonates clearly with a more fundamental change in the nature of local government in recent times from service provider to community leader.[71]

The process of local government modernization began during the 1980s, but gained particular prominence under the Labour government following the introduction of the Local Government Act 2000, which applies in both England and Wales.[72] The main mechanism for the development of local authorities in this new role of community leader is the process of community planning. This involves:

- focusing attention on key community priorities.
- galvanizing a range of stakeholders to contribute to delivering these priorities.
- involving citizens in the process of priority identification and delivery.[73]

The central plank of community planning is the creation of a community strategy in consultation and engagement with local people, in order to 'promote or improve the economic, social and environmental well-being' of the area and 'contribute to the achievement of sustainable development in the United Kingdom.'[74]

Community planning, therefore, provides the vehicle for local authorities to consider the strategic development of the local area, including the regeneration of its more deprived communities. The participation of the public and other local actors is essential to this activity, along with the coordination of the efforts of all those working in the local area. Of particular significance with respect to the notion of sustainable communities, however, is the work of Community First Partnerships.

## Community planning

The framework for community planning in England and Wales is provided by the Local Government Act 2000.[75] However, the original system of community planning has been developed rather differently in Wales from in England as a result of enabling powers in the Local Government and Public Involvement in Health Act 2007. The most significant difference is the emphasis in Wales on the role of the public sector in taking action for the local community. This is part of a wider focus in Wales on public service delivery, which is now central to the Welsh agenda for government. This follows the Beecham Review, which supported the notion of 'citizen-centred' services and the need to join up public services across Wales.[76] A second important issue in considering the role of community planning in the development of sustainable communities is the nature of public participation in the process and the significance of the relationship between community planning and the Communities First initiative in this regard. Finally, it is necessary to consider the extent to which this framework provides a mandate to contribute to local sustainability.

## The significance of the role of the public sector

The initial approach to community planning in England and Wales was through the creation of Local Strategic Partnerships (LSPs), which are made up of local councils, other public sector bodies, business and voluntary organizations, and are still operational in England today.[77] In Wales, however, although the community planning process develops the work of prior partnerships, Local Service Boards (LSBs) are to take a lead.[78] LSBs have a specific role in enabling public service organisations to work together more effectively.[79] Furthermore, the Local Government Measure 2009 in Wales has introduced a statutory duty to support the role of 'community planning partners' in this process. These are defined as public sector bodies representing fire and rescue, health, police and national parks along with community and town councils.[80] This therefore provides community and town councils with a specific duty to take part in the community planning process; and not just to participate in local authority planning but 'to carry out those actions to implement the community strategy that fall within their remit.'[81]

This emphasis on the public sector therefore leaves us to question the place of the voluntary sector in this process. Community-planning guidance is clear that the LSB should include the County Voluntary Council to further a constructive dialogue with the wider third sector.[82] However, historically local government has struggled to engage with the voluntary sector in community planning and, despite recent attention to the role of the voluntary sector, the central approach to community planning in Wales undoubtedly focuses on the public sector's role in the delivery of the strategy.[83] The success of public sector actors is measured by their respective performance management systems; but insufficient attention has also been given to the issue of the accountability of the voluntary sector in sustainable community initiatives.[84]

## Public participation and the relationship with the Communities First Initiative

The Local Government Act 2000 included a statutory duty to 'consult and seek the participation of such persons as (local authorities) consider appropriate' in creating community strategies; but there is some evidence that local authorities in Wales have struggled in doing so.[85] In the context of sustainable communities, however, as outlined above, there is evidence that CFPs have been more successful in this regard.[86] Therefore, it is important to provide a means of feeding in the results of this process to that of community planning. This has indeed been recognized in the guidance on community planning, which advocates frequent communication and liaison between the local authority and CFPs.[87] The exact arrangements are to be a matter of local agreement, but it is suggested that this might involve a formal liaison arrangement such as a board.[88] However, as outlined above, there is some evidence that CFPS are failing to influence the work of other actors in this process.[89]

## Local authority leadership and sustainable development

Local authorities have been tasked with a considerable challenge by the Welsh Government to take the lead in developing a new governance approach to sustainable communities. However, local authorities operate within the legal frameworks for community planning provided by the UK and Welsh governments, neither of which clearly supports sustainable development as the central objective for this work. The Local Government Act 2000 focuses on the role of community planning in improving well-being in society rather than sustainable development. The relationship between well-being and sustainability is unclear, but it would appear that the former, despite the reference to environmental well-being, focuses on individual health and/or social sustainability whilst the latter emphasizes the significance of natural resource to the process of development.[90]

More recently, in England, the name of the process has been changed to sustainable community planning, supported by the introduction of a system for local authorities to apply to the Secretary of State for the funding of activities which they consider would contribute to promoting the sustainability of local communities.[91] This has some consequence as a symbol of political leadership in capturing the process of community planning for local sustainability, but has not been adopted in Wales.[92] Nevertheless, the reality in both England and Wales, to date, has been a constant struggle to ensure that sustainable development is the overriding aim of this process.⁹³ Furthermore, even if sustainable development were to be placed at the heart of the community-planning process, the conflict between the views of UK and Welsh administrations on this issue would make this a very difficult objective for local authorities to take forward in their role as community leaders.

## Conclusions

Many people in Wales live in 'safe, sustainable, attractive communities', but where this is not the case there is global agreement that local people should be empowered to take action to improve their living conditions. The means of ensuring community empowerment is, however, a matter of some debate, and the focus of the sustainable communities initiative in Wales is quite different from that of the flagship programme for the Big Society in England. The Big Society initiative supports direct action by communities, which may be viewed by some as highly significant but undoubtedly raises important questions with regard to accountability.⁹⁴ Following devolution, the Welsh Government has proposed a very different new governance framework for sustainable communities that provides for the participation of local people through CFPs, community and town councils and the voluntary sector, as well as the work of local government.

The main mechanism for ensuring participation of both local actors and the public in community regeneration under the Welsh Government's flagship programme for social justice is the CFP. However, these partnerships are relied upon only to influence the work of others, not to take action themselves. Local government is tasked with ensuring that the work of CFPs and the particular concerns of deprived communities are recognized in strategic planning for the local area with other actors. The roles of community and town councils and the voluntary sector have been highlighted as particularly important in representing the views of local people in this regard. However, the process of community planning, achieved largely through the work of LSBs, focuses on the contribution of public sector bodies. In this context, there is evidence that CFPs are not gaining sufficient influence; that the contribution of community and town councils is as yet unclear because their role in local governance in Wales is still in its infancy; and that the contribution of voluntary organisations and the issues of accountability that this will involve have not been fully appreciated.

The most significant issue for environmentalists, however, is that the new governance framework for sustainable communities in Wales has not adopted an integrated approach to the issue of sustainability. The centrality of social equity to the achievement of sustainable development has been recognized in global agreement, but there is a failure at all levels to acknowledge the potential importance of social sustainability to the wider agenda for environmental citizenship. In Wales, the guidance on Communities First at one time made reference to environmental concerns, including global issues such as climate change; but it has now adopted a target-driven approach that focuses more narrowly on issues of poverty. Furthermore, the framework for community planning as the strategic focus for addressing the concerns of deprived communities is ambiguous about the significance of sustainable development to this process.

## Notes

1 Beckerman, for example, considers the need to address the basic needs of those in the developed world as paramount; e.g. W. Beckerman and J. Pasek, *Justice, Posterity and the Environment* (Oxford: Oxford University Press, 2001).

2 There is long-standing evidence that people (or some people in some places) are psychologically more affected by disorderly behaviour and messy environments than they are by more serious crime. The association of these perceptions with fear of crime . . . has been the subject of academic study and debate, mainly in America, for over thirty years.
E. Burnsey, *Making People Behave: Anti-social Behaviour, Politics and Policy* (London: Willan, 2005), p. 5

3 Environmental citizenship is used here to describe behaviour that is sensitive to the needs of the environment. The means of encouraging environmental citizenship is as contestable as the nature of the subject itself, and Dobson, for example, would argue that education was paramount (A. Dobson, *Citizenship and the Environment*, Oxford: Oxford University Press, 2003). However, the reflexive relationship between the local and global has been identified and explored by Giddens (A. Giddens, *The Consequences of Modernity*, Cambridge: Polity Press, 1990, and *Modernity and Self Identify: Self and Society in the Late Modern Age*, Cambridge: Polity Press, 1991) and specifically in the context of sustainability by O'Riordan (T. O' Riordan (ed.), *Globalism, Localism and Identity: Fresh Perspectives on the Transition to Sustainability*, London: Earthscan, 2001).

4 See further O'Riordan, *Globalism, Localism and Identity*, and R. Lee and E. Stokes (eds.), *Economic Globalization and Ecological Localization: Socio-legal Perspectives* (Oxford: Blackwell, 2009).

5 Agenda 21. This was signed by 198 states in Rio de Janeiro in 1992 along with the Rio Declaration of Principles for Sustainable Development.

6 Agenda 21, Chapter 3.

7 D. Warburton, 'A passionate dialogue: community and sustainable development', in D. Warburton (ed.), *Community and Sustainable Development: Participation in the Future* (London: Earthscan, 2000).

8 Environmental justice is defined in terms of poor local environmental quality and differential access to environmental goods and services which 'have a detrimental effect on the quality of life experienced by members of those communities and groups' (K. Lucas, G. Walker, M. Earnes, H. Fay and M. Poustie, *Environmental and Social Justice: Rapid Research and Evidence Review*, London: Policy Studies Institute, 2004, p. ii). See further M. Eames, *Reconciling Environmental and Social Concerns: Findings from the Joseph Rowntree Foundation Research Programme* (York: Joseph Rowntree Foundation, 2006). This was clearly recognized in the last Sustainable Development Strategy, *Securing the Future: UK Government Sustainable Development Strategy* (London: Defra, 2005), Chapter 6, 'Sustainable communities'. See also N. Gunningham, 'The new collaborative environmental governance: the localization of regulation', *Journal of Law and Society*, 36, 1 (2009), 145–66.

9 Gunningham, 'The new collaborative environmental governance', 146. See also G. de Burca and J. Scott (eds.), *Law and New Governance in the EU and the US* (Oxford: Hart, 2006).

10 Defra, *Mainstreaming Sustainable Development: The Government's Vision and What This Means in Practice* (London: Defra, 2011).
11 A. Parekh and P. Kenway, *Monitoring Poverty and Exclusion in Wales 2011* (York: Joseph Rowntree Foundation, 2011). For example, the statistics indicate that half the improvement in the child poverty rate between the mid-1990s and mid-2000s has been lost in the last five years. Tackling poverty is therefore a distinct priority of the current administration in Wales. See further Welsh Government, *Programme for Government 2011-2016* (Cardiff: Welsh Government, 2011).
12 Government of Wales Act 2006, Section 79. The development of the scheme is supported by a power of well-being, i.e. to do anything to promote or improve one or more of the following – the social, economic or environmental well-being of Wales. The Welsh government is also currently consulting on a Sustainable Development Bill; see further *http://www.wales.gov.uk*.
13 The other objectives are to:

- live within our environmental limits,
- support healthy, biologically diverse and productive ecosystems,
- build a resilient and sustainable economy,
- be a fair, just and bilingual nation.

Welsh Government, *One Wales: One Planet: The Sustainable Development Scheme of the Welsh Assembly Government* (Cardiff: Welsh Government, 2009), p. 17

14 Ibid.
15 Defra, *Living Places: Cleaner, Safer, Greener* (London: Defra, 2002), Section 1.
16 Welsh Government, *One Wales: One Planet – the Sustainable Development Scheme of the Welsh Assembly Government* (Welsh Government, 2009), p. 60.
17 See n. 3 above.
18 Agenda 21, Chapter 3.
19 Defra, *Mainstreaming Sustainable Development*, p. 6.
20 H. Johnson, 'The big Welsh society?', in O. Roberts (ed.), *Key Issues for the Fourth Assembly* (Cardiff: National Assembly for Wales Research Service, 2011), p. 74. The current administration nevertheless believes that the funding implications of the Big Society programme will have a significant impact on the voluntary sector in Wales – which it will find particularly challenging.
21 G. Delanty, *Community* (London: Routledge, 2003), p. 1.
22 See, for example, in considering the problems of social cohesion in American city life, H. Gans, *The Urban Villagers: Group and Class in the Life of Italian-Americans* (New York: Free Press, 1982).
23 Delanty, *Community*, p. 81.
24 See, with reference to U.S. society, R. Putnam, *Bowling Alone* (New York: Simon and Schuster, 2001).
25 This reflects Arnstein's ladder of participation, which seeks to analyse the different methods of participation and their significance in development of participatory governance. See further S. R. Arnstein, 'A ladder of citizen participation', *Journal of the American Institute of Planners*, 35, 4 (1969), 216–24.
26 Localism Act 2011, Neighbourhood Planning, Sections 116–20; Localism Act 2011, Community Right to Challenge, Sections 81–6; and Localism Act 2011, Council Tax, Sections 72–9.
27 Localism Act 2011, Schedule 9. The original Bill included a reference to only three individuals. The express purpose of the neighbourhood forum must be to further the social, economic and/or environmental well-being of individuals living, or wanting to live, in an area that includes the neighbourhood; and/or to promote the carrying on of trades, professions or other business in such an area.

28 Localism Act 2011, Assets of Community Value, Sections 87–108. A similar scheme to the Community Right to Buy operates in Scotland under the Land Reform (Scotland) Act 2003.
29 Localism Act 2011, Section 87.
30 Localism Act 2011, Section 95.
31 Localism Act 2011, Section 95(6).
32 Welsh Government, *A Shared Responsibility: Local Government's Contribution to Improving People's Lives: A Policy Statement from the Welsh Assembly Government* (Cardiff: Welsh Government, 2007), p. 41.
33 For basic information about this programme see further *http://www.communities-first.org*.
34 Ibid.
35 These are defined according to statistics from the Wales Index of Multiple Deprivation available at *http://www.wales.gov.uk*.
36 There is evidence that some partnerships may become dominated rather than led by state actors, such as local government, and fail to provide genuine representation of other groups and strengthen local networks. See, for example, M. Taylor, 'Communities in the lead: power, organisational capacity and social capital', *Urban Studies*, 37 (2000), 1019–35; V. Lowndes and H. Sullivan, 'Like a horse and carriage or a fish on a bicycle: how well do local partnerships and public participation go together?', *Local Government Studies*, 30 (2004), 51–73; and M. Geddes, 'Partnership and the limits to local governance in England: institutional analysis and neo-liberalism', *International Journal of Urban and Regional Research*, 30 (2006), 76–97.
37 See further G. Bristow, T. Entwhistle, F. Hines and S. Martin, 'New spaces for inclusion? Lessons from the "three-thirds" partnerships in Wales', *International Journal of Urban and Regional Research*, 32 (2008), 903–21.
38 This is referred to as 'programme bending'. See further Welsh Government, *Communities First Guidance* (Cardiff: Welsh Government, 2007); D. Adamson and R. Bromiley, *Community Empowerment in Practice: Lessons from Communities First* (York: Joseph Rowntree Foundation, 2008).
39 Adamson and Bromiley, *Community Empowerment in Practice*.
40 *Communities First Vision Framework Poster: Environment*, available at *http://www.wales.gov.uk* (accessed 4 September 2012).
41 J. Colman, *Communities First* (Cardiff: Wales Audit Office, 2009), p. 33.
42 See, for example, ibid. and S. Hincks and B. Robson, *Regenerating Communities First Neighbourhoods in Wales* (York: Joseph Rowntree Foundation, 2010).
43 Welsh Government, *Welsh Government Consultation Document Communities First: The Future* (Cardiff: Welsh Government, 2011).
44 Although it should be added that, sitting outside the Brecon Beacons National Park, it is certainly not formally designated as such.
45 See, for example, 'Older people enjoy new centre by waterfall', *South Wales Evening Post*, 28 September 2011.
46 See, for example, in the context of the USA, Putnam, *Bowling Alone*.
47 J. Lewis, 'Reviewing the relationship between the voluntary sector and the state in Britain in the 1990s', *Voluntas*, 10, 3 (1999), 255–70.
48 Section 114 states that the Welsh Government 'shall make a scheme setting out how it proposes, in the exercise of its functions, to promote the interests of relevant voluntary organisations.'
49 Welsh Government, *The Third Dimension: A Strategic Action Plan for the Voluntary Sector Scheme* (Cardiff: Welsh Government, 2010).
50 See further *http://www.gwirvol.org.uk*.
51 *Third Sector Statistical Resource 2011*, available at *http://www.WCVA.org.uk* (accessed 4 September 2012).

52 See further *http://www.groundwork.org.uk*.
53 M. Clarke and A. Netherwood, 'Beyond volunteering and rhetoric: implications of local Agenda 21 initiatives Wales', in S. Buckingham-Hatfield and S. Percy (eds.), *Constructing Local Environmental Agendas* (London: Routledge, 1999), pp. 42–56.
54 E. James, 'Whither the third sector? yesterday, today and tomorrow', *Voluntas*, 8, 1 (1997), 1–10, quoting p. 4.
55 M. Taylor and D. Warburton, 'Legitimacy and the role of the UK third sector organizations in the policy process', *Voluntas*, 14, 3 (2003), 321–38.
56 *A Shared Responsibility*, para. 7.14.
57 M. Woods, B. Edwards, J. Anderson, G. Gardner and R Hughes, *Research Study into the Role, Functions and Future Potential of Community and Town Councils in Wales* (Cardiff: University of Wales Aberystwyth/Welsh Assembly Government, 2003), p. 17.
58 I. Jones, *Community and Town Councils Survey 2010: Findings Report* (Cardiff: Welsh Assembly Government, 2010).
59 Ibid., p. 19.
60 Local Government Act 1972, Section 27A, as amended by the Local Government Measure 2011. Such a council can similarly be dissolved by such an order but the poll is effective only if 300 or 30 per cent of the electors attend and there is a two-thirds majority vote. The members should be elected but there is a power to co-opt members in the event of insufficient nominations to fill the vacancies [Local Government (Wales) Measure 2011, section 116]. Such a council also has the opportunity to appoint no more than two individuals between the ages of 15 and 26 to act as community youth representatives [Local Government (Wales) Measure 2011, section 118].
61 V. Bogdanor, *The New British Constitution* (Oxford: Hart, 2009).
62 Woods *et al.*, *Research Study*; *Community and Town Councils Survey 2010: Findings Report*.
63 Woods *et al.*, *Research Study*, p. 8. In 2010, only one-third of councils reported that all their councillors were elected. See *Community and Town Councils Survey 2010: Findings Report*, p. 15.
64 Woods *et al.*, *Research Study*, p. 7; although, in 2010, 90 per cent of councils themselves reported having a good relationship with their communities (*Community and Town Councils Survey 2010: Findings Report*).
65 Local Government Act 1972, Section 137. See further Woods *et al.*, *Research Study*, p. 29.
66 Woods *et al.*, *Research Study*, p. 30.
67 See *Community and Town Councils Survey 2010: Findings Report*, p. 32.
68 Explanatory Memorandum on the Local Government (Wales) Measure 2011, para. 3.32. This included provision on developing a better working partnership with local government and introduced a new power for Welsh Ministers with respect to model charter agreements; and new measures to increase the accountability of this sector by providing a power for Welsh Government to introduce a new system of accreditation of quality in community government.
69 Agenda 21, Chapter 28.1.
70 See further V. Bogdanor (ed.), *Joining-up Government* (Oxford: Oxford University Press, 2005) and note 34 above.
71 M. Clarke and J. Stuart, *Community Governance, Community Leadership and the New Local Government* (York: Joseph Rowntree Foundation, 1999).
72 See further D. Wilson and G. Stokes, *British Local Government in the Twentieth Century* (London: Palgrave, 2004).
73 H. Sullivan, *Meta-Evaluation of the Local Government Modernisation Agenda: The State of Governance of Places: Community Leadership and Stakeholder Engagement* (London: Department for Communities and Local Government, 2008).
74 Local Government Act 2001, Section 4(1).

75 It is supported by a general power of 'well-being' to allow local authorities to do anything which they consider is likely to achieve any one or more of the following: the promotion or improvement of the economic, social or environmental well-being of the community [Local Government Act 2000, Section 2(1)].
76 Welsh Government, *Beyond Boundaries: Citizen-Centred Local Services for Wales* (place: Welsh Government, 2006). This currently places significant emphasis on collaborative working given the high number of local councils in Wales. Welsh Government, *Local, Regional, National: What Services Are Best Delivered Where?* (Cardiff: Welsh Government, 2011).
77 See further *http://www.idea.gov.uk*.
78 Welsh Government, *Local Vision Statutory Guidance from the Welsh Assembly Government on Developing and Delivering Community Strategies* (Cardiff: Welsh Government, 2008) and Local Government (Wales) Measure 2011.
79 Ibid., para. 3.1.
80 Welsh Government, *Community Strategies and Planning: Collaborative Community Planning* (Cardiff: Welsh Government, 2010).
81 Ibid.
82 Welsh Government, *Local Vision Statutory Guidance from the Welsh Assembly Government on Developing and Delivering Community Strategies* (Cardiff: WAG, 2008), para. 5.24.
83 Welsh Government, *People, Plans and Partnerships: A National Evaluation of Community Strategies in Wales* (Cardiff: Welsh Government, 2006).
84 Local authorities must respond to performance indicators set out in the Wales Improvement Programme This replaced Best Value in this context and is governed by the Wales Audit Office. See further *http://www.wao.gov.uk*. However, uniquely, an integrated approach to performance assessment is taken in Wales. This is facilitated by a bespoke software system referred to as Ffynonn. See further *http://www.wales.gov.uk*. On the complexity of this issue see further Taylor and Warburton, 'Legitimacy and the role of the UK third sector organizations in the policy process', 321–38.
85 Local Government Act 2000, Section 4(3). In Wales, this is supported by a more detailed legal duty to ensure that arrangements are in place for the consultation of residents, recipients of services in the area, voluntary organizations, businesses and others with an interest in the economic, social and or environmental well-being and improvement of the area. An early analysis of community strategies in Wales found that the model of community planning in Wales was not one of civic renewal, centring on the engagement of citizens and communities to enhance local democracy, but rather adopted a 'rational planning' approach 'based on the rationale that improved vertical and horizontal co-ordination or integration of services, plans and performance management would deliver effective outcomes and make the most efficient use of scarce resources' [H. Sullivan and P. Williams, 'The limits of co-ordination: community strategies as multi-purpose vehicles in Wales', *Local Government Studies*, 35, 2 (2009), 161–80, quoting p. 166]. Thus community strategy methods were 'only consultative rather than empowering' (Wales Voluntary Council quoted in this publication).
86 Adamson and Bromiley, *Community Empowerment in Practice*.
87 *Community Strategies and Planning*, p. 31.
88 Ibid.
89 Adamson and Bromiley, *Community Empowerment in Practice*.
90 V. Jenkins, 'Local government modernisation and sustainable development in Wales and Ireland', *Environmental Law Review*, 11, 1 (2009), 23–40.
91 Sustainable Communities Act 2007. This was introduced under the Labour government, but continues to enjoy the support of the coalition government.
92 On the issue of the symbolic nature of statutory duties in respect of sustainable development, see further V. Jenkins, 'Placing sustainable development at the heart of

government in the UK: the role of law in the evolution of sustainable development as the central organising principle of government', *Legal Studies*, 22, 4 (2002), 578–602. It was decided not to extend the powers under the Sustainable Communities Act 2007 to Wales because LSBs provide a 'platform where discussions on promoting the wellbeing of an area can take place' and Welsh Ministers hold regular meetings with leaders of local authorities at which these issues can be addressed, so there is no need for local authorities to have the power to submit particular proposals on this issue to central government. Furthermore it was pointed out that the public has the ability to petition the National Assembly. See further statement available at *http://www.dataunitwales.gov.uk*. This does not, however, account for the symbolic change noted here.
93 Jenkins, 'Placing sustainable development at the heart of government in the UK'; P. Williams and A. Thomas, *Sustainable Development in Wales: Understanding Effective Governance* (York: Joseph Rowntree Foundation, 2004); and, in England, K. Lucas, A. Ross and S. Fuller, *Local Agenda 21 Community Planning and Neighbourhood Renewal* (York: Joseph Rowntree Foundation, 2003).
94 See further, in the context of participatory democracy, B. Barber, *Strong Democracy: Participatory Politics in a New Age* (Berkeley: University of California Press, 2004).

# Chapter 9

# Climate change law in Wales: realizing the value of participation

*Mark Stallworthy*

What follows seeks a distinctive Welsh legal perspective on efforts to address the challenges of climate change, under the aegis of the UK's 2008 Climate Change Act ('the Act'). The background to the discussion sees a Welsh government operating in a devolved setting, now on track towards increased legal autonomy, and subject to an evolving duty to promote sustainable development in the exercise of its functions.[1] Yet, at the same time, a Welsh 'voice' jostles in a crowded governance terrain; one marked by challenges across multiple levels of authority, presenting complex and multi-faceted problems, which are often resistant to traditional law and policy responses.[2] Following a preliminary scoping of the type of governance quandaries that responding to climate change represents, the chapter contains a review of key developments of climate change law affecting Wales, and identifies more important implications for policy makers thus far. Thereafter the central concern broadens, to address the role of civil society (a notion that remains more inclusive than the now ubiquitous 'stakeholders') as a central driver in procuring meaningful responses to climate change. The argument, applying an analytical framework that draws upon wider public law discourse, offers a rationale for recourse to wider and deeper forms of public participation than have been seen in this field to date. In particular, it will be argued that this can both create positive conditions for securing behavioural change and enhance legitimizing processes, through fuller social engagement, deliberation and acceptance.

## Universal quandaries and a Welsh locus for response

Quandaries presented by climate change offer paradigm illustrations of what can be termed 'wicked problems': identified in particular by their extreme complexity and uncertainty, and by linkage to oppositional cultural perspectives that lead to entrenched conflict.[3] Attempts to counter environmental threats, achieved primarily through regulatory approaches which rely on quality standards and command-and-control, more recently augmented by the introduction of alternative economic approaches, can claim some considerable success.[4] Yet 'wicked' climate-related threats are proving less amenable to regulation. There is much causative diffusion between, on the one hand, those climate risks that are increasingly being acknowledged and, on the other, the basic forms of organization of our traditional human activities (including our habits of production, commerce and consumption). Commitment to solutions is hindered by a general non-immediacy that characterizes such risks, with impacts widely displaced, both spatially and temporally.

Unsurprisingly, given a policy hinterland typically characterized by a lack of coherence and integration, exemplified, for instance, by a traditional separation of environmental and energy law, it is proving hard to develop effective policy responses and reform regulatory structures.[5] Not only can institutional responses to climate change be described as haphazard, but policy and law structures remain often at variance with ecological realities.[6] Contributory factors are a subject for a different paper, but it may be said that the often abstract nature of climate threats can seem normatively and practically removed from us, as a present generation facing seemingly more immediate, systemic and existential demands. Moreover, issues that arise are also closely aligned to lifestyles that are in notable respects a culmination of human aspirations. Likewise, our governing classes encounter spillover political risks in the event that they propose transforming solutions.[7] Yet climate risks ultimately threaten a fundamental destabilization of the sustainability of natural systems upon which we depend.[8] There is, therefore, much else at stake, with significant implications affecting both public and private realms.[9]

Accordingly, while viewed below from the vantage point of the law of England and Wales, the perspectives presented here are part of a much wider climate law canvas, key elements of which are briefly outlined. Following the seminal UN Convention on Climate Change, achieved at the Rio Summit in 1992, that treaty's somewhat generalized and hortatory aspects were given greater specificity under the Kyoto Protocol, most developed states entering into differential commitments to contribute towards greenhouse gas emissions reductions for the purpose of mitigating effects of climate change.[10] Also a party to Kyoto, the EU had to achieve an aggregate emissions reduction of 8 per cent (on 1990 levels). The Kyoto commitment period was set to expire at the end of 2012, and, with no guarantee of a multi-lateral successor, a broad EU agreement has committed unilaterally to continuing reductions (20 per cent by 2020), with legal responsibilities across Member States imposed under an effort-sharing measure.[11] This is supplemented by a putative commitment to further reductions (to 30 per cent) provided that developed states outside the Union meet certain conditions regarding reciprocity.[12]

Mitigation by emissions reductions has dominated the attention of larger institutions of governance, borne out at the EU level in the political capital invested in the flagship Emissions Trading Scheme (EUETS).[13] That focus is maintained as technological solutions assume an increasing role in climate discourse, both as pressed by powerful lobbies, and more pragmatically as a late throw of the policy dice.[14] The EU itself has moved to create a strategy for a regulatory framework, with financial incentives, for the development of carbon capture and storage.[15] Moreover, recognizing that significant impacts are already unavoidable, the Commission has signalled a change, directing its European Climate Change Programme towards more specific adaptation responses.[16] Adaptation has meanwhile a much firmer footing in developing the climate policy agenda within Member States; and in the UK, from the particular perspective of Wales, crucially within devolved policy areas such as land use planning, energy usage, transport and housing.[17]

## Implications of the UK climate law-making framework for Wales

Providing an umbrella measure for regulating UK responses to climate change, the Climate Change Act 2008 offers an important framing for the discussion that follows. It provides a set of organizing principles, determining objectives and trajectories towards meeting identified goals, under which policies and legal mechanisms can be developed and evaluated. Emerging policy approaches must be tested against the Act's requirements: for instance, the Welsh Government's climate change strategy, discussed below, is a specific response to its statutory obligations.[18] On policy content, the Act is largely of an enabling nature, and mainly concerned with aspects of mitigation, with more cursory treatment of adaptation.[19] Its underlying premise is a mandatory goal of a 60 per cent reduction in UK greenhouse gas emissions (from 1990) by 2050. It relies on placing formal obligations on the central government, based on set targets, carbon budgets, reporting requirements and responsiveness to expert advice. The apparently unambiguous nature of those statutory duties amounts to something of a constitutional innovation, and one which in due course is likely to be tested in the courts in relation to the intensity of scrutiny on review that it incorporates.[20] Ancillary procedural arrangements support delivery on commitments, with ministerial duties to produce risk assessments for climate change impacts, and appropriate adaptation programmes.[21] Heavy reliance is placed on the information, monitoring and advice roles of a statutory, non-departmental Committee on Climate Change ('the Committee'), especially concerning budget setting, risk assessment report preparation and annual progress reports to Parliament.[22]

The Welsh government is vested with a range of statutory authorities under explicit sub-national provisions woven into the fabric of the legislation. These are particularly important for capacity building, and include extensive rights to information and access to advice. For purposes of exposition they can be separated into four categories. Accordingly, the Welsh Government is, first, a statutory recipient of reports produced in pursuance of the Act, including the UK risk assessment reports and adaptation programmes, and Committee advice on assessment reports and carbon budgets, as well as its progress reports.[23] Second, it may issue guidance or directions to the Committee in relation to the latter's advisory and reporting functions; the Committee is required (save as regards actual content) to have regard to and comply with such guidance.[24] Third, it has a catch-all power to require the Committee to advise and assist specifically on any Welsh target or budget requirement (whether arising by adoption or otherwise).[25] Fourth, and more generally, regarding any devolved functions under the Act, it may require the Committee to report on progress made in mitigation, adaptation or (in a sweep-up provision) 'any other matter relating to climate change'.[26]

The legislation also imposes, by virtue of what remains a broadly top-down UK governance framework, substantial constraints on the scope for Welsh government action. Significant areas of non-devolved policy are closely tied to progress on climate objectives. Aside from the core reserved area of fiscal policy, the crucial area of energy law and policy, too, is mainly dictated at the UK level. In particular, in relation to large-scale power generation (at above 50 MW), issues relating to construction, extension and operation of capacity require UK government consent, as do arrangements for electricity transmission, distribution and supply.[27] Nuclear energy and installations are included in this reservation (save disposal of very low-level radioactive waste), and similarly energy conservation (apart from encouraging efficiency otherwise than by prohibition or regulation).[28] Furthermore both power generators and larger industrial installations, each of whose 'traded emissions' fall within the EUETS, are largely excluded from further emissions regulation.

And yet significant sub-national opportunities exist for autonomous mitigation and adaptation measures.[29] In relation to mitigation, from a devolved Wales perspective, relevant fields include land use and agriculture, and more especially smaller-scale forms of power generation, with highly pertinent devolved powers affecting these areas – especially in relation to town and country planning (including in respect of electricity generation up to 50 MW capacity in respect of onshore projects); the promotion of energy efficiency; microgeneration policy; and public sector estate management.[30] There is therefore substantive space for particular Welsh contributions, primarily through demand-side measures, and towards encouraging altered behaviours, which include, for instance, smart energy consumption and modal choices between private and public transport.[31]

Furthermore, it is in relation to adaptation efforts that the most meaningful powers vested in the Welsh Government can arguably be found. In particular, it has extensive powers under the Act to issue directions and/or guidance to 'reporting authorities'.[32] These are creatures of the Act, with functions of a public nature (or otherwise deemed a statutory undertaker under planning legislation), which are obliged under the Act to report progress in policy implementation.[33] The statutory provisions will engage those with responsibilities for delivery of 'critical public services', and that are characterized by a shared vulnerability to climate change impacts by reference to either infrastructure or service provision: such as local government, health, water, the natural environment and emergency response.[34] The Welsh Government is authorized to issue directions both to set the parameters for such statutory reports and to impose risk assessment and adaptation-planning duties on these crucial delivery authorities.[35] Once a report is in place each authority must have regard to it in exercising its functions, taking account of relevant guidance as well as statutory reports on climate change impacts and programmes for adaptation.[36] Outcomes will depend on the nature of commitments and related timescales. However, the scheme will be an iterative process; for instance, these bodies are likely to be required to adopt responses to central government climate change risk assessments (the first is expected during 2012) and related sectoral adaptation plans as well.[37]

The devolved settlement therefore predicates the possibility of distinctive Welsh policy development, already further advanced in Scotland, where the devolutionary remit was from the start more radical.[38] As mentioned above, the Welsh Government has produced a climate change strategy, which has an initial emphasis on mitigation, setting an objective for a 40 per cent reduction in Welsh greenhouse gas emissions by 2020 (against 1990), and a target of 3 per cent per annum in areas of devolved competence.[39] Annual progress reports must follow (from 2013), and there is a departure from UK strategy in respect of calculation of net Welsh emissions being exclusive of offsets (in effect, the buying of credits), whilst the central government has chosen to retain a buy-in discretion for potential use in netting off UK obligations.[40] In that the strategy sets targets for Welsh emissions reductions, supplementing those delivered at a UK level, the exercise is of some complexity. UK emissions under EUETS are excluded, and here there is a softer commitment to 'continue to work with energy generators and energy intensive businesses to support them in reducing emissions and report progress'.[41] Yet other included sources – with target ranges for sectoral reductions – contribute 'direct' greenhouse gas emissions in Wales (especially transport, the residential sector, the public sector, waste, agriculture, land use change and business/industry emissions outside EUETS), including end-user electricity consumption within these categories. A related sign of work towards broader behavioural change appears in the commitment to transparency in indirect impacts such as downstream electricity usage.[42] Here uncertainties arise about the potential for double counting; as, for instance, upstream power generators impose payment premiums on customers based on putative allowances required to secure the reduction of emissions under EUETS.[43] Problems of overlap may intensify in the future should (as originally proposed) further UK trading schemes affecting emissions from other sectors, commercial or other, emerge.[44]

Particularly in light of potential problems in separating instances of overlap and differentiation, adaptation may therefore prove more fertile territory for direct Welsh measures, reaping a benefit from proximity to a wide range of actors with public functions, private–public partnerships, and civil society generally.[45] Already the Welsh climate change strategy sets out an initial framework for developing a structured approach to future adaptation.[46] It has key dual features, including, first, capacity building, across organizations and communities, by seeking to introduce adaptation into mainstream decision making whilst taking account of 'competing pressures on our social, natural and economic systems', and, second, communication of impacts and adaptation responses to 'ensure that decision makers at all levels are aware of the impacts of climate change and equipped with the information and tools they need to apply that knowledge in planning and decision making processes'.[47] In aiming to build resilience throughout Wales to climate impacts, the strategy requires a supplementary adaptation delivery plan, offering greater specificity over activities, objectives and outcomes.

It is in respect of adaptation that community engagement has particular salience, in determining issues of risk acceptability and the development of such mechanisms as information sharing and wider public participation.[48] Devolved settings as in Wales can have especial relevance to the task of seeking the negotiated resolution of conflicts between strategic objectives and local perceptions and impacts.[49] The potential benefits of developing effective participation strategies are explored further below.

## Participatory rationales and the potential for behavioural transformations

For progress towards a low-carbon society, the distinctively Welsh response with arguably greatest potential lies in opportunities for securing community buy-in to policies leading to behavioural change.[50] Despite some discrete successes – as in broadly reducing reliance on the most carbon-intensive fuels – a high proportion of Western decarbonization has been achieved through 'leakage', in effect an outsourcing of industrial production facilities to emerging economies in order to feed persistent consumption demands in developed states.[51] Behavioural change poses intractable problems, as citizens in advanced economies pay lip service to green initiatives (such as recycling) but show little inclination towards radical adjustments in lifestyle.[52] Tensions also arise, though not further discussed here, over compatibility with demands for economic growth, and (since the first banking crisis in 2008) the ongoing concerns at the implications of economic recession and related levels of private and public debt.[53] There remains, however, an active discourse about ways to reconfigure growth variously according to 'green' principles.[54] The argument below, in light of those major psychological influences that influence how we respond to risk, considers key rationales for participation strategies in the process of bringing about behavioural change, and then offers an analysis of steps taken towards their introduction in Wales.

There is an extensive literature concerning the nature of participation mechanisms, although a detailed discussion of methodologies is not part of the present purpose.[55] Levels of public involvement can be placed across a wide spectrum, with lower levels reflecting basic rights to information or mere consultative roles, although categories can mean contrasting things from different normative perspectives. It is argued that more deliberative strategies, at the 'higher' end of involvement, offer optimum potential for addressing areas of policy and decision-making that are the most intractable and categorized by conflict.[56] As is the case with wicked problems referred to above, such conflicts can typically lead to political sclerosis and failure to respond to acknowledged harms. Democratic systems are not immune to decision avoidance; as Glendon argues, the greatest obstacle lies not 'in an "inert people" so much as the failure of persons in positions of leadership . . . to work actively to create opportunities for discussion'.[57] However, there is also a symbiotic element at work, whereby the demos itself can be disinclined to press for change. Much of the discourse about our ambiguous notion of sustainable development, 'essentially driven by political and economic processes . . . defined in such a way as to mean almost anything that anybody wants it to mean', has been so coloured.[58] For example, the incoming UK government draft revised planning policy proposed both greater influence for local community views and at the same time a new presumption in favour of 'sustainable development', a term seemingly approximating closely to 'development'.[59] Indeed, a growing sign of differentiation in this respect will be seen in the discussion of sustainable development in Wales below.

Levels of individual and collective engagement with climate-related risks are shaped by those shared human characteristics that encompass cognitive, affective and behavioural psychological elements, which combine to determine 'states of connection'.[60] Insights from cognitive psychology suggest a tendency to cling to valued activities, even at the cost of undervaluing associated non-trivial risks.[61] Moreover, complexities in individual response reflect both personal experience and societal values.[62] These can typically generate a feedback effect from declining support for action, as citizens (and groups) demonstrate aspects of learned helplessness (nothing can be done) and/or adaptive preference (getting used to 'baseline conditions').[63] That said, differing contexts can yield contrasting conclusions: for instance, whilst risk averseness can attend high levels of uncertainty and potential for catastrophe, cultural 'filters' can bring about counterfactual responses, as where potential harms appear unreal, and so divorced from everyday experience and understanding as to amount to 'virtual risk'.[64] Climate law debates often reflect such responses, in particular because of the pervasive scientific uncertainty that provides a backdrop to policy argument.

The conditioning by expectation and experience (or lack of same) of such attitudes towards serious threats of future disaster can also operate collectively. Thus conditions prior to, during and after Hurricane Katrina have been described as demonstrating a persistent 'disturbing cognitive dissonance . . . between what everyone knew to be the case, how government chose to govern, and how everyone chose to live their lives'.[65] Further, apparent shifts can seem sudden and capricious: for instance in respect of a recent widespread acceptance of nuclear power, linked to its role in meeting growing concerns about energy security.[66] This contrasts with a subsequent renewal of scepticism concerning reliance on nuclear safety, in the aftermath of the 2011 tsunami and earthquake in Japan that overwhelmed technical defences at the Fukushima nuclear power plant.[67] Our responses, as in our more rigid expectations of unchanging conditions of cause and effect, appear to mirror the operation of 'positive feedback' in nature, whereby ecosystems, despite their inherent tendency towards stability – or 'system inertia' – can become overwhelmed.[68] This is one aspect of what has been termed the collective action problem, which in part reflects influences by dominant sectoral interests, seeking to ensure that competing approaches 'only achieve a place on the policy agenda if they do not challenge these interests fundamentally'.[69]

What value does a focus on public participation contribute towards overcoming these limitations and resolving policy dilemmas? At their most effective, those participatory processes that maximize public interaction in decision making offer the potential to enhance knowledge and transparency, the adoption of responsibilities to reach agreement (problem buy-in) and ultimately acceptance (solution buy-in).[70] However, extensions in public involvement into institutional structures have yielded mixed results, as for instance recently in the context of pollution permitting. In these processes, there has been a traditional domination of technical features, which thus become largely reserved matters for regulator and regulated.[71] Evidence suggests that more recent statutory consultation opportunities have yielded extremely low reported response rates, with continuing self-exclusion on grounds including perceived lack of understanding. Kirk and Blackstock have concluded that 'the public are not so much apathetic as passive in their approach to the environment', a tendency perhaps exacerbated 'where there are only limited obligations on regulators to inform the public that participatory processes exist'.[72]

In his groundbreaking assessment of planning 'ideologies', McAuslan described a more radical participatory ideology, as a modern counter to the twin established ideologies based respectively on the common law inviolability of private property and more orthodox restraint imposed in the public interest by public administrators.[73] By contrast, he characterized a more radical, third approach as affording opportunities to influence and challenge the exercise of administrative authority in the public interest. Without perhaps achieving such thoroughgoing change, it is the case that in UK public law the planning process has traditionally demonstrated greater formal recognition of participation than has been apparent in other fields of regulation, with long-standing incorporation of more participatory models into legal structures and administrative cultures.[74] This can also be seen in the modern development of the crossover planning/environmental field of environmental impact assessment, where judicial interpretations have resisted merely cursory approaches to opportunities for wider public involvement.[75]

Indeed, the idea of 'collaborative planning' has been particularly identified with the regulation of land use, offering a greater acknowledgement of the potential decision-making contribution of wider networks of social and communicative interaction in the public realm, and a counterbalance to the dangers of ruling expert consensus as reflecting dominant shared assumptions within both the marketplace and public administration.[76] This idea has a close affinity with the recognition of more deliberative processes, which it has been argued can enhance the quality of public engagement, as well as potentially influencing outcomes, improving (in our present context) opportunities for achieving 'a more ecological way of thinking about social policy'.[77] This can become a socially valuable process in three ways: by, first, encouraging societal engagement in the face of the obstacles that follow from scientific uncertainty; second, introducing longer risk timelines that extend beyond present concerns; and, third, supporting goals of environmental justice by establishing commitments to openness and empowerment, and so countering fears of exclusion.[78]

## Legal architectures and behavioural change

Although, in planning-related circumstances, participatory rights can be limited or even excluded, as in the non-availability of third-party rights of appeal against planning determinations, generally these processes continue to afford significant opportunities for oppositional stances to be identified. This can currently be seen in the contested area of renewable energy development.[79] Whilst often perceived as a focus for community resistance, in some highly conflictual situations resolutions have been reached through recognizably deliberative principles, which have engendered greater community confidence in decision-making procedures, even shifts in public opinion as proposals evolve during a more reflexive process and structures are put in place for subsequent community involvement.[80] Furthermore, in an analogous judicial development, despite long-standing House of Lords authority to the effect that governmental policy is generally off limits for inspector scrutiny at the planning inquiry stage (under the so-called *Bushell* doctrine), a reconsideration may now be under way, to take account of situations where material changes occur after formulation of policy.[81] Where decisions therefore have implications for a wider climate change context, cognate policy developments – such as those pursuant to the Climate Change Act – may have to be taken into account in the planning process in a more reflexive way.[82] There has been similar experience in other judicial contexts, in seeking to contextualize material environmental and other planning interests across a broader spatial and temporal range.[83] Opportunities can therefore be found by such means both to clarify opposing views and to equip participants to engage more explicitly with the issue of climate change.[84]

Most participatory decision-making strategies, especially in light of technical complexities, will focus on procedural issues.[85] In that light, the ultimate value of such approaches lies in the generation of confidence in the processes by which decisions are reached, as opposed to the encouragement of unrealistic assumptions concerning neutrality on the part of participants.[86] Chances for acceptance are correspondingly enhanced by institutional commitments to open decision making, preferably from an early stage, with formal assurances as to iterative forms of engagement thereafter.[87] Such inclusive approaches can be contrasted with early experience of strategic reviews of coastline defences, which were seen as exacerbating particular local vulnerabilities to climate change impacts. There, participatory solutions became necessary *ex post* in order to engage stakeholders (not only communities and businesses, but also local authorities) that had originally felt sidelined in the review process.[88] As a consequence, widening levels of participation – and a wider recognition of interests affected – latterly brought about improved levels of engagement with those feeling otherwise powerless and excluded.[89]

For all the undoubted obstacles, therefore, it is in situations where resistance and conflict are most apparent (and typically in respect of the wicked problems that dominate this present context) that the advantages of developing stronger commitments to public participation appear to be most apparent. As climate law evolves, participatory approaches offer valuable opportunities for legitimizing actions, reinforcing accountabilities and furthering just solutions.[90] Moreover, greater commitment to reflexive decision-making as instanced above does not necessarily undermine or curtail the democratic process. On the contrary, the incorporation of environmental interests into the heart of open and transparent processes can contribute to addressing what has been called the green democratic deficit.[91] Indeed as Wilkinson has argued, democracy itself 'is only compatible with a body of ecological law if ecological values are protected from democratic subversion'.[92] Participatory processes, in this light, offer potential for securing reformed administrative arrangements that help 'to transform perceptions of individual and collective interest'.[93] Nevertheless incorporating into law and policy a greater emphasis upon ecological values poses a considerable challenge to any political process, and so *a fortiori* in the context of attempts to address climate change. Thus the above exegesis of extended forms of participation does not equate to local decision making, or local veto, because important strategic objectives continue to require balancing against local impacts. Yet, even where tensions remain between 'populist' as opposed to 'rationalist' perspectives, opportunities are in this way accorded for a wider range of factors to be identified and taken into account in decision-making.[94]

By contrast, and notwithstanding the above possibilities, still generally low levels of individual engagement with climate change reflect wide-ranging social and institutional barriers.[95] Policy makers find themselves at each turn evaluating issues of trade-off between the effectiveness of measures (as in reduction of emissions) and wider public acceptance. To these ends, the declaratory value of law is a key element, succinctly described by Sunstein as representing the 'expressive function' of law, unlocking opportunities for change through a process of 'norm management'.[96] Reflecting the value of law in influencing exercise of rational choices, the challenge for law makers is to fashion regulatory responses in ways that perform a catalysing role in developing wider climate policy discourse across civil society, by maximizing potential for engagement.[97] Such a task requires a radical leap of legislative expertise and imagination, for legislatures can likewise be 'subject to the same heuristics and cognitive distortions as the general public'.[98] The immense challenge of the task of securing behavioural change demands a multiplicity of contributions to cumulative action, including by exploring further extensions in participatory strategies.[99]

Legal controls can affect individual behaviours directly and otherwise, and there is growing debate about the optimum balance for achieving radical change.[100] Possibilities include the deployment of new forms of command-and-control (perhaps more extensive rationing of resource uses), through economic mechanisms such as carbon taxation and property-based cap-and-trade schemes, through softer approaches exemplified by 'nudge' theory.[101] An expanded view of 'choice architecture' is usefully reflected in Gunningham's depiction of a reformed environmental governance, based *inter alia* on 'participatory dialogue and deliberation, devolved decision-making, flexibility . . . inclusiveness, transparency and institutionalised consensus-building . . . [that is] "societal steering" in its broadest sense'.[102] In this way engagement with climate change problems and constructive responses may be increased by an emphasis on participation and a wider shared responsibility 'rather than upon market individualism and technique'.[103] Thus, as seen in the coastal example above, pre-emptive participatory approaches of an open and deliberative nature can not only effect institutional change but also assist towards identifying issues of burden sharing more effectively.[104] Such approaches can also enhance the likelihood of regulatory incursions being embraced, rather than seen as counterintuitive restrictions on pre-set individual expectations.

## Building participation into emerging climate law in Wales

From a participatory perspective, the Climate Change Act, under which UK, English and Welsh strategies fall to be developed, is disappointingly silent (save as regards cross-institutional transparency arrangements). A contrast can be drawn with early experience in Scotland, where the Scottish Parliament has included within its own (partly autonomous) climate change legislation an unambiguous statutory commitment to the participatory process. This has obliged Scottish Ministers in the first instance to produce a public engagement strategy, in accord with two key premises (which in effect address questions about the 'why' and the 'how').[105] Thus, such strategy must, first, specify the steps that are intended to be put into place both to inform persons in Scotland about statutory targets and to encourage their contributions. Second, the developing strategy must in particular, identify actions which persons in Scotland may take to contribute to the achievement of such targets. An initial strategy has subsequently been published, which is to be part of an iterative process, there being a requirement that it be reviewed from time to time, and at no longer than five-yearly intervals.[106] In explicitly seeking to bring about transformational outcomes, the strategy instigates a search for suitable mechanisms that echoes Sunstein's idea of norm management.[107] Its structure is thematic: under heads that include energy, travel, food, consumption (individuals and households), providing substantive markers of intended future direction. Methodologically, there is a generalist setting out of a series of 'engagement principles' (including formal recognition of 'motivational and proactive' aspects), supported by a concise statement of commitment to identified forms of engagement.[108] The particular value of this approach may therefore lie in matching articulated directions of travel alongside emerging substantive policy proposals, whilst at the same time turning attention to suitable methods for securing public engagement and heightened levels of understanding and acceptance.

It can be said, therefore, that, in our climate law and policy context, commitments to enhancing the role of community participation have been developed with a greater degree of specificity in Scotland, in accord with the principles contained in the statutory public engagement strategy. The first significant fruit, and potential indicator of how efforts are likely to evolve, can already be found in the report setting out a discrete public communication strategy related to the development of carbon capture and storage (CCS) capacity in Scotland.[109] Thus, as well as committing to engagement with the research community (of considerable importance, as CCS remains at a still early developmental stage), the report sets out on a detailed interpretation of what should be regarded as 'engagement', with an emphasis on two-way discussion, locality and decision-making context. It further sees the processes of stakeholder engagement as separate from what it describes as the 'pre-condition' of public acceptance: they are 'distinct activities and should be treated as such'.[110] This interesting separation suggests a draughtsman's caution, for the two notions are closely interlinked, the report itself recognizing a need to build on technical explanations by creating favourable social conditions for public mediation and participatory mechanisms, to 'greatly increase the chances of acceptance'.[111]

A key contrast with the Welsh experience is that the Welsh Government, not being subject to statutory constraints along the Scottish lines, appears to have a freer hand. This has resulted in a more *ad hoc* approach thus far. Nevertheless the Welsh Government has consistently demonstrated an awareness of the importance of engagement. For instance, its climate change strategy speaks of a reaching out to communities and individuals, with a stated intention to provide a framework for delivery, to address barriers to progress, and to ensure that responses are based on principles of social equity.[112] The focus in the early stages has largely been premised upon working with those businesses and organizations that deliver public services, manage the natural environment or contribute to the development of social and economic policy. A somewhat fuller reference appears in (nearly contemporaneous) guidance concerned with building resilience to climate change, in respect of (following what is seen as the technical task of 'risk identification') risk management.[113] Thus, a 'consultation' section advises that successful adaptation requires acceptance

> by the people it is likely to directly affect; consequently the wellbeing and health of those people should be its central aims. Consulting those directly affected by an adaptation measure should increase the likelihood that it will be accepted. People should be informed, involved and empowered wherever they come into contact with a reporting authority; this could be at the point of delivery when providing a service or as part of a wider adaptation strategy where the community is more central to a reporting authority's operations.[114]

This amounted to an interesting earnest of intent, and an indication of a more developed 'behavioural change' model has subsequently been produced in a preliminary strategy, indicating goals of 'exemplification', 'support', 'enabling' and 'engagement'.[115]

It is further suggested that evolving Welsh Government commitments to a further legislative elaboration of its sustainable development obligations can provide the stimulus for developing participatory arrangements at the heart of climate change law and policy. The genesis of this can be seen in the Wales Sustainable Development Charter, which was specifically directed at the threefold objectives of living within 'environmental limits', protecting vulnerable groups against disproportionate burdens, and setting out the rationale for making sustainable development 'the central organising principle in how we make decisions and carry out our work'.[116] That said, whilst linking the long-term integration of 'social, economic and environmental outcomes' with emphasis on partnerships with organizations and engagement with people and communities, the charter makes only generalized reference to wider engagement issues. Somewhat abstract about engagement at this early stage, it may be best perceived as the potential catalyst to more substantive subsequent developments.[117] Similarly, efforts to develop a distinctive Welsh approach are now progressing in early consultation on proposals for a Sustainable Development Bill (aiming for legislation by late 2013). At its heart is likely to be, alongside a general commitment to achieving social justice in the development of sustainable law and policy, the placing on the Welsh Government and other public bodies of (yet to be specified) legal obligations to advance goals of building a sustainable Wales, supported by an element of independent control through a new statutory body. The process of consultation is at an early stage but this also includes headline references to engaging citizens and working in partnership.[118]

Two further proposals contain more extensive acknowledgements of the need for wider engagement, including a Green Paper on natural resources management and a White Paper concerned with encouraging 'active travel'. The former, with the general objective of introducing an ecosystem approach to environmental regulation and management, contains sections devoted to the need for a focus on local needs and improvements, and the linkages between sustainable development and engagement, through involving people and communities and encouraging positive choices.[119] The latter paper offers an illustration of the importance of positive messages to stand alongside commitments to behavioural change, specifically linking emissions reductions with health and other benefits for the community, and in seeking to ensure individual and community buy-in, contains the genesis of an operable 'behavioural change model' on the basis already referred to above.[120] More concrete pointers to how wider engagement in decision making and delivery might be progressed have appeared in the first Welsh emissions reduction delivery plan, a supplement to the climate change strategy. This document can be said to bear some comparison with the more extensive Scottish approach as outlined above, in that it contains selective examples of methods of actualizing climate policy goals through 'third sector and community action' and 'wider behaviour change'.[121]

## Conclusions

In the face of the paradigmatic 'wicked' problems that are associated with climate change, to achieve the required scale of institutional and regulatory reforms (or as discussed above, norm management) presents an immense task, and one which requires, according to Garton-Ash:

> not only leadership of a high order, but also citizens demanding such leadership. Would I personally be happy making the changes in my way of life that would be necessary? Almost certainly not. But at least I'd like to know what they would be.[122]

Whilst by far the tougher decisions (about low-carbon transition) have yet to be made, the benefits of an overarching Climate Change Act have included, thus far, a broad willingness by government bodies to accept independent statutory advice over forthcoming carbon budgetary commitments.[123] By analogy, it has been argued here that not only is a commitment to wider public participation essential if there is to be any realistic chance of securing necessary political traction towards behavioural change in response to climate change, but formalization of such processes in legislative form can contribute to the robust arrangements needed to maximize chances for engagement and acceptance.

Meanwhile distinctive Welsh perspectives on climate law are emerging, and these are a key element in the processes of legislative reform under way. They include more explicit recognition of issues of social justice as crucial elements in formulating legal responses to problems of sustainability. Whilst not part of its explicit remit, this appears to have been recognized by the UK's Committee on Climate Change, in its raising of concerns about energy costs and the consequences for 'fuel poverty' (which means devoting more than 10 per cent of household income to domestic fuel costs), as measures to reduce emissions (through pricing and efficiency requirements) are imposed more strictly.[124]

The scale of the challenges discussed above demands that we move further away from ideas of a passive citizenry accepting traditional processes that secure the political–technical legitimacy of policy makers and their disinterested experts. In the face of the difficult decisions that will increasingly confront decision makers, unlike in Scotland, in both England and Wales a powerful legislative underpinning of the development of participatory strategies is lacking. From the perspective of Wales there are clear signs that, alongside securing social justice, the value of consultation and engagement in this area is acknowledged by law makers. Indeed a more explicit deliberative and participatory agenda appears to be emerging, which will need to be linked to future climate law and policy development.

The final conclusion is that, in the task of mitigating and adapting to climate change, legal mechanisms can perform a crucial role: not only instrumentally but also in contributing to changing values. The UK's framework legislation has produced a coherent response to threats from climate change, as in placing law makers under unambiguous obligations about how they are expected to approach key climate goals in the coming decades. Yet no equivalent statutory commitment exists for the encouragement of a greater shared awareness of climate risks or for a wider engagement with emerging law and policy. The development of effective participatory strategies is a necessary element towards realizing meaningful behavioural change in accord with governmental aspirations for a low-carbon economy. Even absent the normative discipline of an express statutory obligation, signs now emerging suggest that the Welsh Government grasps the crucial importance of community engagement with its developing climate change strategies. Moreover, such reciprocities afford potential opportunities for meaningful progress towards achieving a distinctively Welsh framing of efforts, in particular to address the social dimensions of future climate law and policy.

## Notes

1 Government of Wales Act 2006, Section 79. There are current proposals for a Sustainable Development Bill which would apply more extensive duties on the Welsh Government and other public bodies; see *One Wales: One Planet – a Welsh Government Discussion Paper – Sustainable Development Bill* (WG-14084, November 2011).
2 Cf. D. Shearman and J. Wayne Smith, *The Climate Change Challenge and the Failure of Democracy* (London: Praeger, 2007) and R. Kagan, *The Return of History and the End of Dreams* (London: Atlantic, 2008): respectively critiques of performance of state and international structures. See, for example, C. Hilson, 'Going local? EU law, localism and climate change', *European Law Review*, 33 (2008), 194–210, identifying tensions between free movement obligations and environmental agendas.
3 The notion derives from a planning context; see H. Rittel and M. Webber, 'Dilemmas in general theory of planning', *Policy Sciences*, 4 (1973), 155–69.
4 G. Winter, 'The four phases of environmental law', *Journal of Environmental Law*, 1 (1989), 38–47. And when used together such traditional and alternative tools can also conflict: R. Macrory, 'Weighing up the performance', *Journal of Environmental Law*, 23 (2011), 311–7. R. Macrory, 'Regulating in a risky environment', *Current Legal Problems* (2001), 619–48.
5 See J. P. Tomain, *Ending Dirty Energy Policy: Prelude to Climate Change* (Cambridge: Cambridge University Press, 2011), especially pp. 51–6; H. Bulkeley and P. Newell, *Governing Climate Change* (Abingdon: Routledge, 2010), p. 106, discussing the multi-governance dilemma of 'a plurality of sites of action'.
6 R. J. Lazarus, 'Environmental law after Katrina: reforming environmental law by reforming environmental lawmaking', *Tulane Law Review*, 81 (2007), 1019–58, p. 1058; J. Ebbesson, 'The rule of law in governance of complex socio-ecological changes', *Global Environmental Change*, 20 (2010), 414–22.
7 See, for instance, S. Jasanoff, 'Image and imagination: the formation of global environmental consciousness', in C. Miller and P. N. Edwards (eds.), *Changing the Atmosphere: Expert Knowledge and Environmental Governance* (Cambridge, MA: MIT Press, 2001), pp. 333–4, describing institutional systems of governance as 'imagined political communities'.
8 See, for example, J. Cox, *Climate Crash: Abrupt Climate Change and What It Means for Our Future* (Washington, DC: National Academies Press, 2005).
9 See, for example, Department of Environment, Food and Rural Affairs, *Securing the Future: The UK Government Sustainable Development Strategy*, ch. 4, 'Confronting the greatest threat: climate change and energy', Cm 6467 (London, 2005).
10 (1992) 31 ILM 851; (1998) 37 ILM 22. The UK committed to a 12.5 per cent reduction.
11 European Council, Decision No. 406/2009/EC, *On the Effort of Member States to Reduce their Greenhouse Gas Emissions to Meet the Community's Greenhouse Gas Emission Reduction Commitments up to 2020* [2009] OJ L140/136.
12 See European Commission, Communication, 'Limiting global climate change to 2 degrees Celsius: the way ahead for 2020 and beyond', COM (2007) 2 final.
13 European Council, Directive 2003/87/EC, *Establishing a Scheme for Greenhouse Gas Emissions Allowance Trading within the Community* [2003] L275/32.
14 Cf. J. Vidal, 'Huge mirrors and aerosols in space: just science fiction or the earth's last hope?', *The Guardian*, 16 June 2011; F. Harvey, 'Fight climate change with technology – UN', *The Guardian*, 6 June 2011.
15 European Council, Directive 2009/31/EC, *On the Geological Storage of Carbon Dioxide* [2009] OJ L140/114.
16 European Commission, 'Green paper on adaptation', COM (2007) 354 final. It is to engage multiple stakeholders in the policy generation process; see COM (2000) 88 final for its original remit, concerned with compliance with Kyoto obligations.

17 For an overview of emissions reductions (2008, 2009) in devolved administrations, see Committee on Climate Change, *Meeting Carbon Budgets: 3rd Report to Parliament* (London: Committee on Climate Change, June 2011), ch. 6.
18 Welsh Government, *Climate Change Strategy for Wales* (Cardiff: Welsh Government, October 2010).
19 There is an explicit framework for developing new emissions trading schemes: Part 3, and schedules 2–4.
20 It is, however, less extensive than pre-existing, *sui generis* forms of limited entrenchment under the European Communities Act 1972 and the Human Rights Act 1998. Cf. a contrasting duty-based provision (Warm Homes and Energy Conservation Act, 2000, Section 2); cf. *Friends of the Earth, Help the Aged v Secretary of State for Environment, Food and Rural Affairs* [2010] *Environmental Law Reports* 11.
21 The risk assessments are to be five-yearly from 2012 [Climate Change Act 2008, Section 56(1)]. The adaptation programmes are to specify objectives, propose policies and timescales and must be produced as soon as reasonably practicable following risk assessment reports [Section 58(1)].
22 Including, regarding emissions, use of carbon credits (traded and otherwise) and particular sectoral opportunities: Section 34; including a duty to 'publish ... in such manner as it considers appropriate' [Section 34(6)]. See also Section 57(1); with a similar duty to publish, ibid., Section 57(4). Likewise, Section 36(1)(2); concerning performance levels, likely outcomes and whether further measures are required, and to which the Secretary of State is under a duty to respond [Section 37(1)]; see, for example, Committee on Climate Change, *Meeting Carbon Budgets* (2011).
23 Climate Change Act 2008, Sections 56(6), 58(4), 57(3), 34(5), 36(1); the central government is required to consult with the Welsh Government prior to publishing its response to progress reports [Section 37(2)].
24 Ibid., Sections 41(1), 42(1); there are equivalent central government powers [Sections 41(2), 42(2)]. Also Sections 41(5), 42(6)(4).
25 Ibid., Section 38(3); also statistics preparation, and limits set under any carbon-trading scheme [Section 38(2)].
26 Ibid., Section 38(1). The Committee has already issued a progress report on the Welsh Government Climate Change Strategy, its progress in reducing emissions and on adaptation measures and plans: *Reducing Emissions and Preparing for Climate Change in Wales: 2011 Progress Report* (Cardiff: Committee on Climate Change, October 2011).
27 For a short time an alternative to UK government consent was authority of the Infrastructure Planning Commission under an order of the Planning Act 2008; see now the Localism Act 2011.
28 See Government of Wales Act 2006, Section 95(5); draft National Assembly for Wales (Legislative Competence) Order 2010, to amend Schedule 5 of the 2006 Act (especially Part 2, A1, headlined 'Economic development').
29 T. Rayner and A. Jordan, 'Adapting to climate change: an emerging European Union policy', in Jordan, D. Huitema, H. Van Asselt, T. Rayner and F. Berkhout (eds.), *Climate Change Policy in the European Union* (Cambridge: Cambridge University Press, 2010), 145–7.
30 See Committee on Climate Change, 1st Report to Parliament, *Building a Low Carbon Economy: The UK's Contribution to Tackling Climate Change* (London: Committee on Climate Change, December 2008), ch. 14.
31 See Department of Transport, White Paper, *Creating Growth, Cutting Carbon: Making Sustainable Transport Happen*, Cm 7996 (London: The Stationery Office, 1 January 2011).
32 Ibid., Sections 66, 67.

33 Ibid., Section 70(1); the central government has equivalent powers over non-devolved functions (such as energy, transport, and communications) (Sections 61–3). See also Town and Country Planning Act 1990, Part 11.
34 Welsh Government, Consultation Document, *Building Resilience to Climate Change: Approach to Exercising Powers to Issue Guidance and Directions under Part 4 Climate Change Act (Impact of and Adaptation to Climate Change)* (Cardiff: Welsh Government, December 2010), 96.
35 Climate Change Act 2008, Section 70(1).
36 Ibid., Section 68(7); Section 68(1); Sections 56, 58, 68(3).
37 The centre will have to either consult or obtain consent from the devolved authority where functions are exercisable either on a devolved basis or jointly (ibid., Section 64); equivalent provisions apply to the Welsh Government in the exercise of Section 66–7 powers (Section 69).
38 A. Ross and H. Nash, 'European Union environmental law: who legislates for whom in a devolved Britain', *Public Law*, July (2009), 564–94.
39 Welsh Government, *Climate Change Strategy for Wales*. Chapters 7–13 are concerned with, *inter alia*, sectoral emissions (transport, business, agriculture, waste, residential and the public sector). The commitment, from 2011, is set against a baseline of average emissions 2006–10 (selected 'to be as up to date as possible'); see ch. 5 and annex A.
40 Department of Energy and Climate Change, *Impact Assessment: Setting the Limit on the Use of International Carbon Units for the 2nd Budget Period (2013–17)*; available at http://www.decc.gov.uk/assets/decc/What%20we%20do/A%20low%20carbon%20UK/Carbon%20budgets/1777-ia-2nd-carbon-budget-period.pdf (accessed 4 September 2011).
41 Welsh Government, *Climate Change Strategy for Wales*, p. 40.
42 Ibid., pp. 35–7.
43 G. Winter, 'The climate is no commodity: taking stock of the emissions trading system', *Journal of Environmental Law*, 22 (2010), 1–25.
44 Progress is awaited; cf. trading elements of a carbon reduction commitment scheme affecting other large (public and private sector) emissions sources, which were subsequently replaced by a charge or tax (ENDS Report 429, October 2010). See further, Department of Energy and Climate Change, *CRC Energy Efficiency Scheme*; available at http://www.decc.gov.uk/en/content/cms/emissions/crc_efficiency/crc_efficiency.aspx (accessed 4 September 2011).
45 See R. J. T. Klein, S. Huq, F. Denton, T. E. Downing, R. G. Richels, J. B. Robinson and F. L. Toth, 'Inter-relationships between adaptation and mitigation', in M. L. Parry, O. F. Canziani and J. P. Palutikof (eds.), *Climate Change 2007: Impacts, Adaptation and Vulnerability* (Cambridge: Cambridge University Press, 2007).
46 Welsh Government, *Climate Change Strategy for Wales*, ch. 15.
47 Ibid., p. 90.
48 See J. Forrester, *The Deliberative Practitioner: Encouraging Participatory Planning Processes* (Cambridge, MA: MIT Press, 2000).
49 G. Walker, 'Harnessing community energies: explaining and evaluating community-based localism in renewable energy policy in the UK', *Global Environmental Politics*, 7 (2007), 64–82; also see V. Leitch, 'Securing planning permission for onshore wind farms: the imperativeness of public participation', *Environmental Law Review*, 12 (2010), 182–99.
50 See Welsh Government, *One Wales: One Planet, Sustainable Development Charter* (Cardiff: Welsh Government, May 2010), pp. 5–6.
51 See, for example, H. Jacoby, M. Babiker, S. Paltsev, J. M. Reilly, 'Sharing the burden of GHG reductions', in J. Aldy and R. Stavins (eds.), *Post-Kyoto International Climate Policy* (Cambridge: Cambridge University Press, 2009), p. 753.
52 J. Blake, 'Overcoming the "value–action gap" in environmental policy: tensions between national policy and local experience', *Local Environment*, 4 (1999), 257–78.

53 In consequence, J. Lovelock, *The Revenge of Gaia: Why the Earth Is Fighting Back – and How We Can Still Save Humanity* (London: Penguin, 2007), pp. 8–18, argues that the natural system is so locked into dangerous change that we must rely on scientific solutions, and in the meantime radical measures to shift from fossil fuels but maintain levels of energy demand in other ways.
54 See N. Stern, *Economic Impacts of Climate Change* (London: Cabinet Office, 2006); T. Jackson, *Prosperity without Growth? The Transition to a Sustainable Economy* (London: Sustainable Development Commission, 2009); Tomain, *Ending Dirty Energy Policy*, ch. 7–9.
55 For a classic setting out of a hierarchy of approaches, see S. R. Arnstein, 'A ladder of citizen participation', *Journal of the American Planning Association*, 35 (1969), 216–24. In the planning sphere, a UK parliamentary committee variously identified methods aimed at enhancing involvement, to include multi-level consultation, deliberative polling, standing consultative panels, focus groups, citizens' juries, consensus conferences, stakeholder dialogues and internet dialogue (HL Select Committee on Science and Technology, *Science and Society*, 3rd Report, 1999–2000, paras 5.3–5.37).
56 I. Lorenzoni, S. Nicholson-Cole and L. Whitmarsh, 'Barriers perceived to engaging with climate change among the UK public and their policy implications', *Global Environmental Change*, 17 (2007), 445–59.
57 M. A. Glendon, *Rights Talk: The Impoverishment of Political Discourse* (New York: Free Press, 1991), p. 179.
58 J. Porritt, *Playing Safe: Science and the Environment* (London: Thames & Hudson, 2000), p. 104.
59 Department for Communities and Local Government, *Draft National Planning Policy Framework* (London, July 2011), pp. 3–5.
60 Lorenzoni (2007), ibid., 446.
61 R. G. Noll and J. E. Krier, 'Some implications of cognitive psychology for risk regulation', in C. R. Sunstein (ed.), *Behavioural Law and Economics* (Cambridge: Cambridge University Press, 2000), p. 337; also A. Green, 'Self-control, individual choice, and climate change', *Virginia Environmental Law Journal*, 26 (2008), 77–105.
62 A. Irwin and B. Wynne, *Misunderstanding Science? The Public Reconstruction of Science and Technology* (Cambridge: Cambridge University Press, 1996).
63 C. R. Sunstein, 'Endogenous preferences, environmental law', *Journal of Legal Studies* 22 (1992), 217–54.
64 K. Yardley, G. Wright and A. Pearman, 'The social construction of risk aversion', *Risk Decision & Policy*, 2 (1997), 87–100; J. Adams, *Risk* (London: University College Press, 1995); see also M. Douglas and A. Wildavsky, *Risk and Culture: An Essay on the Selection of Technological and Environmental Dangers* (Berkeley: University of California Press, 1983).
65 Lazarus, 'Environmental law after Katrina', p. 1031.
66 Department for Business and Regulatory Reform, *A White Paper on Nuclear Power*, Cm 7296 (London, January 2008), pp. 16–17.
67 See R. Kasperson, O. Renn, P. Slovic, H. Brown, J. Emel, R. Goble, J. Kasperson and S. Ratick, 'The social amplification of risk: a conceptual framework', *Risk Analysis*, 8 (1988), 177–87. In the aftermath of the earthquake and tsunami that devastated eastern Japan in March 2011, questions resurfaced about the 'fundamental vulnerability' of nuclear power plants: R. McKie, 'Tokyo ministers ignored expert's warnings on risk of building reactors that had "fatal flaws"', *The Guardian*, 13 March 2011.
68 See J. Rockstrom *et al.*, 'A safe operating space for humanity', *Nature*, 461 (2009), 472–5.
69 Y. Rydin, *Urban and Environmental Planning in the UK* (Basingstoke: Macmillan, 1998), p. 356

70 For a general overview of such goal seeking, see Global Environmental Change Programme, *The Politics of GM Food: Risk, Science and Public Trust* (Sussex: ESRC, 1999).

71 J. Rowan-Robinson, A. Ross, W. Walton and J. Rothnie, 'Public access to environmental information: a means to what end?', *Journal of Environmental Law*, 8 (1996), 19–42.

72 See E. A. Kirk and K. L. Blackstock, 'Enhanced decision-making: balancing public participation against "better regulation" in British environmental permitting regimes', *Journal of Environmental Law*, 23 (2011), 97–116, pp. 112–3; echoes can be seen in the rejection of the idea of 'inert people' in Glendon, *Rights Talk*. Environmental Permitting (England and Wales) Regulations 2010 SI 2010/675, Schedule 5, para. 6, requires the Environmental Agency to take steps 'it considers appropriate' to inform public consultees and invite representations (reported mechanism of choice is through website postings).

73 P. McAuslan, *The Ideologies of Planning Law* (Oxford: Pergamon, 1980); see also J. Dryzek, *The Politics of the Earth* (Oxford: Oxford University Press, 1997), ch. 4 and 5.

74 See, for instance, M. Purdue, 'An overview of the law on public participation in planning law and whether it complies with the Aarhus Convention', *Environmental Law and Management*, 17 (2005), 107–14; E. Fisher, P. Pascual and W. Wagner, 'Understanding environmental models in their legal and regulatory context', *Journal of Environmental Law*, 22 (2010), 251–83, identifying *inter alia* 'institutional mandate' models both of regulation and as a source of dispute; also, *R (Edwards) v Environment Agency* [2008] UKHL 22.

75 *Berkeley v Secretary of State for the Environment* [2001] Env Law Rep 16.

76 P. Healy, *Collaborative Planning: Shaping Places in Fragmented Societies* (London: Macmillan, 1997), highlighting opportunities from introducing a reflexive dialogue into the public realm; see J. Habermas, *The Theory of Communicative Action, volume 1: Reason and the Rationalisation of Society* (Cambridge: Polity Press, 1984).

77 See Glendon, *Rights Talk*, p. 137. M. Lee and C. Abbot, 'The usual suspects? Public participation under the Aarhus Convention', *Modern Law Review*, 66 (2003), 80–108, p. 87, emphasizing the distinctive feature of deliberation as going beyond the more traditional technocratic/consultative role 'primarily to provide information for decision-makers'. For a discussion containing a perceptive review of the literature concerned with deliberation, see J. Steele, 'Participation and deliberation in environmental decision-making: exploring a problem-solving approach', *Oxford Journal of Legal Studies*, 21 (2001), 415–42.

78 Steele, 'Participation and deliberation', pp. 426, 434–5; Lee and Abbot, 'The usual suspects?', p. 82; E. T. Freyfogle, 'Owning the land: four contemporary narratives', *Journal of Land Use and Environmental Law*, 13 (1998), 279–307.

79 D. Toke, 'Explaining wind power planning outcomes', *Energy Policy*, 33 (2005), 1527–39.

80 Leitch, 'Securing planning permission for onshore wind farms', pp. 193–5; cf. B. E. Olsen, 'Wind energy and local acceptance: how to get beyond the Nimby effect', *European Energy and Environmental Law Review*, 19 (2010), 239–51.

81 *Bushell v Secretary of State for the Environment* [1981] AC 75; also *Barbone v Secretary of State for Transport* [2009] EWHC 463 (Admin). See *R (Hillingdon LBC) v Sec of State for Transport and Transport for London* [2010] EWHC 626 (Admin), Carnwath LJ, especially paras. 63, 94.

82 *Hillingdon*, para. 51, where policy concerning a new Heathrow Terminal 6 and Runway 3 pre-dated the statutory targets enshrined in Climate Change Act 2008, Section 1.

83 See *Gray v Minister for Planning* (2006) 152 *LGERA* 258, concerning a proposal for a mining development, where it was ruled that the requirement for an environmental impact assessment must extend to consideration of potential effects from

greenhouse gas emissions. Cf. intergenerational benefits of a wind farm proposal: *Taralga Landscape Guardians Inc v Minister for Planning* (2007) 161 *LGERA* 1; both cases (in New South Wales Land and Environment Court) are discussed by J. Peel, 'Climate change law: the emergence of a new legal discipline', *Melbourne University Law Review*, 32 (2008), 922–79.

84  R. C. Paehlke, 'Democracy, bureaucracy, environmentalism', *Environmental Ethics*, 10 (1988), 294–5.

85  W. Howarth, 'Aspirations and realities under the Water Framework Directive: proceduralisation, participation and practicalities', *Journal of Environmental Law*, 21 (2009), 391–418.

86  A much contested area: see, for example, J. D. Nyhart and M. M. Carrow, *Law and Science in Collaboration: Resolving Regulatory Issues of Science and Technology* (Lexington, MA: D. C. Heath, 1983), ch. 11; cf. B. G. Wynn and S. Mayer, 'How science fails the environment', *New Scientist*, 138 (1993), 33–5; S. Foster, 'Justice from the ground up', *California Law Review*, 86 (1998), 775–841, pp. 834–5; Steele, 'Participation and deliberation', p. 435, in aphoristic mode, offers: 'The last thing that would help resolve questions of sustainability is a committee of unsituated and selfless individuals'.

87  A point made by S. Owens and R. Cowell, *Land and Limits: Interpreting Sustainability in the Planning Process* (Abingdon: Routledge, 2002), albeit recognizing the more dominant influence of more entrenched 'commitments to particular patterns of growth' (p. 60). See, for example, B. A. Williams and A. R. Matheny, *Democracy, Dialogue, and Environmental Disputes: The Contested Languages of Social Regulation* (New Haven, CT: Yale University Press, 1995), pp. 201–2; B. G. Rabe, *Beyond Nimby: Hazardous Waste Siting in Canada and the United States* (Washington, DC: Brookings Institution, 1994), ch. 3.

88  See Environment Agency, *Understanding the Risks, Empowering Communities, Building Resilience: The National Flood and Coastal Erosion Risk Management Strategy for England* (London, 2011), which has a section (3.3.2) concerned with developing policy 'to reduce the likelihood of harm to people and damage to the economy, environment and society'.

89  E. J. Treby and M. J. Clark, 'Refining a practical approach to participatory decision making: an example from coastal zone management', *Coastal Management*, 32 (2004), 353–72, pp. 355–8; also J. Glicken, 'Getting stakeholder participation "right": a discussion of participatory processes and possible pitfalls', *Environmental Science and Policy*, 3 (2000), 305–10.

90  R. Eckersley, *The Green State: Rethinking Democracy and Sovereignty* (Cambridge, MA: MIT Press, 2004).

91  M. Lee, *EU Environmental Law: Challenges, Change and Decision-Making* (Oxford: Hart, 2004), ch. 5; see also A. Giddens, *Beyond Left and Right: The Future of Radical Politics* (Cambridge: Polity, 1994), p. 113.

92  D. Wilkinson, 'Using environmental ethics to create ecological law', in J. Holder and D. McGillivray (eds.), *Locality and Identity: Environmental Issues in Law and Society* (Aldershot: Dartmouth, 1999), p. 17.

93  W. M. Lafferty and J. Meadowcroft (eds.), *Democracy and the Environment: Problems and Prospects* (Cheltenham: Edward Elgar, 1996), p. 3; also W. Achterberg, 'Sustainability and associative democracy', in Lafferty and Meadowcroft, ibid., p. 291.

94  C. Hilson, 'Planning law and public perceptions of risk: evidence of concern or concern based on evidence?', *Journal of Planning Law* (2004), 1638–48; N. Stanley, 'Public concern: the decision-maker's dilemma' *Journal of Planning Law* (1998), 919–34.

95  D. E. Blake, 'Contextual effects on environmental attitudes and behaviour', *Environment and Behaviour*, 33 (2001), 708–25.

96 See C. R. Sunstein, 'Social norms and social roles', *Columbia Law Review*, 96 (1996), 903–68.
97 C. R. Sunstein and C. Jolls, 'Debiasing through law', *Journal of Legal Studies*, 85 (2006), 199–241, p. 234; M. D. Zinn, 'Adapting to climate change: environmental law in a warmer world', *Ecology Law Quarterly*, 34 (2007), 61–105, pp. 82–3.
98 Lazarus, 'Environmental law after Katrina', pp. 1043–4.
99 See R. Atfield 'Mediated responsibilities, global warming, and the scope of ethics', in R. Irwin (ed.), *Climate Change and Philosophy: Transformational Possibilities* (London: Continuum, 2010), pp. 189–90; also HL Select Committee on Science and Technology, 2nd Report 2010-11, *Behaviour Change* (July 2011), ch. 8. Cf. A. Gedicks, *The New Resource Wars* (Boston: South End, 1993), p. 204, describing a need to secure a shift from how projects are developed 'to *who* will be involved in the decision-making process'.
100 Though problems in identifying individual emissions arise: M. Vandenbergh, 'From smokestack to SUV: the individual as regulated entity in the new era of environmental law', *Vanderbilt Law Review*, 57 (2004), 515–628, pp. 537–40.
101 R. H. Thaler and C. R. Sunstein, *Nudge: Improving Decisions about Health, Wealth, and Happiness* (New Haven, CT: Yale University Press, 2008).
102 N. Gunningham, 'Environmental law, regulation and governance: shifting architectures', *Journal of Environmental Law*, 21 (2009), 179–212, p. 203; also Thaler and Sunstein, *Nudge*. See HL Select Committee on Science and Technology, *Behaviour Change*, ch. 2, citing Nuffield Council of Bioethics, *Public Health: The Ethical Issues* (London: Nuffield Council of Bioethics, 2007). The HL Select Committee takes issue with the adequacy of 'nudge theory' as being insufficient in the face of the scale of the challenges faced.
103 S. Hinchliffe, 'Helping the Earth begins at home: the social construction of socio-environmental responsibilities', *Global Environmental Change*, 6 (1996), 53–62, p. 54.
104 G. Torres, 'Environmental burdens and democratic justice', *Fordham Urban Law Journal*, 21 (1994), 431–60, p. 460.
105 Climate Change (Scotland) Act 2009, Section 91(1)(2).
106 Scottish Government, *Low Carbon Scotland: Public Engagement Strategy* (Edinburgh: Scottish Government, December 2010); Climate Change (Scotland) Act 2009, Section 91(3).
107 Scottish Government, *Low Carbon Scotland*, p. 5, setting out benefits of a low-carbon society.
108 Ibid., pp. 9–12.
109 J. Hammond and S. Shackley, *Towards a Public Communication Engagement Strategy for Carbon Dioxide Capture and Storage Projects in Scotland*, SCCS Working Paper (Edinburgh: Scottish Centre for Carbon Capture, 2010).
110 Ibid., p. 13.
111 Ibid., pp. 3–4.
112 Welsh Government, *Climate Change Strategy for Wales*, especially ch. 2.
113 Welsh Government, draft *Guidance Document, Building Resilience to Climate Change: Statutory Guidance for Reporting Authorities* (Cardiff: Welsh Government, December 2010).
114 Ibid., para. 3.2.4.4, para 3.3.1.
115 Welsh Government, *Climate Change Engagement Strategy* (Cardiff: Welsh Government, November 2011).
116 Welsh Government, *Sustainable Development Charter*, p. 5.
117 E.g. Welsh Assembly Government, *National Energy and Efficiency Savings Plan* (Cardiff: Welsh Government, 2011), pp. 10–16, which identifies approaches to developing behavioural change programmes (e.g. 'energy behaviours'), including support and funding for selected community projects.

118 Welsh Government, *One Wales: One Planet – A Welsh Government Discussion Paper – Sustainable Development Bill* (Cardiff: Welsh Government, November 2011), pp. 3–4.
119 Welsh Government, *Consultation Document, Sustaining a Living Wales: A Green Paper on a New Approach to Natural Resource Management in Wales* (Cardiff: Welsh Government, 30 January 2012), paras 2, 3, 8.
120 Welsh Government, *White Paper: Consultation on Active Travel (Wales) Bill* (Cardiff: Welsh Government, May 2012), especially paras 5, 6, 54–5, 71.
121 Welsh Assembly Government, *Climate Change Strategy for Wales: Delivery Plan for Emissions Reduction* (Cardiff: Welsh Assembly Government, October 2010), pp. 37–40, adopting the 'social marketing' language of the Scottish strategy.
122 T. Garton Ash, '2009 brings hard choices over the future of capitalism', *The Guardian*, 1 January 2009.
123 For the response to Committee on Climate Change, *Meeting Carbon Budgets*, detailing carbon budget objectives up to 2027, see HM Government, *Implementing the Climate Change Act 2008: The Government's Proposal for Setting the 4th Carbon Budget, Policy Statement* (London: HM Government, May 2011), though at the Treasury's behest subject to a further Government review in 2014.
124 E.g. Committee on Climate Change, *The 4th Carbon Budget: Reducing Emissions through the 2020s* (London: Committee on Climate Change, December 2010), ch. 8, 'Wider economic and social considerations', pp. 337–40 (impacts on fuel poverty); see also B. Boardman and A. Darby, *Effective Advice: Energy Efficiency and the Disadvantaged*, Research Report 24 (Oxford: Environmental Change Institute Oxford University, 2000); Department of Energy and Climate Change, *The UK Low Carbon Transition Plan: National Strategy for Climate and Energy* (London: The Stationery Office, July 2009), distributional impacts, pp. 73–7.

# Chapter 10

# Made in Wales: devolving and evolving environmental policy making

*Elen Stokes*

## Introduction

In supermarkets and corner shops across Wales, consumers are charged at least 5 p for every carrier bag used.[1] Cross the border into England, however, and bags are given away for free with the purchase of goods. The example might seem trivial but it gives some indication of the shape of things to come, with Wales showing an increasing willingness to do things differently. In the aftermath of the referendum, in which Wales voted 'yes' to direct law-making powers, one might expect the disparities between policies in Wales and England to grow in both number and size. Yet, as this chapter suggests, although Wales has shown huge ambition in improving policies in a range of fields, most notably environmental protection, there may be good reasons for taking stock of some of the practical implications of a distinctly Welsh approach.

The chapter begins by looking at the story so far, introducing some of the areas in which differences of approach have emerged between the Welsh Government (formerly the Welsh Assembly Government) and the national and/or other regional administrations. In order to give a flavour of the capacity for divergence, an overview of some of the differences is presented in relation to sustainable development policy, waste law, marine protection and the planning system. The chapter then proceeds to look at some of the problems encountered when a Welsh approach is pursued, particularly where (prior to the recent expansion of the Welsh Government's law-making facilities) devolved powers were sought primarily from UK Acts.[2] Amongst the difficulties arising were a lack of scrutiny and, particularly early on, a high degree of complexity, lack of clarity of purpose, multiple accountabilities and insufficient leadership. Broadly speaking, the significance of these problems has diminished following recent and considerable changes to the Welsh legislative landscape. Environmental policy making in

Wales is now far less constrained by the challenges it faced in the past, and the Welsh agenda has gained new momentum. However, the chapter concludes by highlighting that the Welsh project should be approached with care and caution. If too little is distinctive about environmental policy in Wales, supporters will be left disappointed and disillusioned. Yet, if too much is done, there is a danger that the Welsh ambition, admirable though it is, will begin to outstrip resource capacity and undermine efforts to promote an improved and more holistic approach to environmental legislation.

## Welsh stance

Environmental policy is a sphere densely packed with different types of protective measures and, importantly, one in which governments in devolved administrations have expressed a preference for forms of quasi-legislation.[3] In keeping with this trend there have been significant opportunities to deploy secondary powers following the devolution settlement. For instance, the powers originally transferred using the Transfer of Functions Order under Section 22 of the Government of Wales Act 1998 were wide ranging, the most significant exceptions being for the development of natural energy resources and nuclear power. These powers were used extensively in the first term of the Assembly, as evidenced by the thirty-two pieces of secondary legislation on the environment passed.[4] However, much of the environmental legislation either was identical to its English counterpart or mirrored it very closely.

Replication can also be seen to occur in the transposition of EU requirements, and it has been suggested that legislation from EU sources is more likely than measures first enacted at UK level to be cut and pasted directly into Welsh policy. When he was Secretary of State, John Gummer famously stated that 80 per cent of British environmental policy came from the EU.[5] The extent to which this is an accurate assessment can be questioned, but it is undoubtedly true that EU measures have proved a dominant feature of UK environmental legislation. It follows that in Wales, as elsewhere in the UK, many environment measures transpose EU environmental directives using powers under Section 2(2) of the European Communities Act and the relevant designation orders, which empower the Welsh Ministers in areas such as air, quality, waste management and localized pollution such as noise or contaminated land.

Jenkins makes the point that notwithstanding the extrapolation of legislative content, sometimes referred to as the 'copying-out' technique, the possibility of a distinctively Welsh approach to the implementation of provisions nonetheless remained.[6] Towards the end of the first term, the Assembly adopted quite different regulatory regimes in respect of nitrate pollution and access to the countryside.[7] These measures probably reflect greater sensitivity than their English equivalents to the needs of agricultural landowners, which in turn points towards the more extensive rural environment in Wales. A more significant source of difference, however, was the use of 'Wales only' provisions in UK statutes. Examples can be found in the Water Act 2003 (in relation to membership of flood defence committees), the Waste and Emissions Trading Act 2003 and the Household Waste Recycling Act 2003. These waste statutes certainly contributed to a more distinctive approach in Wales, explored further below.

This begins to paint a picture of a Welsh agenda growing in prominence but with fairly small windows of opportunity to see this through to distinct legislation. With time, and as the administration has developed confidence, these opportunities are beginning to be taken, resulting in a regulatory landscape that is no doubt complex but one where Welsh features have gradually been carved out.

## Sustainable development

To some extent the potential for divergence has stemmed from the presence of clear policy visions and structures. Wales has for some time had in place an institutional and governance framework for sustainable development. This derives in no small part from the Government of Wales Act 2006, which imposes a duty on the Welsh Government to promote sustainable development, to ensure a scheme for its implementation and to keep that scheme under review.[8] The Act makes Wales one of very few jurisdictions in the world to have a distinctive statutory duty of this kind.[9] The duty is non-delegable and the aim a hugely ambitious one: to embed sustainable development as the central organizing principle of Welsh government.[10] There is no accountability to or monitoring of the process by the UK government in relation to either the scheme or its delivery. The review of the scheme remains within Wales, further strengthening the sense of Welsh ownership and oversight.

Two possible effects may have emerged from the existence and observance of such duties. First, it could mean that sustainability policy is better developed in Wales than in Westminster. One crude indication of this is that the policy instruments, particularly the Environment Strategy for Wales and the sustainability indicators, are more detailed than in the UK equivalent documents.[11] The second effect is that there is a legitimacy at the heart of Welsh policy. Given the inclusive process of developing the scheme and the task of integrating sustainability principles into all policy-making activities, it is difficult for the Welsh Government to stray much beyond the sustainable development agenda. In light of this, environmental initiatives, which constitute one of the pillars of sustainability, should develop differently in Wales. This is reflected in the policy literature, which leaves little doubt that the Welsh Government sees the formulation of sustainability as offering a distinctive Welsh approach.[12]

## Waste

The UK is charged with compliance with EU law by altering the way it manages waste from an over-reliance on landfill disposal to a more sustainable integrated waste management system. The Waste Framework Directive, together with its daughter directive the Landfill Directive, requires all Member States to move towards a system of reduction, reuse and recycling, whilst at the same time following the principles of self-sufficiency and proximity.[13] Severe financial penalties attach to any infractions, and targets for diversification away from landfill are generally accepted as tough. The UK's current system of devolved governance has resulted not in one waste strategy but four; Scotland, Wales and Northern Ireland have all issued their own separate waste management policies and strategies.

Welsh waste strategy has always recognized that waste is Wales's 'biggest environmental problem' and that Wales must improve its approach to waste management.[14] The underpinning intention is:

> to move Wales from an over-reliance on landfill to a position where it will be a model for sustainable waste management. It will achieve this by adopting and implementing a sustainable, integrated approach to waste production, management and regulation . . . that minimises the production of waste and its impact on the environment, maximises the use of unavoidable waste as a resource.[15]

The Welsh waste strategy has two primary objectives. The first is to make Wales a model for sustainable waste management; the second is to comply with the requirements of relevant EU directives in promoting options of disposal.

Waste strategy in Wales strongly espouses the proximity principle. The Wales Waste Strategy strongly favours 'solutions that meet the needs and aspirations of local communities' that 'waste should be recovered or disposed of as close as possible to where it has been produced in order to reduce the environmental impact of transporting it'.[16] A sustainable transportation of mixed waste streams is favoured, as these should be dealt with as near as possible to the source of production. Finally, areas should be self-sufficient; that is, there should be sufficient capacity in terms of waste management facilities to manage the wastes produced in any given area.

If the 'distinctiveness' of environmental law and policy in Wales were to rest on any one sector, it would be waste. In this area more than others, the Welsh Government has shown that it seeks to adopt a stronger, more stringent stance than what might be perceived as a minimal approach taken in other administrations.[17] The most compelling evidence of this commitment comes from the fact that the first measure to be passed under the Environment Legislative Competence Order was the Waste (Wales) Measure 2010 (which, among other things, requires retailers to impose charges for single-use carrier bags).[18] The Measure provides the legislative frame on which Wales's Waste Strategy, *Towards Zero Waste*, can hang and the practical means by which the long-term goal, which is that Wales becomes a zero-waste country by 2050, can be realized. A zero-waste approach seeks to encourage a shift away from waste disposal and towards waste prevention; however, where it cannot be eliminated it ought to be reused or recycled. Whereas, elsewhere in the EU, the definition of waste and the weight attached to different levels of the 'waste hierarchy' (prevention, recovery and reuse, disposal) have caused considerable confusion, the Welsh policy (if not the practice) is refreshingly focused on prevention and, where this is not possible, on recovery. This finds support in the policy emphasis on material resource efficiency and on the creation of jobs in the environmental industry sector.[19]

Similar pledges can, of course, be found in the policies of other administrations elsewhere in the UK.[20] The suggestion that the Welsh approach exhibits different characteristics becomes more convincing, however, on a closer look at the finer detail of legislative content. For instance, the 2010 Measure has been used in Wales to extend the reach of environmental permitting regulations in order to exert greater control over the deposit of waste to landfill, irrespective of whether or not that waste is capable of causing environmental pollution.[21]

A further example of difference arises from the Landfill Allowance Schemes, which transpose elements of the Landfill Directive. Unlike the scheme in England, Wales's Landfill Allowance Scheme does not allow the trading of landfill allowances.[22] Under the Landfill Allowance Trading Scheme, waste disposal authorities in England were given individual targets although they were able to trade those allowances in a cost-effective way. Although the initial aim was to introduce a degree of flexibility to the meeting of targets, the idea was resisted in Wales from the outset:

> The Welsh Assembly Government wished to see each local authority investing in BMW [biodegradable municipal waste] diversion from the outset. It was perceived that 'buying' allowances rather than investing in diversion would postpone the necessary investment and waste money. If Welsh local authorities were to buy surplus allowances from English local authorities there would be, in effect, a flow of funding from Welsh to English local authorities and no tangible BMW diversion in Wales to show for it. This conflicts with several of the tenets of the Wales waste strategy.[23]

These limits have also been recognised more recently in a UK government review of waste policy, in which it announces its decision to end landfill allowance trading in England. It has been noted that, 'While LATS [Landfill Allowance Trading Schemes] has undoubtedly been effective in kick starting significant efforts to divert waste away from landfill, the rising level of Landfill Tax means it is now by far the more significant driver'.[24]

The approach in Wales is clearly paying off, as recent evidence has shown.[25] Recent results, for instance, show that all twenty-two local authorities in Wales achieved their 2010/11 allowance obligations. In total, 458,2641 tonnes of biodegradable municipal waste was sent to landfill in 2010/11 compared with an overall Wales allowance of 630,000 tonnes. This was 27 per cent less than the allowance.[26]

Divergences show signs of emerging in other respects besides, and it need not be the result of proactive policy making. It can also stem from the lessons learned from the experiences of other regional administrations. For example, under the Clean Neighbourhood Act 2005, Wales has indicated that it intends to develop more stringent Site Waste Management Plans than those in England. It has been suggested that Wales is now in a strong position to draft more effective plans because it has been able to observe and learn from the implementation of the Site Waste Management Plans Regulations 2008 in England.[27]

Yet, in spite of its laudable aims, there have been times when the Welsh Government's progress has been held back by its (at the time limited) legislative competences. One example of this arises in relation to the Climate Change Act, under which five local authorities in England were allowed to pilot a waste reduction scheme introducing rebates and incentives for households that reduced their waste quantities.[28] That provision does not, however, apply to Wales. In line with its stringent waste aims, the Welsh Government explored the possibility of imposing direct and variable charges ('pay as you throw') on households if they throw away a greater volume of waste than is prescribed or place recyclable materials in non-recyclable waste streams. The problem facing the Welsh Government at the time was that Section 46(1) of the Environmental Protection Act does not permit local authorities to charge for certain waste disposals. Although, under the Environmental Protection Act 1990, local authorities can implement charging, the Environment Legislative Competence Order 2009 does not bestow these powers on the Welsh Government. As a result, the issue remains in the hands of individual local authorities instead of forming part of a coherent, all-Wales approach. This serves to show that, whilst there might have been a will, there was not always a way.

## Marine protection

Wales's intention to take a different approach to certain aspects of marine protection became acutely evident during the negotiation of the Marine and Coastal Access Bill. Instead of pursuing a broad framework of Assembly legislative powers (deriving from clauses in Westminster Bills), the Welsh Government agreed to the devolution of a lengthy list of executive powers. A Written Cabinet Statement noted that this decision was taken as a result of the 'complex mix of devolved and non-devolved powers in the marine environment. In some cases it may be more appropriate to seek the devolution of functions directly to Welsh Ministers on the face of the Bill.'[29] Where legislative powers were conferred, however, it was in relation to a narrow slice of the legislative remit: coastal access. The First Minister commented:

> As this is not just a marine Bill, but a marine and coastal access Bill, it will empower the Assembly to pass legislation in this area. We are taking it forward now, through an improvement programme, but we can now give that legislative backing, so that we can provide the path infrastructure at the coast, in partnership with each of our coastal local authorities. It also enables us to clarify public access rights, which is a vexed issue in certain areas of the Welsh coast, and to identify additional areas of coastal land that will be available to the people of Wales for recreational access.[30]

Following this statement, one of the questions raised was whether, had this been a Marine Bill only (without any focus on coastal access), any legislative powers would have been conferred to Wales at all.[31]

Since it was enacted, a number of distinctly Welsh practices have emerged. For instance, in England, Sea Fisheries Committees were replaced under the Act by Inshore Fisheries and Conservation Authorities (IFCAs) whereas in Wales this function was taken into the Welsh Government, becoming subject to separate Welsh Government procedures including its own processes of consultation, stakeholder engagement and impact assessment. Similarly, in England licensing is delegated to the Marine Management Organisation but in Wales these powers are exercised by the Welsh Government. However, it is not unreasonable to suppose that an organizational separation might eventually lead to divergent practices. One explanation for the retention of such a function by the Welsh Government is its pursuit, at the time, of an anti-quango agenda. Since the marine planning process is still in its early stages of development, it is too early to discern any operational differences between the Marine Management Organisation and the Welsh Government. The real difference here lies in the delivery mechanism rather than the locus of power (since licensing powers still ultimately reside with the Secretaries of State for England and Wales respectively).

Differences are also beginning to emerge through the secondary legislation promulgated under the Marine and Coastal Access Act 2009, which sets out how that Act is to be implemented. Some of this secondary legislation is applicable throughout the UK; some applies to England and Wales; some applies to England only or to Wales only. On fees, for example, there is a statutory instrument setting out fee arrangements for the Marine Management Organisation; there are separate statutory instruments setting out different marine licensing fee arrangements in Wales and Scotland. There is a real possibility that divergences will continue to emerge, given that the Marine and Coastal Access Act is an enabling measure that will be implemented through further guidance.

## Planning

The final example is the capacity for difference in the planning regime. For instance, the Welsh Technical Advice Notes, which are equivalent to Planning Policy Statements in England, are more distinctive in certain areas such as sustainable buildings and waste.[32] Differences may also emerge, not because the system in Wales changes tack but because the approach in England looks set to take a different course. One effect of the 'localism agenda' in England, for example, might be a pared-back, liberalized planning regime whereas the regime in Wales is likely to continue to apply along more traditional and prescriptive lines. Although this may lead to an initial divergence in planning cultures, recent findings that the planning application process in Wales is 'under stress' and that 'very few are happy with its operation or impact' could if anything create pressure for a deregulated approach like the one envisaged in England.[33] Yet, notwithstanding the perceived weaknesses of the current approach in Wales, the emphasis appears still to be on the opportunities for continued difference:

> Most, however, saw the opportunity for a distinctly Welsh response – because of the opportunity presented by the small number of planning authorities and because of the different issues and challenges faced. The scope this presented for Wales to use the planning system as a lever for further economic development and investment was also highlighted.[34]

## Difficulties so far

Whilst there can be no disputing the political will and ambition of the Welsh Government, a number of factors have hampered efforts to improve environmental policy making in Wales. The first limit relates to the resource base, the problem being that political intention might not always benefit from the support of an adequate resource infrastructure. In particular there is no effective outlet for treatment and disposal of hazardous wastes in Wales.[35] Moreover, like elsewhere in the UK, current disposal to landfill is unsustainable and landfill capacity is declining.

Wales also faces particular problems related to its geography and underpinning economy. Only 3 per cent of the Welsh land is urbanized, while 79 per cent of land is used for agriculture, affecting both the composition and source of waste streams.[36] The most urbanized area of Wales is the south east, with the greatest density of both population and industrial development. There is, therefore, great divergence between areas in relation to varying employment rates, skills level and general infrastructure. Surveys reveal an unequal distribution of landfill capacity.[37] Half of all licensed waste management facilities operating in Wales are located in South Wales.[38]

The economic characteristics of a country can have major implications on how successfully it can implement its policies. The dominance in Wales of small to medium-sized enterprises (SMEs) has a number of implications. To implement the waste strategy successfully, businesses are encouraged to develop innovative product designs, which will ensure that products are more durable, more easily reusable and recyclable and therefore less disposable. They are encouraged to implement appropriate and, where necessary, innovative waste management systems and to invest in resource productivity, thereby achieving an improved economy without squandering natural resources. These approaches require research and development and new technologies, skills, expertise and a desire to undertake innovation. These are generally lacking in many businesses in Wales, in light of such factors as its traditional industrial base and the structure of its economy. From this we might conclude that the physical, economic and environmental characteristics of a region impact on the success or failure of waste strategies, forming the reality in which the policies and strategies must operate. Without a clear and detailed understanding of these characteristics, strategies can falter and fail to meet their objectives.

Other problems may arise in relation to the share of responsibilities within the Welsh Government and the Assembly, as well as the three regulatory agencies with which they liaise: the Forestry Commission for Wales (FCW), Environment Agency Wales (EAW) and Countryside Council for Wales (CCW).[39] One study reports of complexity, lack of clarity of purpose, multiple accountabilities, insufficient leadership and inadequate integration between policy formulation and implementation. Interorganizational relationships were said to be deficient in several areas, particularly between the Welsh Assembly and local government, and the Welsh Assembly and Assembly-sponsored public bodies. The report found that good progress had been made but that there was much more to do.[40] Elsewhere it has been found that, in spite of the multiple decision-making bodies present, there is a clear sense of roles and responsibilities, particularly amongst the regulatory agencies operating in Wales (EAW, CCW, FCW). In other words, the current arrangements have been relatively effective. A proposal to merge the agencies and create an all-Wales environment body is currently being considered.[41] This is seen as a resource-saving exercise rather than a response to any perceived problem with the decision-making process as it stands. It raises the broader point, however, that Welsh policy can be only as progressive as its resource base allows.

A final difficulty encountered in the years preceding the referendum relates to the scrutiny of Welsh provisions in UK Bills.[42] UK Bills have been the primary route for the devolution of powers to the Welsh Government, rather than Transfer of Function Orders and Legislative Competence Orders. The problem appears to be twofold. The first issue is the infrequency of opportunities for scrutiny. The second is that, where those opportunities arise, the procedures of scrutiny (including the depth of scrutiny and, importantly, the location of scrutiny) have been inadequate. There is no routine procedure for stakeholder consultation on the Welsh provisions.[43] Moreover, the process for agreeing devolved powers for Wales in UK Bills has been described as 'closed', comprising a series of negotiations between Welsh Government officials and Ministers, and Whitehall and UK Ministers.[44] Whilst provisions for Wales are scrutinized as part of the UK Parliamentary Bill process, the extent to which Welsh provisions are considered in detail is variable. It was also suggested that the absence of any consultation and/or approval process in Wales for Welsh provisions also creates difficulties for Welsh stakeholders in engaging with relevant processes at Westminster.

There have, of course, been instances in which the pre-legislative scrutiny of Welsh provisions has been thorough, and the negotiation of the Marine Bill is often cited as one such example.[45] It seems, however, that much of this success was attributable to the hard work, good will and cooperation of individuals rather than the rigour of any scrutiny process formally in place. It may also turn on context and in particular the political visibility of a particular issue in Wales. For instance, the Marine Bill had a long gestation period involving a wide range of stakeholders, including non-governmental organizations (NGOs), who proved to be critical in flagging up issues that arose generally as well as those that impacted specifically on Wales. In areas that benefited less from the time and efforts of key individuals and organizations, however, the lack of a structured scrutiny process has proved to be one of the most fundamental problems afflicting Welsh policy making. Numerous reasons for the scrutiny deficit are cited, including the lack of appropriate information on how powers conferred to Welsh Ministers would be implemented, and a low level of expertise amongst members of the Westminster Joint Committee responsible for scrutinizing the Bill in respect of its importance in Wales. It could also be caused, at least in part, by the fact that there has been very little change to the pre-devolution organization of committees at Westminster, with the exception of the Welsh Grand and Welsh Select Committees, which were introduced to scrutinise draft legislation as it applies to Wales.[46] As the Welsh Affairs Committee notes, however, the heavy reliance on Westminster did prove to be a problem:

> We are concerned that framework powers are not scrutinised to the same degree as proposed Legislative Competence Orders, either within Parliament or the National Assembly for Wales. We suggest that it is appropriate for this Committee to provide more parliamentary oversight of such powers and will investigate the most effective way of doing this. It is not appropriate for two legislatures to be entirely beholden to their executives in order to converse formally, and the National Assembly for Wales should have the opportunity to make observations on any proposal to legislate at Westminster in relation to devolved matters. It is our intention to explore the development of practice in this area.[47]

These concerns are shared by other stakeholders and there have been countless calls for improved procedure:

> WEL [Wales Environment Link] is aware that the Assembly Committees have packed agendas, and it is unsurprising that scrutiny of draft UK Bills is not given the highest priority ... It is important to ensure that, where UK Bills provide duties and powers for Welsh Ministers they are the right ones, and that sufficient recognition is given to the role of the Assembly which will ultimately hold Welsh Ministers to account.
>
> Therefore, we would urge the [Subordinate Legislation] Committee to consider how the opportunity presented by the publication of draft Bills can be effectively harnessed by the Assembly. We would recommend a formalised procedure for the relevant Assembly committee to review impacts of UK legislation at the draft stage, taking evidence from stakeholders, and input directly into Westminster pre-legislative scrutiny. This would mean a departure from the standard timescales for the Committees to report, and ministers to respond. It would also require an agreement to be established with the UK Parliament, so that the importance of evidence gathered by the Assembly Committees can be adequately recognised.[48]

## New horizons

The referendum in May 2011 not only injected new momentum into the Welsh agenda but has also provided the opportunity to overcome perceived shortfalls in the old approach. The implications of reformed arrangements will be that the Assembly will no longer require approval from Westminster in order to pass primary legislation, with the familiar system of Legislative Competence Orders being replaced by Welsh Bills and Acts. Recognizing some of the problems that have bedevilled Welsh policy making previously, a new, improved approach to scrutiny has been introduced on the basis that 'It is important to reflect upon and learn lessons from our experiences over the past four years in taking legislation forward'.[49] A number of priorities have been identified, including improving stakeholder engagement, allowing sufficient scrutiny time for committees, improving the quality of information in explanatory memoranda and regulatory impact assessments, improving transparency in the choice of procedure for statutory instruments, providing a greater opportunity for Assembly Members to scrutinize the transfer of executive powers to Welsh Ministers, and earlier notice of Ministers' intention to legislate. Amongst the priorities is ensuring innovative stakeholder engagement, including the use of Green and White Papers, so that the Welsh public can influence proposals at the policy development stage, before the decision to legislate has even been taken.

It is to be expected that these recent developments and the renewed emphasis on better legislation will result in a flurry of policy making in Wales, particularly in the sphere of environmental protection, where Wales has developed a strong vision. One of the issues facing policy makers, however, is the extent to which Wales can and should seek to follow a different path from other administrations, particularly England, where responsibility for physical environments is typically shared across the border. The question is: how distinctly Welsh can Wales afford to be?

This question is a complex one, which may be answered properly only with the benefit of time, once Welsh policies have been allowed to take root. However, some initial observations can be made about concerns as they relate to the pre-referendum settlement, since they are likely to become only more prominent when the first seeds of direct law making in Wales are sown. The first concern relates to the rationale for distinctly Welsh policies, with suggestions that a Welsh approach is sometimes pursued simply for the sake of establishing difference. To some extent this trait is to be expected in any fledgling regime, so that legislative activity helps to legitimize its own existence and dispel any notion of a 'glorified local government'.[50] Too great a readiness to secure a Welsh position without proper consideration of its likely impacts, however, will not only feed the suspicions of many who remain wary, in Wales as well as Westminster, about the added value of the devolved model but also lead to excessive and less credible policy.

As the possibility of an increasingly complex patchwork of environmental policy looks ever more likely, questions of coherence and consistency also come to the fore. The Welsh ambition may be no bad thing except that, if it takes the form of independence in policy, then it can be difficult to coordinate and integrate sustainability strategy vertically to produce orchestrated policy for the UK as a whole.[51] The differences of approach under devolution have been recognized by Defra, which has pointed nonetheless to the need to satisfy international commitments and UK-wide aspirations.[52] The question is often whether policy ought to be implemented according to political or naturally occurring boundaries. Illustrating the demands for efficiency, the Environment Agency (EA)'s operational boundaries were changed last year so that they now reflect political, rather than water catchment, boundaries. Previously, there were parts of Wales governed by EA in England; likewise, parts of England fell under the remit of EA Wales's administration. Alteration has enabled Environment Agency Wales to focus its attention and resources on environmental policy matters in Wales. However there are also persuasive arguments against such an approach, since there are fairly obvious reasons for not wishing to see pollution controls vary too greatly between England and Wales. The first is that pollution can be trans-boundary in its nature, especially where one is dealing with water-based pollution.[53] Indeed, for this reason, the EU Water Framework Directive envisages water management by reference to river basin catchment areas rather than political or administrative boundaries.[54] The second is that, to the extent that pollution controls govern business activity, one would not wish to engender some form of regulatory arbitrage on the part of business looking to locate in England or in Wales. A broadly level playing field of regulation is surely desirable. The third is that, because pollution is often diffuse, improving the environment depends on jurisdictions working towards similar standards. Finally, there are efficiencies in the provision of regulation if both regulatory and regulated entities are working to broadly harmonized standards and procedures.

Clearly, then, there is a balance to be had between, on the one hand, different kinds of judgement and, on the other, policy logistics. This is not to say that the commitment shown towards environmental legislation in Wales ought to reflect a compromise between rhetoric and reality, but it does call for Welsh policy makers to exercise care and caution in deciding which policy battles to fight.

## Conclusion

However else we may describe government in the United Kingdom, it can no longer be labelled unitary. The emerging, distinct and particular models of national government in Northern Ireland, Scotland and Wales have seen to that. Although national government in Wales has, until recently, operated under the more limited model of devolution, it may offer some of the greater surprises to environmental lawyers. This is because we are used to a mainly unified legal system for England and Wales, although that notion is beginning to erode. There are areas, most notably waste policy, in which Wales has started to forge its own path and, in some respects, establish itself as leader of the regional pack. In other areas, the Welsh vision has been far less sharp, owing to over-stretched resources rather than a lack of ambition, and as a result Welsh policy is often different only in name. The transference of legislative capacity should enhance confidence in the approach to environmental challenges ahead and encourage innovation in the development of environmental policy. However, as the chapter has sought to point out, the fundamental question is not whether there is the political appetite but whether those intentions can be translated into workable tools and real means of securing a better Welsh environment and a better Wales.

## Notes

1 The Single Use Carrier Bags Charge (Wales) Regulations 2010. The regulations cover single-use carrier bags as defined in regulation 3.
2 On these issues, the chapter draws on my research for the UK Environmental Law Association 'Aim 5' project. See UKELA and King's College London, *The State of UK Environmental Legislation in 2011: Is There a Case for Reform? Interim Report* (London: UKELA/KCL, 2011); for final report see UKELA, KCL and BRASS Cardiff University, *The State of UK Environmental Law in 2011–2012: Is There a Case for Legislative Reform?*

(London: UKELA, 2012). My thanks go to the project team for providing valuable support and guidance.
3 R. Lee, 'Devolution and the environment: Wales', in N. Faris and S. Turner (eds.), *Public Law and the Environment: New Directions?*, Proceedings of the UKELA Conference, Belfast, 16–18 April 1999 (London: UKELA, 1999), p. 85.
4 V. Jenkins, 'Environmental law in Wales', *Journal of Environmental Law*, 17, 2 (2005), 207–27, pp. 215–216.
5 Select Committee on Environmental Audit, *Minutes of Evidence* taken on 21 July 1998, Examination of Witnesses Mr Nigel Haigh and Mr Derek Osborn, Session 1997–98, Question 11.
6 UKELA and King's College London, *The State of UK Environmental Legislation in 2011: Is There a Case for Reform? Interim Report*, August 2011 (London: UKELA/KCL, 2011), hereafter referred to as UKELA/KCL Interim Report, p. 25; Jenkins, 'Environmental law in Wales', p. 216.
7 See Commission on the Powers and Electoral Arrangements of the National Assembly for Wales, *Report of the Richard Commission*, Written Evidence to the Richard Commission, Sue Essex AM, Minister for Environment, Annex 4 (Norwich: The Stationery Office, 2004).
8 Government of Wales Act 2006, Section 79, formerly Section 121 of the Government of Wales Act 1998. For the latest review see Welsh Assembly Government, *One Wales: One Planet – the Sustainable Development Annual Report 2009–2010* (Cardiff: WAG, 2010). The sustainable development scheme was last revised in 2009 when WAG issued *One Wales: One Planet – the Sustainable Development Scheme of the Welsh Assembly Government* (Cardiff: WAG 2009).
9 Northern Ireland has a similar duty contained in the Northern Ireland (Miscellaneous Provisions) Act 2006, Section 25.
10 See WAG, *Sustainable Development Annual Report 2009–2010*, p. 5.
11 Compare with, for example, UK Government, *Securing the Future: Delivering the UK Sustainable Development Strategy* (2005), Cm 6467.
12 This may be reflected in the titles given to the schemes: see National Assembly for Wales, *A Sustainable Wales – Learning to Live Differently* (Cardiff: NAW, 2000) and the follow-up report *Starting to Live Differently* (Cardiff: NAW, 2004).
13 Directive 2008/98/EC on waste [2008] OJ L312/3; Directive 99/31/EC on the landfill of waste [1999] OJ L182/1.
14 Welsh Assembly Government, *Wise about Waste: A Waste Strategy for Wales* (Cardiff: WAG, 2002), p. v.
15 Ibid. p. vii.
16 Ibid., para. 2.21; para. 2.18.
17 See note 34 below.
18 The National Assembly for Wales (Legislative Competence) (Environment) Order 2010.
19 Welsh Assembly Government, *Capturing the Potential: A Green Jobs Strategy for Wales* (Cardiff: WAG, 2009).
20 See, for example, Defra, *Government Review of Waste Policy in England 2011* (London: Defra, 2011).
21 Waste (Wales) Measure 2010, Section 9. For a fuller explanation, see Explanatory Memorandum to the proposed Waste (Wales) Measure 2010.
22 The Welsh scheme was introduced through Landfill Allowances Scheme (Wales) Regulations 2004. Note that the Waste Review has announced the ending of the Landfill Allowance Trading Scheme (LATS) after the 2012/13 scheme year in England.
23 Welsh Assembly Government/Welsh Local Government Association, Protocol on Identifying Concern and the Imposing of Penalties under the Landfill Allowance Scheme (Wales) Regulations 2004 (2010).

24 Defra, *Government Review of Waste Policy in England 2011*, p. 47.
25 See, for example, Environment Agency, *Comparative Analysis of the Landfill Allowance Schemes in England, Wales, Scotland and Northern Ireland*, available at *http://archive.defra.gov.uk/environment/waste/localauth/lats/documents/lats-comparanalysis.pdf*. Figures show that Wales achieved the lowest percentage of biodegradable content of municipal waste.
26 Environment Agency Wales, *Report on the Landfill Allowances Scheme (LAS) Wales 2010/11* (Cardiff: EAW, 2011).
27 UKELA/KCL Interim Report, pp. 54–5.
28 Ibid.
29 Environment, Planning and Countryside Commission Paper EPC(2) 17–06 (p3) Cabinet Written Statement: Carwyn Jones, Minister for Environment, Planning and Countryside: 'Response to the report of the Environment, Planning and Countryside Committee's consideration of Defra's consultation on a Marine Bill', 22 November 2006.
30 National Assembly for Wales, Constitutional Affairs Committee, Bills which will include provisions for Welsh Ministers, SLC(3)-01-09 (p2) (Annex).
31 R. W. Jones and R. Scully (eds.), *Wales Devolution Monitoring Report* (London: Constitution Unit, 2009), p. 26.
32 Technical Advice Note 22; Technical Advice Note 21.
33 Welsh Assembly Government, *Study to Examine the Planning Application Process in Wales* (Cardiff: WAG, 2010), p. iii.
34 National Assembly for Wales, Members' Research Service Research Paper: *Waste Management in Wales* (Cardiff: NAW, 2008).
35 Environment Agency, 'Evidence to the Environment Planning and Countryside Committee on: The Wales Spatial Plan – Environmental and Funding Issues', EPC(2) 16–06 (p5), para. 2.2.
36 S. Russell, 'Status and changes in the UK's ecosystems and their services to society: Wales', in *UK National Ecosystem Assessment, The UK National Ecosystem Assessment Technical Report* (Cambridge: UNEP-WCMC, 2011), p. 1030.
37 National Assembly for Wales, *Waste Management in Wales* (Cardiff: NAW, 2008), p. 28.
38 Welsh Assembly Government, *Wise about Waste: A Waste Strategy for Wales*, p. 75.
39 See Chapter 5 of this volume.
40 P. Williams and A. Thomas, *Sustainable Development in Wales: Understanding Effective Governance* (York: Joseph Rowntree Foundation, 2004).
41 Welsh Assembly Government, Consultation: *A Living Wales – A New Framework for Our Environment, Our Countryside and Our Seas* (Cardiff: NAW, 2010).
42 UKELA/KCL Interim Report, p. 166.
43 Ibid., p. 90.
44 Ibid., p. 88.
45 Ibid., pp. 89–90.
46 House of Commons, *An Introduction to Devolution in the UK*, Research Paper 03/84, p. 33.
47 Welsh Affairs Committee, *Wales and Whitehall: Eleventh Report*, HC Report (Session 2009–10), no. 246, para. 159.
48 National Assembly for Wales, *Subordinate Legislation Committee (SLC), Inquiry into the Scrutiny of Subordinate Legislation and Delegated Powers* (Cardiff: NAW, 2009), Wales Environment Link, Written Evidence SLC4, see Annex 5. Note that the Subordinate Legislation Committee is now the Constitutional Affairs Committee. Wales Environment Link is a network of environmental NGOs in Wales. It is the designated intermediary body between the government and the environmental NGO sector in Wales.

49 Record of proceedings, National Assembly for Wales, 15 March 2011, available at *http://www.assemblywales.org/bus-home/bus-chamber/bus-chamber-third-assembly-rop.htm?act=dis&id=212756&ds=3/2011*.
50 D. T. Lloyd, *Writing on the Edge: Interviews with Writers and Editors of Wales* (Amsterdam: Rodopi, 1997), p. 21.
51 R. Steurer and A. Martinuzzi, 'Towards a new pattern of strategy formation in the public sector: first experiences with national strategies for sustainable development in Europe', *Environment and Planning C: Government and Policy*, 23, 3 (2005), 455–72.
52 See Defra, *Consultation Paper – Taking It On: Developing UK Sustainable Development Strategy Together* (London: Defra, 2004).
53 While, by virtue of Section 94 of the Government of Wales Act 2006, Assembly Measures can have effect only in Wales.
54 Directive 2000/60/EC establishing a framework for the Community action in the field of water policy [2000] OJ L327/1.

# Bibliography

Achterberg, W., 'Sustainability and associative democracy', in W. M. Lafferty and J. Meadowcroft (eds.), *Democracy and the Environment: Problems and Prospects* (Cheltenham: Edward Elgar, 1996).
Ackerman, F. and Heinzerling, L., 'Pricing the priceless: cost–benefit analysis of environmental protection', *University of Pennsylvania Law Review*, 150 (2002), 1553–84.
Adams, J., *Risk* (London: University College Press, 1995).
Adamson, D. and Bromiley, R., *Community Empowerment in Practice: Lessons from Communities First* (York: Joseph Rowntree Foundation, 2008).
Aldrich, J., 'Correlations genuine and spurious in Pearson and Yule', *Statistical Science*, 10, 4 (1990), 364–76.
Ambler-Edwards, S., Bailey, K., Kiff, A., Lang, T., Lee, R., Marsden, T., Simons, D. and Tibbs, H., *Food Futures, Rethinking UK Strategy* (London: Chatham House, 2009).
Angelo, M., 'Harnessing the power of science in environmental law: why we should, why we don't, and how we can', *Texas Law Review*, 86 (2008), 1527–32.
Arnstein, S. R., 'A ladder of citizen participation,' *Journal of the American Planning Association*, 35, 4 (1969), 216–24.
Atfield, R., 'Mediated responsibilities, global warming, and the scope of ethics', in R. Irwin (ed.), *Climate Change and Philosophy: Transformational Possibilities* (London: Continuum, 2010).
Babich, A., 'Too much science in environmental law', *Columbia Journal of Environmental Law*, 28 (2003), 119–75.
Barber, B., *Strong Democracy: Participatory Politics in a New Age* (Berkeley: University of California Press, 2004).
Barker, G. F. R., 'Scarlett, James, first Baron Abinger (1769–1844)', rev. Elisabeth A. Cawthon, *Oxford Dictionary of National Biography* (Oxford: Oxford University Press, 2004).
Barker, T. C. and Harris, J. R., *A Merseyside Town in the Industrial Revolution: St Helens 1750–1900* (Liverpool: University of Liverpool Press, 1954; 3rd impression, Abingdon: Frank Cass, 1993).
Beatson, J., 'Reforming an unwritten constitution', *Law Quarterly Review*, 126 (2010), 48–71.
Beckerman, W. and Pasek, J., *Justice, Posterity and the Environment* (Oxford: Oxford University Press, 2001).

Bell, S. and McGillivray, D., *Environmental Law*, 7th edn (Oxford: Oxford University Press, 2008).
Bennett, R. and Willis, K., 'The value of badger populations and control of tuberculosis in cattle in England and Wales: a note', *Journal of Agricultural Economics*, 58, 1 (2007), 152–6.
Birnie, P., Boyle, A. and Redgewell, C., *International Law and the Environment*, 3rd edn (Oxford: Oxford University Press, 2009).
Blake, D. E., 'Contextual effects on environmental attitudes and behaviour', *Environment and Behaviour*, 33 (2001), 708.
Blake, J., 'Overcoming the "value-action gap" in environmental policy: tensions between national policy and local experience', *Local Environment*, 4 (1999), 257–78.
Boardman, B. and Darby, A., *Effective Advice: Energy Efficiency and the Disadvantaged*, Research Report 24 (Oxford: Environmental Change Institute Oxford University, 2000).
Bogdanor, V., *The New British Constitution* (Oxford: Hart, 2009).
Bogdanor, V., 'Our new constitution', *Law Quarterly Review*, 120 (2004), 242–62.
Bourlakis, M. A. and Weightman, P. W. H., *Food Supply Chain Management* (Oxford: Blackwell Publishing, 2004).
Bradbury, J. and Mitchell, J., 'Devolution: between governance and territorial politics', *Parliamentary Affairs*, 58, 2 (2005), 287–301.
BRASS, *Food and Drink Strategy for Wales: Work Package 1a, Food Sector Data* (unpublished, 2010).
BRASS, *Food and Drink Strategy for Wales, Work Package 1c, Best Practice Review* (unpublished, 2009).
BRASS, *Food and Drink Strategy for Wales: Work Package 2, Strategic Options – Discussion Paper* (unpublished, 2010).
Bristow, G., Entwistle, T., Hines, F. and Martin, S., 'New spaces for inclusion? Lessons from the "three-thirds" partnerships in Wales', *International Journal of Urban and Regional Research*, 32 (2008), 903–21.
Bulkeley, H. and Newell, P., *Governing Climate Change* (Abingdon: Routledge, 2010).
de Burca, G. and Scott, J. (eds.), *Law and New Governance in the EU and the US* (Oxford: Hart, 2006).
Burnsey, E., *Making People Behave: Anti-social Behaviour, Politics and Policy* (London: Willan, 2005).
Butler, S. H., 'Headwinds to a clean energy future: nuisance suits against wind energy projects in the United States', *California Law Review*, 97, 5 (2009), 1337–75.
Cabinet Office Strategy Unit, *Food Matters: Towards a Strategy for the Twenty First Century* (London: Cabinet Office, 2008).
Callon, M., 'Some elements of a new sociology of translation', in J. Law (ed.), *Power Action and Belief: a New Sociology of Knowledge* (London: Routledge, 1986).
Campbell, D., 'Of Coase and corn: a (sort of) defence of private nuisance', *Modern Law Review*, 63, 2 (2000), 197–215.
Campbell, D. and Lee, R. G., 'Carnage by computer: the blackboard economies of the 2001 foot and mouth epidemic', *Social and Legal Studies*, 12, 4 (2003), 425–59.
Campbell, D. and Lee, R., *Environmental Law and Economics* (Farnham: Ashgate, 2007).
Cane, P., 'Tort law as regulation', *Common Law World Review*, 31, 4 (2002), 305–31.
Cane, P., *Tort Law and Economic Interests* (Oxford: Clarendon Press, 1996).
Carson, R., *Silent Spring* (Boston, MA: Houghton Mifflin, 1962).
Carter, S., Delahay, R., Smith, G., Macdonald, D., Riordan, P., Etherington, T., Pimley, E., Walker, N. and Cheeseman, C., 'Culling-induced social perturbation in Eurasian badgers *Meles meles* and the management of TB in cattle: an analysis of a critical problem in applied ecology', *Proceedings of the Royal Society B*, 274 (2007), 2769–70.
Chambers, M. *et al.*, 'Bacillus Calmette–Guérin vaccination reduces the severity and

progression of tuberculosis in badgers', *Proceedings of the Royal Society B*, 1953 (2010), 1–8.

Chinkin, C., 'The challenge of soft law: development and change in international law', *International and Comparative Law Quarterly*, 38 (1989), 850–66.

Clapp, B. W., *An Environmental History of Britain* (London: Longman, 1994).

Clarke, M. and Netherwood, A., 'Beyond volunteering and rhetoric: implications of local Agenda 21 initiatives Wales', in S. Buckingham-Hatfield and S. Percy (eds.), *Constructing Local Environmental Agendas* (Abingdon: Routledge, 1999).

Coase, R. H., 'The problem of social cost', *Journal of Law & Economics*, 3 (1960), 1–44.

Cole, A., *Beyond Devolution and Decentralisation: Building Regional Capacity in Wales and Brittany* (Manchester: Manchester University Press, 2006).

Committee on Climate Change, *Meeting Carbon Budgets: 3rd Report to Parliament* (London: Committee on Climate Change, 2011).

Committee on Climate Change, 1st Report to Parliament, *Building a Low Carbon Economy: The UK's Contribution to Tackling Climate Change* (London: Committee on Climate Change, 2008).

Committee on Climate Change, *Reducing Emissions and Preparing for Climate Change in Wales: 2011 Progress Report* (Cardiff: Committee on Climate Change, 2011).

Committee on Climate Change, *The 4th Carbon Budget: Reducing Emissions through the 2020s* (London: Committee on Climate Change, 2010).

Cox, J., *Climate Crash: Abrupt Climate Change and What It Means for Our Future* (Washington DC: National Academies Press, 2005).

Craddock, P. T., 'Bronze age metallurgy in Britain', *Current Archaeology*, 99 (1986), 106–9.

Culley, K., 'Has Texas nuisance law been blown away by the demand for wind power', *Baylor Law Review*, 61 (2009), 943–72.

Defra, *Consultation Paper – Taking It On: Developing UK Sustainable Development Strategy Together* (London: Defra, 2004).

Defra, *Government Review of Waste Policy in England 2011* (London: Defra, 2011).

Defra, *Mainstreaming Sustainable Development: The Government's Vision and What This Means in Practice* (London: Defra, 2011).

Delanty, G., *Community* (Abingdon: Routledge, 2003).

Department for Business and Regulatory Reform, *A White Paper on Nuclear Power*, Cm 7296 (London, January 2008).

Department for Communities and Local Government, *Draft National Planning Policy Framework* (London, 2011).

Department for Food, Environment and Rural Affairs, *UK Food Security Assessment* (London: Defra, 2009; updated 2010).

Department of Energy and Climate Change, *The UK Low Carbon Transition Plan: National Strategy for Climate and Energy* (London: The Stationery Office, 2009).

Department of Transport, White Paper, *Creating Growth, Cutting Carbon: Making Sustainable Transport Happen*, Cm 7996 (London: The Stationery Office, 2011).

Dobson, A., *Citizenship and the Environment* (Oxford: Oxford University Press, 2003).

Donald, M. B., *Elizabethan Copper: The History of the Company of Mines Royal 1568–1605* (London: Pergamon, 1955).

Doremus, H., 'Science plays defense: natural resource management in the Bush Administration', *Ecology Law Quarterly*, 32 (2005), 249–305.

Doremus, H., 'Scientific and political integrity in environmental policy', *Texas Law Review*, 87 (2008), 1601–20.

Doremus, H. and Tarlock, D., 'Science, judgement, and controversy in natural resource regulation', *Public Land and Resources Law Review*, 26 (2005), 1–2.

Douglas, M. and Wildavsky, A., *Risk and Culture: An Essay on the Selection of Technological and Environmental Dangers* (Berkeley: University of California Press, 1983).

Dryzek, J., *The Politics of the Earth* (Oxford: Oxford University Press, 1997).

Dube, S., 'Small abattoirs at risk from FSA costs blow', *Western Mail*, 16 November 2010.
Eames, M., *Reconciling Environmental and Social Concerns: Findings from the Joseph Rowntree Foundation Research Programme* (York: Joseph Rowntree Foundation, 2006).
Ebbesson, J., 'The rule of law in governance of complex socio-ecological changes', *Global Environmental Change*, 20 (2010), 414–22.
Eckersley, R., *The Green State: Rethinking Democracy and Sovereignty* (Cambridge, MA: MIT Press, 2004).
Edley, C., 'The governance crisis, legal theory, and political ideology', *Duke Law Journal*, 3 (1991), 561–77.
Enticott, G., 'Calculating nature: the case of badgers, bovine tuberculosis and cattle', *Journal of Rural Studies*, 17 (2001), 149–55.
Environment Agency, *Understanding the Risks, Empowering Communities, Building Resilience: The National Flood and Coastal Erosion Risk Management Strategy for England* (London, 2011).
Environment Agency Wales, *Report on the Landfill Allowances Scheme (LAS) Wales 2010/11* (Cardiff: EAW, 2011).
Environment, Food and Rural Affairs Committee, *Securing Food Supplies up to 2050: The Challenges for the UK* (Fourth Report of Session 2008–09, HC 213, 21 July 2009).
Esty, D. C., 'Toward optimal environmental governance', *New York University Law Review*, 74 (1999), 1495–1574.
Etherington, L., '"Mandatory guidance" for dealing with contaminated land: paradox or pragmatism?', *Statute Law Review*, 23, 3 (2002), 203–26.
European Commission, *Common Implementation Strategy for the Water Framework Directive (2000/60/EC)*.
European Commission, *Our Life Insurance, Our Natural Capital: An EU Biodiversity Strategy to 2020*, COM (2011) 244 final.
Evans, J., Smith, E., Banerjee, A. and Smith, R., 'Cluster of human tuberculosis caused by *Mycobacterium bovis*: evidence for person to person transmission in the UK', *The Lancet*, 369 (2007), 1270–6.
Fisher, E., Lange, B., Scotford, E., and Carlane, C., 'Maturity and methodology: a debate about environmental law scholarship', *Journal of Environmental Law*, 21 (2009), 213–50.
Fisher, E., Pascual, P. and Wagner, W., 'Understanding environmental models in their legal and regulatory context', *Journal of Environmental Law*, 22 (2010), 251–83.
Fitzmaurice, M. A., 'International protection of the environment', in *Collected Courses of The Hague Academy of International Law*, 293 (Leiden: Martinus Nijhoff Publishers, 2001).
Foresight, *The Future of Food and Farming* (London: Government Office for Science, 2011).
Forrester, J., *The Deliberative Practitioner: Encouraging Participatory Planning Processes* (Cambridge, MA: MIT Press, 2000).
Foster, S., 'Justice from the ground up', *California Law Review*, 86 (1998), 775–841.
Freyfogle, E. T., 'Owning the land: four contemporary narratives', *Journal of Land Use and Environmental Law*, 13 (1998), 279–307.
Fuller, L., 'The forms and limits of adjudication', *Harvard Law Review*, 92, 2 (1978), 353–409.
Funtowicz, S., Shepherd, I., Wilkinson, D. and Ravetz, J., 'Science and governance in the European Union: a contribution to the debate', *Science and Public Policy*, 27 (2000), 327–36.
Gans, H., *The Urban Villagers: Group and Class in the Life of Italian-Americans* (New York: Free Press, 1982).
Garton Ash, T., '2009 brings hard choices over the future of capitalism', *The Guardian*, 1 January 2009.
Geddes, M., 'Partnership and the limits to local governance in England: institutional analysis and neo-liberalism', *International Journal of Urban and Regional Research*, 30 (2006), 76–97.
Gedicks, A., *The New Resource Wars* (Boston: South End, 1993).

# Bibliography

Giddens, A., *Beyond Left and Right: The Future of Radical Politics* (Cambridge: Polity Press, 1994).
Giddens, A., *Modernity and Self Identify: Self and Society in the Late Modern Age* (Cambridge: Polity Press, 1991).
Giddens, A., *The Consequences of Modernity* (Cambridge: Polity Press, 1990).
Glendon, M. A., *Rights Talk: The Impoverishment of Political Discourse* (New York: Free Press, 1991).
Glicken, J., 'Getting stakeholder participation "right": a discussion of participatory processes and possible pitfalls', *Environmental Science and Policy*, 3 (2000), 305–10.
Global Environmental Change Programme, *The Politics of GM Food: Risk, Science and Public Trust* (Sussex: ESRC, 1999).
Gordon, S., 'Bovine TB: stopping disease control would block all live exports', *Nature*, 456 (2008), 700.
Graham, N., *Lawscape: Property, Environment and Law* (Abingdon: Routledge-Cavendish, 2010).
Green, A., 'Self-control, individual choice, and climate change', *Virginia Environmental Law Journal*, 26 (2008), 77–105.
Gunningham, N., 'Environmental law, regulation and governance: shifting architectures', *Journal of Environmental Law*, 21 (2009), 179–212.
Gunningham, N., 'The new collaborative environmental governance: the localization of regulation', *Journal of Law and Society*, 36, 1 (2009), 145–66.
Gunningham, N., Grabovsky, P. and Sinclair, D., *Smart Regulation: Designing Environmental Policy* (Oxford: Oxford University Press, 1998).
Habermas, J., *The Theory of Communicative Action, volume 1: Reason and the Rationalisation of Society* (Cambridge: Polity Press, 1984).
Hale, B., 'Power giant buys town to avoid pollution lawsuits', *The Times*, 14 May 2002, 27.
Hammond, J. and Shackley, S., *Towards a Public Communication Engagement Strategy for Carbon Dioxide Capture and Storage Projects in Scotland*, SCCS Working Paper (Edinburgh: Scottish Centre for Carbon Capture, 2010).
Harvey, F., 'Fight climate change with technology – UN', *The Guardian*, 6 June 2011.
Healy, P., *Collaborative Planning: Shaping Places in Fragmented Societies* (London: Macmillan, 1997).
Hilson, C., 'Going local? EU law, localism and climate change', *European Law Review*, 33 (2008), 194–210.
Hilson, C., 'Planning law and public perceptions of risk: evidence of concern or concern based on evidence?', *Journal of Planning Law* (2004), 1638–48.
Hinchliffe, S., 'Helping the Earth begins at home: the social construction of socio-environmental responsibilities', *Global Environmental Change*, 6 (1996), 53–62.
Hincks, S. and Robson, B., *Regenerating Communities First Neighbourhoods in Wales* (York: Joseph Rowntree Foundation, 2010).
HL Select Committee on Science and Technology, 2nd Report 2010–11, *Behaviour Change* (2011).
HL Select Committee on Science and Technology, *Science and Society*, 3rd Report (1999–2000).
HM Government, *Implementing the Climate Change Act 2008: The Government's Proposal for Setting the 4th Carbon Budget, Policy Statement* (May 2011).
Hockin, L. E., 'The British approach to the control of industrial emissions to the atmosphere', *Annals of Occupational Hygiene*, 15 (1972), 399–406.
Houck, O., 'Tales from a troubled marriage: science and law in environmental policy', *Science*, 302 (2003), 1926–9.
House of Commons, *An Introduction to Devolution in the UK*, Research Paper 03/84.
Howarth, W., 'Aspirations and realities under the Water Framework Directive: proceduralisation, participation and practicalities', *Journal of Environmental Law*, 21 (2009), 391–418.

Irwin, A. and Wynne, B., *Misunderstanding Science? The Public Reconstruction of Science and Technology* (Cambridge: Cambridge University Press, 1996).
Jack, B., 'Enforcing member state compliance with EU environmental law: a critical evaluation of the use of financial penalties', *Journal of Environmental Law*, 23 (2011), 73–95.
Jackson, T., *Prosperity without Growth? The Transition to a Sustainable Economy* (London: Sustainable Development Commission, 2009).
Jacoby, H., Babiker, M., Paltsev, S. and Reilly, J. M., 'Sharing the burden of GHG reductions', in J. Aldy and R. Stavins (eds.), *Post-Kyoto International Climate Policy* (Cambridge: Cambridge University Press, 2009).
James, E., 'Whither the third sector? Yesterday, today and tomorrow', *Voluntas*, 8, 1 (1997), 1–10.
Jasanoff, S., 'Image and imagination: the formation of global environmental consciousness', in C. Miller and P. N. Edwards (eds.), *Changing the Atmosphere: Expert Knowledge and Environmental Governance* (Cambridge, MA: MIT Press, 2001).
Jenkins, H., Woodroffe, R. and Donnelly, C., 'The duration and effects of repeated widespread badger culling on cattle tuberculosis following the cessation of culling', *Plos One*, 5, 2 (2010), 1–5.
Jenkins, H., Woodroffe, R. and Donnelly, C., 'The effects of annual widespread badger culls on cattle tuberculosis following the cessation of culling', *International Journal of Infectious Diseases*, 12 (2008), 457–65.
Jenkins, V., 'Environmental law in Wales', *Journal of Environmental Law*, 17, 2 (2005), 207–27.
Jenkins, V., 'Local government modernisation and sustainable development in Wales and Ireland', *Environmental Law Review*, 11, 1 (2009), 23–40.
Jenkins, V., 'Placing sustainable development at the heart of government in the UK: the role of law in the evolution of sustainable development as the central organising principle of government', *Legal Studies*, 22, 4 (2002), 578–602.
Jewell, T. and Steele, J., *Law in Environmental Decision-making: National, European and International Perspectives* (Oxford: Clarendon Press, 1998).
Jolowicz, J. A., 'Liability for accidents', *Cambridge Law Journal*, 26, 1 (1968), 50–63.
Jolowicz, J. A., 'Should courts answer questions? Does statutory authority to build confer immunity from liability for use?', *Cambridge Law Journal*, 40, 2 (1981), 226–30.
Jones, J., 'Regulatory design for scientific uncertainty: acknowledging the diversity of approaches in environmental regulation and public administration', *Journal of Environmental Law*, 19, 3 (2007), 347–65.
Jones, R. W. and Scully, R. (eds.), *Wales Devolution Monitoring Report* (London: Constitution Unit 2009).
Kagan, R., *The Return of History and the End of Dreams* (London: Atlantic, 2008).
Kasperson, R., Renn, O., Slovic, P., Brown, H., Emel, J., Goble, R., Kasperson, J. and Ratick, S., 'The social amplification of risk: a conceptual framework', *Risk Analysis*, 8 (1988), 177–87.
Kelly, B., 'The Planning Bill: implications of the proposals for a new regime for major infrastructure for democracy and delivery', *Journal of Planning and Environment Law*, 13 (2008), 1–12.
Kirk, E. A. and Blackstock, K. L., 'Enhanced decision-making: balancing public participation against "better regulation" in British environmental permitting regimes', *Journal of Environmental Law*, 23 (2011), 97–116.
Klein, R. J. T., Huq, S., Denton, F., Downing, T. E., Richels, R. G., Robinson, J. B. and Toth, F. L., 'Inter-relationships between adaptation and mitigation', in M. L. Parry, O. F. Canziani and J. P. Palutikof (eds.), *Climate Change 2007: Impacts, Adaptation and Vulnerability* (Cambridge: Cambridge University Press, 2007).
Krebs, J., Anderson, R., Clutton-Brock, T., Morrison, I., Young, D., Donnelly, C., Frost, S. and Woodroffe, R., *Bovine Tuberculosis in Cattle and Badgers* (London: MAFF Publications, PB3423, 1997).

## Bibliography

Lacey, H., *Is Science Value Free? Values and Scientific Understanding* (London: Routledge, 2004).

Lafferty, W. M. and Meadowcroft, J. (eds.), *Democracy and the Environment: Problems and Prospects* (Cheltenham: Edward Elgar, 1996).

Langdon-Down, G., 'How more devolved powers in Wales could affect the law', *Law Society Gazette*, 20 January 2011.

Last, K. V., 'Habitat protection: has the Wildlife and Countryside Act 1981 made a difference?', *Journal of Environmental Law*, 11, 1 (1999), 15–34.

Latour, B. and Woolgar, S., *Laboratory Life: The Social Construction of Scientific Facts* (London: Sage, 1979).

Law, J., *Organising Modernity* (Oxford: Blackwell, 1994).

Lazarus, R. J., 'Environmental law after Katrina: reforming environmental law by reforming environmental lawmaking', *Tulane Law Review*, 81 (2007), 1019–58.

Lee, M. and Abbot, C., 'The usual suspects? Public participation under the Aarhus Convention', *Modern Law Review*, 66 (2003), 80–108.

Lee, M., *EU Environmental Law: Challenges, Change and Decision-Making* (Oxford: Hart, 2004).

Lee, R. G., 'Devolution and the environment: Wales', in N. Faris and S. Turner (eds.), *Public Law and the Environment: New Directions?*, Proceedings of the UKELA Conference, Belfast, 16–18 April 1999 (London: UKELA, 1999).

Lee, R. G. and Stallworthy, M., 'From the criminal to the consensual: the shifting mechanisms of environmental regulation', in J. Coggon, A. Kessel and A. Viens (eds.), *Criminal Law, Philosophy and Public Health* (Cambridge: Cambridge University Press, forthcoming).

Lee, R. G. and Stokes, E. (eds.), *Economic Globalization and Ecological Localization: Socio-legal Perspectives* (Oxford: Blackwell, 2009).

Leopold, A., *A Sand County Almanac* (Oxford: Oxford University Press, 1949).

Lewis, J., 'Reviewing the relationship between the voluntary sector and the state in Britain in the 1990s', *Voluntas*, 10, 3 (1999), 255–70.

Lloyd, D. T., *Writing on the Edge: Interviews with Writers and Editors of Wales* (Amsterdam: Rodopi, 1997).

Lorenzoni, I., Nicholson-Cole, S. and Whitmarsh, L., 'Barriers perceived to engaging with climate change among the UK public and their policy implications', *Global Environmental Change*, 17 (2007), 445–59.

Lovelock, J., *The Revenge of Gaia: Why the Earth is Fighting Back – and How We Can Still Save Humanity* (London: Penguin, 2007).

Lowndes, V. and Sullivan, H., 'Like a horse and carriage or a fish on a bicycle: how well do local partnerships and public participation go together?', *Local Government Studies* (2004), 51–73.

Lucas, K., Walker, G., Eames, M., Fay, H. and Poustie, M., *Environmental and Social Justice: Rapid Research and Evidence Review* (London: Policy Studies Institute, 2004).

Lucas, K., Ross, A. and Fuller, S., *Local Agenda 21 Community Planning and Neighbourhood Renewal* (York: Joseph Rowntree Foundation, 2003).

McAllister, L., 'The Welsh devolution referendum: definitely, maybe?', *Parliamentary Affairs*, 51, 2 (1998), 149–65.

McAuslan, P., *The Ideologies of Planning Law* (Oxford: Pergamon, 1980).

McKie, R., 'Tokyo ministers ignored expert's warnings on risk of building reactors that had "fatal flaws"', *The Guardian*, 13 March 2011.

McLaren, J. P. S., 'Nuisance law and the industrial revolution: some lessons from social history', *Oxford Journal of Legal Studies*, 155 (1983), 194–5.

Macrory, R., 'Regulating in a risky environment', *Current Legal Problems* (2001), 619–48.

Macrory, R., 'Weighing up the performance', *Journal of Environmental Law*, 23 (2011), 311–7.

Marsden, T., Banks, J. and Bristow, G., 'Food supply chain approaches: exploring their role in rural development', *Sociologia Ruralis*, 40 (2000), 424–38.

Micheals, D. and Monforton, C., 'Scientific evidence in the regulatory system: manufacturing uncertainty and the demise of the formal regulatory system', *Journal of Law and Policy*, 17 (2005), 17–35.

Morag-Levine, N., 'Is precautionary regulation a civil law instrument? Lessons from the history of the Alkali Act', *Journal of Environmental Law*, 23, 1 (2011), 1–43.

Morgan, K. and Sonnino, R., 'Empowering consumers: the creative procurement of school meals in Italy and the UK', *International Journal of Consumer Studies*, 31, 1 (2007), 19–25.

Morgan, K., *The Public Plate* (Brass Working Paper 43, 2007).

Morgan, K., Marsden, T. and Murdoch, J., *Worlds of Food: Place, Power, and Provenance in the Food Chain* (Oxford: Oxford University Press, 2006).

Morrow, K., 'Actualising sustainability in the United Kingdom: recent developments in devolved and local government', in K. Bosselmann, R. Engel and P. Taylor (eds.), *A Guide to Governance for Sustainability: Issues, Challenges and Successes*, Environmental Policy and Law Paper No. 70 (Bonn: IUCN, The World Conservation Union, 2008).

Muirhead, R., Gallagher, J. and Burn, K., 'Tuberculosis in wild badgers in Gloucestershire: epidemiology', *Veterinary Record*, 95 (1974), 552–5.

National Assembly for Wales, *Starting to Live Differently* (Cardiff: NAW, 2004).

National Assembly for Wales, *A Sustainable Wales: Learning to Live Differently* (Cardiff: NAW, 2000).

National Assembly for Wales, Subordinate Legislation Committee, *Inquiry into the Scrutiny of Subordinate Legislation and Delegated Powers* (Cardiff: NAW, 2009).

National Assembly for Wales, *Waste Management in Wales* (Cardiff: NAW, 2008).

Newark, F. H., 'The boundaries of nuisance', *Law Quarterly Review*, 65 (1949), 480–90.

Noll, R. G. and Krier, J. E., 'Some implications of cognitive psychology for risk regulation', in C. R. Sunstein (ed.), *Behavioural Law and Economics* (Cambridge: Cambridge University Press, 2000).

Nyhart, J. D. and Carrow, M. M., *Law and Science in Collaboration: Resolving Regulatory Issues of Science and Technology* (Lexington, MA: D. C. Heath, 1983).

O'Riordan, T. (ed.), *Globalism, Localism and Identity: Fresh Perspectives on the Transition to Sustainability* (London: Earthscan, 2001).

Owens, S. and Cowell, R., *Land and Limits: Interpreting Sustainability in the Planning Process* (Abingdon: Routledge, 2002).

Paehlke, R. C., 'Democracy, bureaucracy, environmentalism', *Environmental Ethics*, 10 (1988), 294–5.

Palmer, R. C., 'Personal injury in private nuisance: the historical truth about actionability of "bodily security"', *Environmental Law and Management*, 21, 6 (2009), 302–11.

Parekh, A. and Kenway, P., *Monitoring Poverty and Exclusion in Wales 2011* (York: Joseph Rowntree Foundation, 2011).

Peel, J., 'Climate change law: the emergence of a new legal discipline', *Melbourne University Law Review*, 32 (2008), 922–79.

Pigou, A. C., *The Economics of Welfare*, 4th edn (London: Macmillan, 1932).

Porritt, J., *Playing Safe: Science and the Environment* (London: Thames & Hudson, 2000).

Pouyat, R., 'Science and environmental policy: making them compatible', *Bioscience*, 49, 4 (1999), 281–2.

Proud, A., 'Some lessons from the history of the eradication of bovine tuberculosis in Great Britain', *Government Veterinary Journal*, 16, 1 (2006), 11–18.

Purdue, M., 'An overview of the law on public participation in planning law and whether it complies with the Aarhus Convention', *Environmental Law and Management*, 17 (2005), 107–14.

Putnam, R., *Bowling Alone* (New York: Simon and Schuster, 2001).

## Bibliography

Rabe, B. G., *Beyond Nimby: Hazardous Waste Siting in Canada and the United States* (Washington, DC: Brookings Institution, 1994).

Ravetz, J., 'The post-normal science of precaution', *Futures*, 36 (2004), 347–57.

Ravetz, J., 'What is post-normal science?', *Futures*, 31 (1999), 647–53.

Rayner, T. and Jordan, A., 'Adapting to climate change: an emerging European Union policy', in A. Jordan, D. Huitema, H. Van Asselt, T. Rayner and F. Berkhout (eds.), *Climate Change Policy in the European Union* (Cambridge: Cambridge University Press, 2010).

Rees, R., *King Copper: South Wales and the Copper Trade 1584–1895* (Cardiff: University of Wales Press, 2000).

Rittel, H. and Webber, M., 'Dilemmas in general theory of planning', *Policy Sciences*, 4 (1973), 155–69.

Roberts, R. O., 'The development and decline of the non-ferrous metal smelting industries in South Wales', in W. E. Minchinton (ed.), *Industrial South Wales 1750–1914: Essays in Welsh Economic History* (London: Frank Cass, 1969).

Rockstrom, J. et al., 'A safe operating space for humanity', *Nature*, 461 (2009), 472–5.

Rosneau, J., 'Environmental challenges in a global context', in S. Kamieniecki (ed.), *Environmental Politics in the International Arena: Movements, Parties, Organizations and Policy* (Albany: State University of New York Press, 1993).

Ross, A., 'Why legislate for sustainable development?', *Journal of Environmental Law*, 20 (2008), 35–68.

Ross, A. and Nash, H., 'European Union environmental law and who legislates for whom in a devolved Great Britain', *Public Law*, July (2009), 564–94.

Rowan-Robinson, J., Ross, A., Walton, W. and Rothnie, J., 'Public access to environmental information: a means to what end?', *Journal of Environmental Law*, 8 (1996), 19–42.

Royles, E., *Revitalizing Democracy? Devolution and Civil Society in Wales* (Cardiff: University of Wales Press, 2007).

Rydin, Y., *Urban and Environmental Planning in the UK* (Basingstoke: Macmillan, 1998).

de Sadeleer, N., *Environmental Principles: From Political Slogans to Legal Rules* (Oxford: Oxford University Press, 2002).

Schlemminger, H. and Martens, C.-P., *German Environmental Law for Practitioners* (The Hague: Kluwer Law International, 2004).

Schofield, R. and Shaoul, J., 'Food safety regulations and the conflict of interest: the case of meat safety and *E. coli* 0157', *Public Administration*, 78, 3 (2000), 531–54.

Senden, L., *Soft Law in the European Community* (Oxford: Hart, 2004).

Sheail, J., 'The National Parks and Access to the Countryside Act of 1949: its origins and significance', in T. C. Smout (ed.), *Nature, Landscape and People since the Second World War* (East Linton: Tuckwell Press, 2001).

Shearman, D. and Wayne Smith, J., *The Climate Change Challenge and the Failure of Democracy* (London: Praeger, 2007).

Simpson, A. W. B., 'Victorian judges and the problem of social cost: *Tipping v. St Helens Smelting Company*', in A. W. B. Simpson (ed.), *Leading Cases in the Common Law* (Oxford: Clarendon Press, 1995).

Smith, N. and Clifton-Hadley, R., 'Bovine TB: don't get rid of the cat because the mice have gone', *Nature*, 456 (2008), 700.

Stanley, N., 'Public concern: the decision-maker's dilemma', *Journal of Planning Law* (1998), 919–34.

Steele, J., 'Participation and deliberation in environmental decision-making: exploring a problem-solving approach', *Oxford Journal of Legal Studies*, 21 (2001), 415–42.

Stern, N., *Economic Impacts of Climate Change* (London: Cabinet Office, 2006).

Steurer, R. and Martinuzzi, A., 'Towards a new pattern of strategy formation in the public sector: first experiences with national strategies for sustainable development in Europe', *Environment and Planning C: Government and Policy*, 23, 3 (2005), 455–72.

## Bibliography

Sullivan, H., *Meta-Evaluation of the Local Government Modernisation Agenda: The State of Governance of Places: Community Leadership and Stakeholder Engagement* (London: Department for Communities and Local Government, 2008).

Sunstein, C. R. and Jolls, C., 'Debiasing through law', *Journal of Legal Studies*, 85 (2006), 199-241.

Sunstein, C. R., 'Endogenous preferences, environmental law', *Journal of Legal Studies*, 22 (1992), 217-54.

Sunstein, C. R., 'Social norms and social roles', *Columbia Law Review*, 96 (1996), 903-68.

Sustainable Development Commission, *Food Security and Sustainability: The Perfect Fit* (SDC Position Paper, July 2009).

Tarlock, D., 'Environmental law: ethics or science?', *Duke Environmental Law and Policy Forum*, 7 (1996), 193-5.

Tasker, J., 'Renewed call to tackle food inflation', *Farmers Weekly*, 22 July 2011.

Taylor, M. and Warburton, D., 'Legitimacy and the role of the UK third sector organizations in the policy process', *Voluntas*, 14, 3 (2003), 321-38.

Taylor, M., 'Communities in the lead: power, organisational capacity and social capital', *Urban Studies*, 37 (2000), 1019-35.

Thaler, R. H. and Sunstein, C. R., *Nudge: Improving Decisions about Health, Wealth, and Happiness* (New Haven, CT: Yale University Press, 2008).

Tierney, S., 'Giving with one hand: Scottish devolution within a unitary state', *International Journal of Constitutional Law*, 5, 4 (2007), 730-53.

Toke, D., 'Explaining wind power planning outcomes', *Energy Policy*, 33 (2005), 1527-39.

Tomain, J. P., *Ending Dirty Energy Policy: Prelude to Climate Change* (Cambridge: Cambridge University Press, 2011).

Torgerson, P. and Torgerson, D., 'Public health and bovine tuberculosis: what's all the fuss about?', *Trends in Microbiology*, 18, 2 (2010), 67-9.

Torres, G., 'Environmental burdens and democratic justice', *Fordham Urban Law Journal*, 21 (1994), 431-60.

Treby, E. J. and Clark, M. J., 'Refining a practical approach to participatory decision making: an example from coastal zone management', *Coastal Management*, 32 (2004), 353-72.

Tromans, S., 'Nuisance: prevention or payment?', *Cambridge Law Journal*, 41, 1 (1982), 87-109.

UK Government, *Securing the Future: Delivering the UK Sustainable Development Strategy* (2005), Cm 6467.

UKELA and King's College London, *The State of UK Environmental Legislation in 2011: Is There a Case for Reform? Interim Report*, August 2011 (London: UKELA/KCL, 2011).

Vandenbergh, M., 'From smokestack to SUV: the individual as regulated entity in the new era of environmental law', *Vanderbilt Law Review*, 57 (2004), 515-628.

Vidal, J., 'Huge mirrors and aerosols in space: just science fiction or the earth's last hope?', *The Guardian*, 16 June 2011.

Wagner, W., 'The "bad science" fiction: reclaiming the debate over the role of science in public health and environmental regulation', *Law and Contemporary Problems*, 66 (2003), 63-76.

Wald, P., 'Analysts and policymakers: a confusion of roles', *Stanford Law and Policy Review*, 17 (2006), 241-74.

Walker, G., 'Harnessing community energies: explaining and evaluating community-based localism in renewable energy policy in the UK', *Global Environmental Politics*, 7 (2007), 64-82.

Warburton, D., 'A passionate dialogue: community and sustainable development', in D. Warburton (ed.), *Community and Sustainable Development: Participation in the Future* (London: Earthscan, 2000).

Warren, L. M., 'Law and policy for marine protected areas', in C. P. Rodgers (ed.), *Nature Conservation and Countryside Law* (Cardiff: University of Wales Press, 1996).

Welsh Affairs Committee, *Wales and Whitehall: Eleventh Report*, HC Report (Session 2009-10) no. 246.

Welsh Assembly Government, *A Shared Responsibility: Local Government's Contribution to Improving People's Lives: A Policy Statement from the Welsh Assembly Government* (Cardiff: Welsh Government, 2007).

Welsh Assembly Government, *Capturing the Potential: A Green Jobs Strategy for Wales* (Cardiff: WAG, 2009).

Welsh Assembly Government, *Consultation: A Living Wales – A New Framework for Our Environment, Our Countryside and Our Seas* (Cardiff: NAW, 2010).

Welsh Assembly Government, *Food for Wales, Food from Wales 2010-2020* (Cardiff: WAG, 2010)

Welsh Assembly Government, *Food for Wales, Food from Wales 2010-2020: Summary of Responses to the Welsh Assembly Government Consultation on the Food Strategy for Wales* (Cardiff: WAG, 2010).

Welsh Assembly Government, *National Energy and Efficiency Savings Plan* (Cardiff: WAG, 2011).

Welsh Assembly Government, *One Wales: One Planet – the Sustainable Development Annual Report 2009-2010* (Cardiff: WAG, 2010).

Welsh Assembly Government, *One Wales: One Planet – the Sustainable Development Scheme of the Welsh Assembly Government* (Cardiff: WAG, 2009).

Welsh Assembly Government, *Study to Examine the Planning Application Process in Wales* (Cardiff: WAG, 2010).

Welsh Assembly Government, *Towards Zero Waste – One Wales: One Planet* (Cardiff: WAG, 2010).

Welsh Assembly Government, *Wise about Waste: A Waste Strategy for Wales* (2002).

Welsh Government, *Climate Change Engagement Strategy* (Cardiff: Welsh Government, 2011).

Welsh Government, *Climate Change Strategy for Wales* (Cardiff: Welsh Government, 2010).

Welsh Government, *Consultation Document Communities First: The Future* (Cardiff: Welsh Government, 2011).

Welsh Government, *Consultation Document, Building Resilience to Climate Change: Approach to Exercising Powers to Issue Guidance and Directions under Part 4 Climate Change Act (Impact of and Adaptation to Climate Change)* (Cardiff: Welsh Government, 2010).

Welsh Government, draft *Guidance Document, Building Resilience to Climate Change: Statutory Guidance for Reporting Authorities* (Cardiff: Welsh Government, 2010).

Welsh Government, *Local Vision Statutory Guidance from the Welsh Assembly Government on Developing and Delivering Community Strategies* (Cardiff: Welsh Government, 2008).

Welsh Government, *Local, Regional, National: What Services Are Best Delivered Where?* (Cardiff: Welsh Government, 2011).

Welsh Government, *One Wales: One Planet, Sustainable Development Charter* (Cardiff: Welsh Government, 2010).

Welsh Government, *The Third Dimension: A Strategic Action Plan for the Voluntary Sector Scheme* (Cardiff: Welsh Government, 2010).

Which, *The Rising Cost of Food* (London: Which, July 2011).

Wilde, M. and Smith, C. 'R. v. Pease', in C. Mitchell and P. Mitchell (eds.), *Landmark Cases in the Law of Tort* (Oxford: Hart, 2010).

Wilkinson, D., 'Using environmental ethics to create ecological law', in J. Holder and D. McGillivray (eds.), *Locality and Identity: Environmental Issues in Law and Society* (Aldershot: Dartmouth, 1999).

Williams, B. A. and Matheny, A. R., *Democracy, Dialogue, and Environmental Disputes: The Contested Languages of Social Regulation* (New Haven, CT: Yale University Press, 1995).

Williams, P. and Thomas, A., *Sustainable Development in Wales: Understanding Effective Governance* (York: Joseph Rowntree Foundation, 2004)

Wilson, D. and Stokes, G., *British Local Government in the Twentieth Century* (London: Palgrave, 2004).

Winter, G., 'The climate is no commodity: taking stock of the emissions trading system', *Journal of Environmental Law*, 22 (2010), 1–25.

Winter, G., 'The four phases of environmental law', *Journal of Environmental Law*, 1 (1989), 38–47.

Woods, M., Edwards, B., Anderson, J., Gardner, G. and Hughes, R., *Research Study into the Role, Functions and Future Potential of Community and Town Councils in Wales* (Cardiff: University of Wales Aberystwyth/Welsh Assembly Government, 2003).

Wynn, B. G. and Mayer, S., 'How science fails the environment', *New Scientist*, 138 (1993), 33–5.

Yardley, K., Wright, G. and Pearman, A., 'The social construction of risk aversion', *Risk Decision & Policy*, 2 (1997), 87–100.

Zinn, M. D., 'Adapting to climate change: environmental law in a warmer world', *Ecology Law Quarterly*, 34 (2007), 61–105.

# Index

Agenda 21 (UN action plan) 123, 124, 126, 132
agriculture 66, 85, 108, 110, 111–12, 115, 168
   exclusion from planning controls 66
   exports 85
   food strategies and 108, 111
   greenhouse gases, as a source of 147
   intensification of 66
   research 115
   rising costs of 115
   subsidies 110, 111–12
   Wales, percentage of land used for 174
   *see also* bovine tuberculosis
Alkali Inspectorate 43, 46
Animal Health Act 1981 90–2, 96
animal welfare 85
Asiantaeth yr Amgylchedd Cymru 9
Assembly measures 16–18, 170

Badger (Control Area) (Wales) Order 2011 90, 91
badger culling *see* bovine tuberculosis
Badger Trust 89, 91–2, 95–6
   *Badger Trust v. The Welsh Ministers* 89, 91–2, 95–6
banking crisis (2008) 148
Berne Convention on the Conservation of European Wildlife and Natural Habitats 1979 70
Better Governance for Wales 10
Big Society (UK Govt. initiative) 126, 127, 135
biodiversity 63, 66, 68, 70, 76–7, 129

bovine tuberculosis 1, 83–98
   badger culling to prevent 83–4, 86–98
   badgers, existence in 87
   compensation for losses caused by 84–5
   economic costs of 84–6, 94
   exports, potential effect on 85
   history of 84
   human health, threat to 84–5
   Intensive Action Pilot Area (IAPA) 90–1, 96
   Jenkins, Helen, et al., study by 89, 95–7
   King Report on 93–5, 97
   Krebs report on 86–7
   pathology of 84
   randomised badger-culling trial (RBCT) 87, 88–90, 93–5, 97
   Strategic Framework for Bovine TB Eradication in Wales 98
   vaccination against 87, 98
   Welsh Government response to 83–5, 93, 95, 97–8
bovine spongiform encephalopathy (BSE) 85

carbon reduction *see* greenhouse gases
carbon taxes 153
child poverty 129
   *see also* sustainable development
Clean Air Act 47
Clean Neighbourhood Act 2005 172
climate change 1, 124, 129, 135, 143–57
   emerging economies, role of 148

European Union response to 144–5
public engagement with, barriers
  to 149–50, 153
Welsh Government powers
  pertaining to 145–7
Welsh responses to 147
Scottish response to 154, 156
*see also* carbon taxes; Climate
  Change Act 2008; Emissions
  Trading Scheme; greenhouse
  gases
Climate Change Act 2008 143, 145–7, 151, 153, 156, 172
coal mining 28
coastal access 173
  *see also* Marine and Coastal Access Act 2009
Commission Communication on Sustainable Development 107
Committee on Climate Change 145–6, 157
Common Agriculture Policy 111–12
common law 25–7, 30, 38, 43, 47–8, 51, 52–3, 54, 55, 56
  regulation versus 25–7, 38, 43, 51, 53
Communities First (Welsh Govt. programme) 124, 127–9, 132–3, 134–5
Community First Partnerships *see* Communities First
compensation 26, 44, 47–50, 53, 54, 56
  for farmers affected by bovine tuberculosis 84–5
compulsory purchase 71
conservation *see* nature conservation
Conservation (Natural Habitats, etc.) Regulations 1994 71, 73
Conservation of Wild Creatures and Wild Plants Act 1975 64
consultation 20
contamination (of land) 5, 34, 107, 168
  *see also* pollution
Convention for the Protection of the Marine Environment of the North East Atlantic (OSPAR Convention) 70, 78
Convention on Biological Diversity 70
Convention on International Trade in Endangered Species (CITES) 5
copper industry 25–38, 48, 49, 54, 55
  decline of 37–8
  history of 28–30
  pollution from 25, 27, 29–38

regulation of 25, 37–8, 55
*St Helens Smelting v. Tipping* 26, 27–8, 31, 35–7, 38, 48, 49, 54
Council of Europe 70
Council of Ministers (EU) 112
Countryside Agency 74
Countryside and Rights of Way Act 2000 66, 71
Countryside Commissions 73, 74
Countryside Council for Wales 71, 76, 175
County Voluntary Councils 130, 133
Court of Appeal 5, 37, 47–9, 57, 89, 90–2, 96
crime prevention 131

Defra *see* Department for Environment, Food and Rural Affairs
Department for Energy and Climate Change 56
Department for Environment, Food and Rural Affairs 12, 95, 178
Department for Transport, Local Government and the Regions 12
devolution vii, ix, 2, 3–4, 7–21, 56, 63, 66, 167–79
  climate change, in respect to 146–8
  energy policy, in respect to 146
  marine environment, in respect to 172–3
  nature conservation, in respect to 72, 73–6, 78
  planning, in respect to 174
  soft law, in respect to 105, 107
  UK Bills, Welsh provisions in 175–7
  voluntary sector, in respect to 129
Dublin Summit (1972) 106

Emissions Trading Scheme 145, 147
employment issues 19
energy 16, 27, 44, 53, 55–7, 115, 144, 145, 146, 147, 148, 151, 154, 157, 168
  coal 44
  fuel poverty, definition of 157
  nuclear 27, 53, 56, 146, 150, 168
  wind 27, 55–6
English Nature 74
environment, impact of human activity on 83
  *see also* climate change; pollution
Environment Agency for England and Wales 9, 74

Environment Agency Wales 74, 76, 175, 178
Environment LCO (2010) *see* Legislative Competence Orders
Environmental Protection Act 1990 172
Environment Protection Agency (Scotland) 74
Environment Strategy for Wales (2006) 17, 169
environmental impact assessments 45, 55, 151
environmental law 1-6, 14-15, 52, 167-79
  common law and 52
  EU Directives 14, 66, 68-9, 70, 71-3, 77-8, 79, 170, 178-9
  international cooperation in 4, 178
  methodological challenges of 1-6
  public participation in the formulation of 150-7, 177
  reform of 78
  regional implementations of 14, 75-6, 167-79
  science and 83-4, 86-98
  United Kingdom and 14-15
  Wales-only provisions in UK 169, 175-7
  *see also* nature conservation
Environmental Protection Act 1990 52, 73, 74, 172
environmental resource management 63, 70, 77, 90, 111, 114, 124, 156, 175
European Climate Change Programme 145
European Commission 68, 106, 107, 145
European Court of Justice 15
European Parliament 112
European Union 1-5, 14-15, 112, 129, 144-5, 168, 170-1
  climate-change commitments 144
  environmental law and 14-15, 106-7, 168
  food regulation and 112
  nature conservation and 66, 68-9, 70, 71-3, 74, 77-8
  soft law and 106-7
  trade and 116

farming *see* agriculture
fisheries 74, 173
  *see also* marine environment
flood defence 9, 169

food 105-18
  in the developing world 115
  economic development, contribution to 108
  education about 108-9, 112-13, 114, 115, 117
  importing of 116
  labelling of 111-12
  local branding of 111-12, 113, 114, 116
  organic production of 111
  price of 115, 116
  production of 105, 108, 111, 115
  supply of 107, 112, 113, 114, 115, 118
  sustainability and 109-11, 114, 115
  tourism and 110, 113, 116, 117
Food and Drink Partnership 115, 116
food safety 116
food security 115-16, 118
food strategies 105, 108-9
  international, compared 108-9
Food Strategy for Wales 105, 106, 108-18
  consultations on 116-17, 118
  as soft law 105, 109, 110, 112, 113-18
foot and mouth disease 95
Forestry Commission Wales 76, 175

Good Agricultural and Environmental Conditions (GAEC) 15
Government of Wales Act (1998) 9, 10, 129, 130, 168
Government of Wales Act (2006) 3, 10-12, 14, 16-18, 118, 169
greenhouse gases 56, 115, 144-5, 147-8
  carbon capture and storage (CCS) 154
  emissions trading 145, 147-8, 153
  reduction of 153, 156, 157
  sources of, in Wales 147
  targets for reduction of 144-5, 147
  *see also* climate change; Emissions Trading Scheme
Groundwork (organisation) 130

House of Commons Welsh Affairs Select Committee 17
House of Lords 17, 26, 36, 44, 49-51, 53, 54, 151
  Constitution Committee 17
  decision in *Allen v. Gulf Oil Refining Ltd.* 49-51, 53, 54

Household Waste Recycling Act 2003  169

Independent Scientific Group on Cattle TB  85–6, 87, 89, 93–5, 97
Industrial Revolution  25, 27–9, 36
industrialization  25–6, 51, 174
    environmental effects of  26, 29–30, 31, 32, 33, 34, 35, 45, 49
    health effects on livestock  29, 33–4
    health effects on people  45–6, 49, 54

Joint Nature Conservation Committee  73, 75

Kyoto Protocol  144

Landfill Allowance Schemes  171
Landfill Directive (EU)  170
Legislative Competence Orders  11, 14, 16–17, 21, 56, 118, 170, 172, 175, 176, 177
    National Assembly for Wales (Legislative Competence) (Environment) Order 2010  16–17, 21, 56, 170
Law Commission  78
Lisbon Treaty  16
local authorities  9, 21, 46, 74, 113, 124, 127–8, 130–5, 147, 152, 171–2, 175
    community and town councils  130–1, 135
    community planning and  132–6
    elections for  131
Local Government Act 1972  130
Local Government Act 1984  130
Local Government Act 2000  132–3, 134
Local Government and Public Involvement in Health Act 2007  133
Local Government Measure 2009  133
Local Government Measure 2011  131
Local Service Boards  133, 135
Local Strategic Partnerships  133
Localism Act 2011  127

Marine and Coastal Access Act 2009  75, 173
marine environment  19, 66, 70, 71–2, 75–6, 78, 172–3
    devolution of powers relating to  172–3, 176
    Inshore Fisheries and Conservation Authorities (IFCAs)  173

Marine Conservation Zones  71–2, 75–6, 79
Marine Management Organisation  173
Marine Protected Areas  70, 75, 78
Marine Nature Reserves  71
Scotland and  73–4, 75
UK Marine Policy Statement  76
Wales and  75–6, 172–3
Millennium Development Goals  70
Mines Royal Society  28
mussel farming  18–19

National Assembly for Wales  4, 9–10, 11, 14, 16–18, 19, 21, 74, 76, 90, 117, 118, 129, 130, 168, 175, 176–7
National Parks  64–5
    National Parks and Access to the Countryside Act 1949  64–6
    National Parks Commission  64
    Nature Reserves, compared with  64–5
Natura 2000  68–9
Natural England  74, 75
Natural Environment and Rural Communities Act 2006  66, 73
Natural Environment Framework (A Living Wales)  63, 76–9
Natural Resource Wales (Green Paper)  79
Natural Resources Wales (body)  vii
*Nature* (journal)  95
Nature Conservancy  65
Nature Conservancy Council  73
nature conservation  63–79, 110
    birds, protection of  63–4, 68, 69, 73, 78
    conservation law, evolution of  63–9
    devolution and  72, 73–6, 78
    ecosystems  63, 76, 77, 78
    EU Directives  66, 68–9, 70, 71–3, 74, 77–8, 79
    habitat protection  68–9, 70
    international agreements  70, 77
    legislation  64–6, 67 *table*
    listed species, protection of  69, 72–3
    potentially damaging operations (PDO)  71
    protected areas, creation of  64–6, 68, 70, 71, 78
    recreation and  64–5, 68, 73, 74, 173
    Scotland, special environmental legislation in  73–4

Special Nature Conservation
    Orders 71
  see also biodiversity; Sites of Special
    Scientific Interest; Wildlife and
    Countryside Act 1981
Nature Reserves 64–5, 71
nrg4SD (organisation) 13
nuclear power 27, 53, 56
  Nuclear Installations Act 1965 53
nuisance law 25–6, 27, 31, 32–6, 37,
    43–57
  character of the neighbourhood
    test 26, 27, 48–9, 51, 54
  copper industry and 25–38
  limitations in respect of
    environmental harm 26
  locality doctrine 36, 54
  oil-refining industry and 43–57
  public utility 31, 35–6
  railways and 44, 47
  statutory authority defence 26, 43–5,
    47–51, 52, 54–5, 56
  statutory nuisance 52–3, 56
nuisances 17, 44, 45, 46–7, 49, 52–3, 56

oil refining 25–6, 43–57
  *Allen v. Gulf Oil Refining Ltd.* 26, 27,
    43, 44, 45–51, 55, 56
  pollution from 43–4, 45–7, 49, 51
  risks associated with 48
*One Wales: One Planet see* Welsh
    Sustainable Development Scheme
Orders in Council 11
OSPAR Convention *see* Convention
    for the Protection of the Marine
    Environment of the North East
    Atlantic

penalties 18, 170
planning 18, 20, 26–7, 44, 45, 46, 49,
    51–4, 55, 56, 65–6, 74, 75, 107, 127,
    145, 150–1, 174
  marine environment and 75, 174
  Planning Act 2008 27, 55, 56
  Planning Policy Statements 174
  rural development 65, 74, 108, 114,
    115
  Technical Advice Notes 174
  urban development 66, 108, 114
planning applications 18, 74, 174
pollution 4, 5, 17, 25, 27, 29–38, 43–4,
    45–7, 49, 51, 54, 55, 65, 106, 150, 168,
    171, 178–9

  alkali industry and 29, 37–8, 43
  copper smelting and 25, 27, 29–38
  oil refining and 43–4, 45–7, 49, 51
  power generation and 44, 45; *see also*
    climate change
  visual 51
  water 178–9
poverty *see* sustainable development
power generation 9, 44
precautionary principle 4
privatization 5
Protected Food Names (EU) 112
Protection of Birds Act 1967 64
Public Health Acts 43, 47
public health inspectors 47
public–private partnerships 3, 114, 117,
    148

railways 44, 45, 47–8
recycling 17–18, 21, 148, 170, 171, 172,
    175
resource management *see* environmental
    resource management
Richard Commission 10
rights of way 15
Rio Summit (1992) 144
Rio+20 summit *see* World Summit on
    Sustainable Development (2002)
Rural Development Commission 74

*Securing the Future* 124
single-use carrier bag charge 17, 167, 170
Sites of Special Scientific Interest 65–6,
    68, 70, 71, 73
social sustainability 109, 115, 123
soft law 105–18
  definitions of 106
Special Areas of Conservation 68–9, 71
Special Protection Areas 68, 69
'statutory authority' defence 43–5
sustainable development 4, 12–13, 17,
    20, 66, 77, 109, 118, 123–36, 149, 155,
    169, 178
  climate change and 149, 155–6
  coalition government approach
    to 125, 126
  economic growth and 125
  local communities and 123–36
  poverty and 123, 125–9, 135–6
  public sector, Welsh emphasis on role
    of 130, 133–4, 135
  regeneration and 124, 128
  social justice and 124, 125

voluntary sector and 124, 127–30, 133, 135
  in Wales (compared with England and UK) 126–8, 134, 169
Sustaining a Living Wales (Green Paper) 78–9

taxation 2, 127, 153, 171
tourism 74, 110, 113, 116, 117
*Towards Zero Waste* 17, 171
Town and Country Planning Act 1947 65
Transfer of Function Orders 175
transportation 110, 113, 115, 131, 145, 146, 147, 170
  *see also* railways
Tuberculosis Eradication (Wales) Order 2009 90

United Nations vii, 13, 144
UN Framework Convention on Climate Change 144

voluntary sector *see* devolution; sustainable development

Wales vii–viii, ix
  compared with Scotland and Northern Ireland 7–8
  environmental challenges for vii
  environmental case law in 19
  environmental policy in 19–20, 147, 167–79
  greenhouse gas reduction targets for 147
  institutional framework of 9–12
  legal proceedings, venue for 19
  Legislative Competence Orders 14, 16–17, 21, 56, 118
  limitations on autonomy of 3–4, 146
  nrg4SD, role in 13
  policy divergence from UK 3–4, 8, 9, 126–7, 167–79
  referendum (2011), implications of 20–1, 118, 167, 177
  socio-economic structure of 174–5
  *see also* devolution
Wales Environment Link 177
Wales Spatial Plan 9
Wales Waste Strategy 170
Wales Sustainable Development Charter 155
Waste and Emissions Trading Act 2003 169
Waste Framework Directive (EU) 170
waste management 17–18, 52–3, 57, 110, 114, 147, 168, 169, 170–2, 174–75, 179
  hazardous waste, disposal of 174
  landfills 170, 171-2, 174
  marine 17
  Site Waste Management Plans 172
  Welsh strategies for 17–18, 170–2, 175, 179
Waste (Wales) Measure 2010 17–18, 21, 170–1
Water Act 2003 169
Water Framework Directive (EU) 178–9
Welsh Assembly *see* National Assembly for Wales
Welsh Assembly Government *see* Welsh Government
Welsh Government 8, 9–10, 11, 12–13, 16–18, 20, 21, 74, 75, 77, 78, 109, 113, 116–18, 124–5, 127–9, 131, 134, 135, 143, 145–7, 155–6, 157, 167, 169, 170–6
  bovine tuberculosis, response to 83–5, 93, 95, 97–8
  climate-change strategy of 147–8, 155–6, 157
  sustainable-development duty of 12–13, 125, 143, 155, 169
Welsh Office 8
Welsh Sustainable Development Scheme 12–13, 17, 125
Westminster 9–11, 14, 16, 18, 20–1, 75, 76, 78, 169, 172, 176–7, 178
  Welsh Committees at 176
Whitehall 8, 11–12, 176
Wild Birds Protection Act 1880 64
Wildlife and Countryside Act 1981 64, 66, 68, 70, 71, 72, 74
wind farms 27, 55–6
  environmental impact of 56
World Summit on Sustainable Development (2002) 13, 70
World Summit on Sustainable Development (2005) 70